LEARN, TEACH...

SUCCEED...

With **REA's PRAXIS II: Biology**
test prep, you'll be in a class all your own.

WE'D LIKE TO HEAR FROM YOU!
Visit **www.rea.com** to send us your comments

PRAXIS II® BIOLOGY
CONTENT KNOWLEDGE (0235)

TestWare® Edition

Laurie Ann Callihan, M.S.
Rebekah Warner, M.S.

Research & Education Association

Planet Friendly Publishing
✔ Made in the United States
✔ Printed on Recycled Paper
Text: 10%   Cover: 10%
Learn more: www.greenedition.org

GREEN EDITION®

At REA we're committed to producing books in an Earth-friendly manner and to helping our customers make greener choices.

Manufacturing books in the United States ensures compliance with strict environmental laws and eliminates the need for international freight shipping, a major contributor to global air pollution.

And printing on recycled paper helps minimize our consumption of trees, water and fossil fuels. This book was printed on paper made with **10% post-consumer waste**. According to the Environmental Paper Network's Paper Calculator, by using this innovative paper instead of conventional papers, we achieved the following environmental benefits:

Trees Saved: 4 • Air Emissions Eliminated: 836 pounds
Water Saved: 810 gallons • Solid Waste Eliminated: 247 pounds

Courier Corporation, the manufacturer of this book, owns the Green Edition Trademark.
For more information on our environmental practices, please visit us online at **www.rea.com/green**

Research & Education Association
61 Ethel Road West
Piscataway, New Jersey 08854
E-mail: info@rea.com

Praxis II® Biology: Core Content Knowledge (0235) Test with TestWare® on CD

Published 2012
Copyright © 2011 by Research & Education Association, Inc. All rights reserved. No part of this book may be reproduced in any form without permission of the publisher.

Printed in the United States of America

Library of Congress Control Number 2010926297

ISBN-13: 978-0-7386-0774-0
ISBN-10: 0-7386-0774-6

REA® and TestWare® are registered trademarks of
Research & Education Association, Inc.

About Research & Education Association

Founded in 1959, Research & Education Association is dedicated to publishing the finest and most effective educational materials—including software, study guides, and test preps—for students in middle school, high school, college, graduate school, and beyond.

Today, REA's wide-ranging catalog is a leading resource for teachers, students, and professionals.

Acknowledgments

We would like to thank Larry Kling, Vice President, Editorial, for his editorial direction; Pam Weston, Vice President, Publishing, for setting the quality standards for production integrity and managing the publication to completion; John Cording, Vice President, Technology, for coordinating the design, development, and testing of REA's TestWare®; Diane Goldschmidt, Senior Editor, Alice Leonard, Senior Editor, and Wallie Hammond, Senior Editor, for pre-flight editorial review; Kathleen Casey, Senior Editor, for project management; Heena Patel, Technology Project Manager, for software testing; Christine Saul, Senior Graphic Artist, for cover design; and Rachel DiMatteo, Graphic Artist, for post-production file mapping.

We also gratefully acknowledge Maria Malzone for copyediting; DataStream Content Solutions, LLC for typesetting; and Terry Casey for indexing the manuscript.

About the Authors

Laurie A. Callihan is a doctoral candidate in Science Education at Florida State University with an expected graduation date of December 2010. She has a B.S. in Biology and extensive training in the natural sciences and teacher education. She is the author of several Biology test preparation books, including several books for REA, and has many years' experience as a classroom teacher. She currently resides in Tallahassee, Florida.

Rebekah Warner has been a Registered Nurse (RN) since May 2004, when she graduated from the nursing program at Roberts Wesleyan College in Rochester, New York, with a Baccalaureate of Science in Nursing (BSN).

While in nursing school, Rebekah was inducted into Delta Sigma Tai, the Honor Society for Nurses. Rebekah became a member of the American Association of Critical Care Nurses (AACN) in 2005. Over her career as a Registered Nurse, Rebekah has worked in various nursing areas, including Medical, Surgical, Orthopedic and Progressive care.

Since August of 2007, Rebekah and her family have been living in Colorado Springs, Colorado. She is currently working on a busy Medical/Cardiac floor of a Catholic hospital in the area. Rebekah and her husband have a three-year-old daughter, Eden, and a 12-month-old son, Caedmon. The Warner family loves living in the beautiful state of Colorado and the very family-friendly environment of Colorado Springs.

Prior to this book Rebekah authored other various works, including the NCLEX-PN Flashcard Book published by REA.

CONTENTS

Introduction

ABOUT THIS BOOK AND TESTWARE®

If you're looking to secure certification as a biology teacher, you'll find that many states require you to pass the Praxis II: Biology Core Content Knowledge (0235) test. Think of this book as your toolkit to pass the test. It will take the mystery and anxiety out of the testing process by equipping you with the best information, and ultimately, with the confidence to succeed alongside your peers across the United States.

Our test prep pulls together all the critical information you need to know to pass the test. We will provide you with the touchstones that will allow you to do your very best come test day and beyond. In this test prep, we offer in-depth, up-to-date, objective coverage, with test-specific modules devoted to targeted review and realistic practice exams. We also include a quick-view answer key, detailed answer explanations, and a competency-categorized progress chart to enable you to pinpoint your strengths and weaknesses. However, this test preparation guide is not intended as an all-inclusive source of biology knowledge, and it is not a substitute for college coursework in the subject area. The reference list, while helpful, is not exhaustive, and the sample items are not intended to be exact representations of actual exam items. Instead, the guide is intended to help test-takers prepare for the Praxis II Biology exam by providing a content overview and sample questions in similar format and likeness to the Praxis exam questions.

Our TestWare CD contains the practice tests from this book with automatic scoring and timed testing conditions to help you to become comfortable as you prepare for the actual exam. We strongly suggest that you begin your preparation with the TestWare tests, to get a good understanding of the material tested on the Praxis II Biology exam.

ABOUT THE PRAXIS SERIES

Praxis is Educational Testing Service's (ETS) shorthand for Professional Assessments for Beginning Teachers. The series is a group of teacher licensing and certification tests that ETS developed in concert with states across the nation. There are three categories of tests in the series: Praxis I, Praxis II and Praxis III. Praxis I includes the paper-based Pre-Professional Skills Tests (PPST) and the Praxis I Computer-Based Tests (CBT). Both versions cover essentially the same subject matter. These exams measure reading, mathematics, and writing skills and are often a requirement for admission to a teacher education program.

Praxis II embraces Subject Assessment/Specialty Area Tests, of which the Praxis II: Biology Core Content Knowledge (0235) is a part. Most Praxis II examinations cover the subject matter that teacher certification candidates typically study in teacher education courses such as language acquisition, school curriculum, methods of teaching, and other professional development courses. In most teacher-training programs, teacher candidates take these tests after having completed their classroom training, the coursework, and practicum.

Praxis III is different from the multiple-choice and essay tests typically used for assessment purposes. With this assessment, ETS-trained observers evaluate an instructor's performance in the classroom, using nationally validated criteria. The observers may videotape the lesson, and other teaching experts may critique the resulting tapes.

Who Takes the Test?

Thirty states require teacher certification candidates to pass the Praxis II: Biology Core Content Knowledge (0235) for certification as a beginning teacher of biology in a secondary school. Check with your state's education agency to determine which Praxis examination(s) you should take; the ETS Praxis website (www.ets.org/Praxis/) and registration bulletin may help you determine the test(s) you need to take for certification. You should also consult your education program for its own test requirements. Colleges and universities often require Praxis examinations for entry into programs, for graduation, and for the completion of a teacher certification program. These requirements may differ from the baseline requirements the state has for teacher certification.

When and Where Can I Take the Test?

ETS offers the Praxis II: Biology Core Content Knowledge test seven times a year at a number of locations across the nation. The usual testing day is Saturday, but examinees may request an administration on an alternate day if a conflict—such as a religious obligation—exists.

How Do I Get More Information on the ETS Praxis Exams?

To receive information on upcoming administrations of the Praxis II: Biology Core Content Knowledge test, or any other test, consult the ETS registration bulletin or website, or contact ETS at:

Educational Testing Service
Teaching and Learning Division
P.O. Box 6051
Princeton, NJ 08541-6051
Phone: (609) 771-7395
Website: www.ets.org/Praxis
E-mail: Praxis@ets.org

Special accommodations are available for candidates who are visually impaired, hearing impaired, physically disabled, or specific learning disabled. For questions concerning disability services, contact:

ETS Disability Services: (609) 771-7780
TTY only: (609) 771-7714

Provisions are also available for examinees whose primary language is not English. The ETS registration bulletin and website include directions for those requesting such accommodations. You can also consult ETS with regard to available test sites; reporting test scores; requesting changes in tests, centers, and dates of test; purchasing additional score reports; retaking tests; and other important test information.

Is There a Registration Fee?

To take a Praxis examination, you must pay a registration fee, which is payable by check, money order, or with American Express, Discover, MasterCard, or Visa credit cards. In certain cases, ETS offers fee waivers. The registration bulletin and website give qualifications for receiving this benefit and describe the application process. Cash is not accepted for payment.

Can I Retake the Test?

Some states, institutions, and associations limit the number of times you can retest. Contact your state or licensing authority to confirm their retest policies.

HOW TO USE THIS BOOK AND TESTWARE®

What Do I Study First?

Read our subject reviews and suggestions for test taking. Studying the review chapters thoroughly will reinforce the skills you need to do well on the exam. Take Practice Test 1 on CD to determine your strengths and weaknesses, and then restudy the material, focusing on your specific problem areas. Do the practice questions in this book so that you will be familiar with the format and procedures involved with taking the actual test.

When Should I Start Studying?

It is never too early to start studying; the earlier you begin, the more time you will have to sharpen your skills. Do not procrastinate! Cramming is not an effective way to study because it does not allow you the time needed to learn the test material.

FORMAT OF THE TEST

The Praxis II: Biology Core Content Knowledge test runs for two hours and consists of 150 multiple-choice questions that address your knowledge of the biological sciences, the basic principles of science, and the issues and applications concerning science, technology, and society.

The questions are derived from topics typically covered in an introductory college-level biology course. The test questions address a variety of abilities and knowledge, and include definition of terms and comprehension of critical concepts. You will also be expected to use application and analysis to address and solve problems. It is possible that some of the questions on the test are being assessed for use in future tests and may not count toward your score.

CONTENT CATEGORY	APPROXIMATE NUMBER OF QUESTIONS	APPROXIMATE PERCENTAGE OF QUESTIONS
I. Basic Principles of Science	12	8%
II. Molecular and Cellular Biology	38	25%
III. Classical Genetics and Evolution	23	15%
IV. Diversity of life, Plants, and Animals	45	30%
V. Ecology	22	15%
VI. Science, Technology, and Society	10	7%

You should spend less than one minute on each multiple-choice question on each of the practice tests—and on the real exam, of course. The review chapters in this book will help you sharpen the basic skills needed to approach the exam and offer strategies for answering the questions. By using the reviews in conjunction with the practice tests, you will better prepare yourself for the actual test.

You have learned through your course work and your practical experience in schools most of what you need to know to answer the questions on the test. In your education classes, you gained the expertise to make important decisions about situations you will face as a teacher. You should have acquired the knowledge you will need to teach this specific content in your content courses.

The review chapters in this book will help you fit the information you have acquired into its specific testable category. Reviewing your class notes and textbooks along with systematic use of this book will give you an excellent springboard for passing the Praxis II: Biology Core Content Knowledge exam.

SCORING THE TEST

The number of raw points awarded on the Praxis II: Biology Core Content Knowledge test is based on the number of correct answers given. Most Praxis examinations vary by edition, which means that each test has several variations that contain different questions. The different questions are intended to measure the same general types of knowledge or skills. However, there is no way to guarantee that the questions on all editions of the test will have the same degree of difficulty.

To avoid penalizing test takers who answer questions that are more difficult, the initial scores are adjusted for difficulty by using a statistical process known as equating. To avoid confusion between the adjusted and unadjusted scores, ETS reports the adjusted scores on a score scale that makes them clearly different from the unadjusted scores. Unadjusted scores or "raw scores" are simply the number of questions answered correctly. Adjusted scores, which are equated to the scale ETS uses for reporting the scores are called "scaled scores." For each edition of a Praxis test, a "raw-to-scale conversion table" is used to translate raw to scaled scores.

The easier the questions are on a test edition, the more questions must be answered correctly to earn a given scaled score. The college or university in which you are enrolled may set passing scores for the completion of your teacher education program and for graduation. Be sure to check the requirements in the catalogues or bulletins. You will also want to talk with your advisor. The passing scores for the Praxis II tests vary from state to state. To find out which of the Praxis II tests your state requires and what your state's set passing score is, contact your state's education department directly.

Score Reporting

When Will I Receive My Examinee Score Report and in What Form Will It Be?

ETS mails test-score reports six weeks after the test date. There is an exception for computer-based tests and for the Praxis I examinations. Score reports will list your current score and the highest score you have earned on each test you have taken over the last 10 years. Along with your score report, ETS will provide you with a booklet that offers details on your scores. For each test date, you may request that ETS send a copy of your scores to as many as three score recipients, provided that each institution or agency is eligible to receive the scores.

STUDYING FOR THE TEST

It is critical to your success that you study effectively. Throughout this test prep, you will find Praxis Pointers that will give you tips for successful test taking. Here are a few tips to help get you going:

- Choose a time and a place for studying that works best for you. Some people set aside a certain number of hours every morning to study; others may choose to study at night before going to sleep. Only you know what is most effective for you.

- Use your time wisely and be consistent. Work out a study routine and stick to it; don't let your personal schedule interfere. Remember, seven weeks of studying is a modest investment to put you on your chosen career path.

- Don't cram the night before the test. You may have heard many amazing tales about effective cramming, but don't kid yourself: most of them are false. Cramming is not an effective way to study because it does not allow you ample time to learn and absorb the material tested on the exam. Trying to cram the night before the test may actually increase your test-anxiety.

- When you take the practice tests in this book, try to make your testing conditions as much like the actual test as possible. Turn off your television, radio, and telephone. Sit down at a quiet table free from distraction.

- As you complete each practice test, score your test and thoroughly review the explanations to the questions you answered incorrectly.

- Take notes on material you will want to go over again or research further.

- Keep track of your scores. By doing so, you will be able to gauge your progress and discover your strengths and weaknesses. You should carefully study the material relevant to your areas of difficulty. This will build your test-taking skills and your confidence!

STUDY SCHEDULE

The following study schedule allows for thorough preparation to pass the Praxis II: Biology Core Content Knowledge test. This is a suggested seven-week course of study. However, you can condense this schedule if you are in a time crunch or expand it if you have more time. You may decide to use your weekends for study and preparation and go about your other business during the week. You may even want to record information and listen to your mp3 player or tape as you travel in your car. However you decide to study, be sure to stick to the schedule that works best for you.

WEEK	ACTIVITY
1	After reading this chapter to understand the format and content of the Praxis II: Biology test, take the first practice test on CD. The score will indicate your strengths and weaknesses. Make sure you simulate real exam conditions when you take the test. Afterward, score the practice test and review the answer explanations, especially for questions you answered incorrectly.
2	Review the explanations for the questions you missed on the practice test, and read through the appropriate review chapters. Useful study techniques include highlighting key terms and information, taking notes as you review each section, and putting new terms and information on note cards to help retain the information.
3 and 4	Reread all your note cards and refresh your understanding of the material tested on the exam. Study the review chapters in this book, especially those that cover the areas in which you feel weak. Review your college textbooks and read over notes you took in your college classes. This is also the time to consider any other supplementary materials that your counselor or your state education agency suggests. Make additional notes as you study each chapter.
5	Condense your notes and findings. A structured list of important facts and information, based on your note cards will help you thoroughly review for the test. Study our review chapters and focus on any areas that are confusing or you feel you need improvement.
6	Have someone quiz you using the note cards you created. Take the second full-length practice test on CD.
7	Using all your study materials, review areas of weakness revealed by your score on the second practice tests. Study the detailed answer explanations for the questions you answered incorrectly. Then retake sections of the practice tests to give you extra practice before exam day.

THE DAY OF THE TEST

Before the Test

- Dress comfortably in layers. You do not want to be distracted by being too hot or too cold while you are taking the test.

- Check your registration ticket to verify your arrival time.

- Arrive at the test center early. This will allow you to collect your thoughts and relax before the test. Your early arrival will also spare you the anguish that comes with being late. If you arrive late, you may not be admitted to the test, and your registration and test fees will be forfeited.

- Bring your admission ticket with you and two forms of identification, one of which must contain a recent photograph, your name, and your signature (e.g., a driver's license). You will not gain entry to the test center without proper identification.

- Bring several sharpened No. 2 pencils with erasers for the multiple-choice section; pens if you are taking another test that might have essay or constructed-response questions. You will not want to waste time searching for a replacement pencil or pen if you break a pencil point or run out of ink when you are trying to complete your test. The proctor will not provide pencils or pens at the test center.

- Wear a watch to the test center so you can monitor your testing time. You may not, however, wear a watch that makes noise or that will otherwise disturb the other test takers.

- Leave all dictionaries, textbooks, notebooks, calculators, briefcases, and packages at home. You may not take these items into the test center.

- Cell phones, BlackBerry devices, PDAs and any other electronic or photographic devices are not permitted at the test center. If you bring such devices to the test center, you will be dismissed from the test, your registration and test fees will be forfeited and your scores will be canceled. Test center staff is not permitted to collect or store devices.

- Do not eat or drink too much before the test. The proctor will not allow you to make up time you miss if you have to take a bathroom break. You will not be allowed to take materials with you, and you must secure permission before leaving the room.

- On occasion, weather conditions, or other circumstances beyond the test administrator's or ETS's control may require a delayed start or the rescheduling of your test appointment.

During the Test

- *Pace yourself*. ETS administers the Praxis II: Biology Core Content Knowledge (0235) test in one two-hour sitting with no breaks. Follow all of the rules and instructions that the test proctor gives you. Proctors will enforce these procedures to maintain test security. If you do not abide by the regulations, the proctor may dismiss you from the test and notify ETS to cancel your score.

- *Listen closely* as the test instructor provides the directions for completing the test. Follow the directions carefully. Be sure to *mark only one answer* per multiple-choice question, erase all unwanted answers and marks completely, and fill in the answers darkly and neatly. There is no penalty for guessing at an answer, *do not leave any answer ovals blank*. Remember: a blank oval is scored as wrong, but a guessed answer has a chance of being right!

- *Take the test and do your best*! Afterward, make notes about the multiple-choice questions you remember. You may not share this information with others, but you may find that the information proves useful on other exams that you take. Go home and relax—you deserve it!—and wait for that passing score to arrive.

Basic Principles of Science

HISTORY AND NATURE OF SCIENCE

Nature of Scientific Knowledge and Inquiry

While science is fundamentally an intellectual endeavor, it has a distinct social component that is recognized and appreciated by modern scientists and philosophers. It has been particularly important in recent years for those teaching science to help students understand that while science as a way of knowing is an important method of intellectual pursuit, it is not the only method by which individuals or societies gain knowledge. Indeed there are other ways of knowing besides the "scientific way of knowing." That being said, the science classroom should focus on scientific ways of knowing and students in the science classroom should be taught to distinguish between science and pseudoscience.

Science is an ongoing study of the universe, and as such the knowledge gained in the endeavor of learning through science is subject to change over time. Scientific ideas are tested and retested over time through methodical processes which have been sometimes referred to as the scientific method . . . however, in truth there is more than one scientific method. There are many valuable ways to investigate the natural world in a scientific manner through methods such as **direct observation**, **modeling**, **testing hypotheses**, etc. The socioscientific methods of gathering knowledge are subject to careful scrutiny by the body of knowledgeable individuals that belong to the scientific community. While there is no one set of steps that defines the one scientific method, there are general methods and acceptable practices that characterize a scientific approach. Among these practices are a foundation of reliance on empirical **observations**, **testing**, healthy **skepticism**, and **naturalistic** (based on observation and empirical testing) explanations.

The foundational method of gathering scientific knowledge is through **inquiry**. Science is based on inquiry that looks at the natural world and develops questions. These questions form the basis of developing ideas and answers about how the natural world works. All accumulated knowledge of the natural world has come about through this practical process of scientific inquiry over the ages. Inquiry results in a quest for evidence. Science is unique in its demand for **empirical evidence** as its basis for knowing. Scientists from various disciplines use a multitude of different types of methods to gather many kinds of evidence. Scientists use a combination of logic and imagination to explain and predict why any given evidence may explain a particular phenomenon.

Conducting scientific inquiry also includes the process of identifying and avoiding bias as completely as possible. In addition, an important goal of scientific inquiry is to structure scientific knowledge in the form of **theories** and **laws**. Both of these terms have very specific definitions in the scientific world. Scientific laws are universal generalizations related to an aspect of how the natural world behaves under certain conditions. A scientific law must be testable, internally consistent, and compatible with available evidence and phenomena. For example, Newton's Laws of Motion are well established as scientific laws. A theory is an explanation of a particular phenomenon of the natural world. Theories explain aspects of laws, but not all laws have corresponding theories. Theories do not become laws with increasing testing or evidence. Rather, theories are a separate type of explanation.

One way scientists construct theories is by using models to describe objects or phenomena in the natural world. Models allow scientists to describe aspects of natural phenomena that may not be directly observable. Models use physical, visual, mathematical, written, or computational means to represent scientific concepts. For example, the Watson-Crick model of the DNA molecule revolutionized molecular biology by enabling scientists to understand how many facets of genetics and cellular processes functioned.

It is the nature of scientific pursuit to search for the best theory to fit the observations available. Therefore, as more information becomes available, whether through more testing, developing technology, or increased access, theories may develop and change. No matter how well a theory might fit a given set of observations, a new theory might be developed that fits as well or better or that might fit with a greater set of observations.

For example, in 1687 Newton revolutionized the study of science in publishing *Mathematical Principles of Natural Philosophy,* which for the first time in history applied empirical mathematics to the understanding of the natural world. Newton's Laws of Motion, including the understanding of gravity and the ability to explain it and other concepts by mathematical terms and equations dominated the physical sciences into the 20th century. For the first time, physics and chemistry, and the physical world could be described and manipulated empirically. Then in the 20th century, Einstein developed quantum and relativity theories as he recognized that Newtonian physics did not apply to situations of very small mass or very high velocity. The world of physics and chemistry were faced with a major paradigm shift as a theoretical challenge was leveled at the theories of physical science. The scientific world adapted and changed to include the new evidence as it became available and it was clear that Einstein's claims were true. Einstein's theories of relativity and quantum mechanics have yet to be fully explored, as they have led to string theory and concepts of complexity and chaos theory. However, while Newtonian physics clearly explains a large part of how the universe works, there is no longer any doubt that Newtonian physics is limited in its scope.

In the mid-19th century the biological sciences underwent a revolution similar to the Newtonian shift when Darwin introduced his concept of **Natural Selection**. Followed in the 20th century by Watson and Crick's discovery of the molecular nature of genes and DNA, the biological sciences were finally empirically explained by evidentiary claims of phylogenetic history and genetic coding.

These historical adjustments in the realm of scientific knowledge bring to light two important characteristics of the **Nature of Scientific Knowledge**—namely **durability** and **tentativeness**. While much scientific knowledge is maintained through historical testing and retesting, it remains and is durable knowledge that stands the test of time—it is also true that new or extended understanding and observations are made possible through the development of new technologies or the perseverance of continued observation and testing. In this way, scientific knowledge is also tentative; its durability is dependent upon future testing and open to scrutiny that new technologies and understanding may allow.

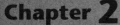

Historical Perspectives

The broadest goal of scientific inquiry is to produce knowledge that results in the ability to **explain phenomena** and **predict outcomes**. The Project 2061 Benchmarks: Science for All Americans documents (AAAS, 2009) identify ten historical inquiries that were monumental in adding to the advancement of scientific perspectives. These ten events provide an appropriate historical outline of scientific achievements:

1) *Understanding the Solar System*
   Aristotle - 350 BCE – Earth-centered (geocentric) universe
   Ptolemy - 140 CE – mathematical model of geocentric universe with spherical orbits
   Copernicus - 1530 CE – Earth spinning on its axis; sun-centered (heliocentric) universe
   Galileo - 1564–1642 – invented telescope; used investigative inquiry methods; confirmed heliocentric model; discovered details about moon, sun, planets
   Kepler - 1571–1630 – proposed mathematical model for elliptical heliocentric orbits of planetary motion with varying speeds

2) *Understanding Gravity and Motion*
   Isaac **Newton** (1643–1727) – *Mathematical Principles of Natural Philosophy* – explained the **Three Laws of Motion** (law of inertia, law of acceleration on force and mass, and law of action and reaction) and the law of universal gravitation

3) *Looking Back in Geologic Time*
   Charles **Lyell** (1797–1875) – *Principles of Geology* – considered rock and sediment layering patterns as well as fossil placement in mountains and various locations on Earth, proposing a much older earth than had been previously considered; set the stage for the ideas of natural selection later proposed by Darwin.

4) *Theory of Relativity*
   Albert **Einstein** (1879–1955) – *Theories of Relativity* – Newton's laws of motion did not hold true in cases of high velocity (approaching the speed of light) or very small mass; $E = mc^2$; important inferences:

a) mass and energy are equivalent and b) the speed of light (c^2) in a vacuum is equal for all observers, regardless of their relative motion or of the motion of the source of light; implications of this theory are just beginning to be investigated to their full potential in the 21st century

5) *Plate Tectonics*

Ideas regarding plate tectonics progressed throughout the 1900's – Alfred **Wegener** proposed moving continents; with recognition of the increase of volcanic and earthquake activity around "ring of fire," the idea of plate tectonics developed

Figure 2.1 Tectonic Plates

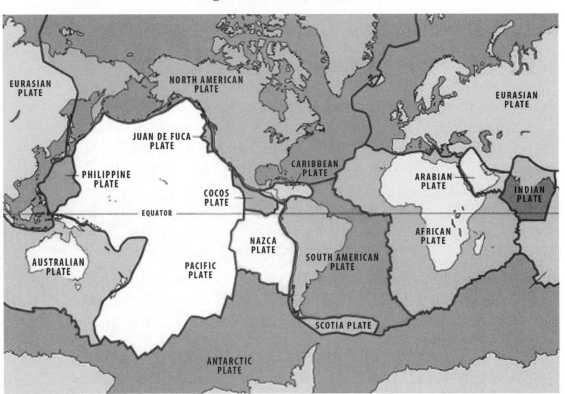

6) *The Conservation of Matter*

Antoine **Lavoisier** and John **Dalton** (among others) (1700–1800's) – develop chemistry as a distinct field of science with experimental data describing atomic and elemental nature of matter, as well as bonding

7) *Radioactivity and Nuclear Fission*

Several scientists (including Marie and Pierre **Curie**, Ernest **Rutherford** and Enrico **Fermi** discover and experiment with the radioactive nature of some elements resulting in the development of nuclear power and nuclear weapons

8) *The Evolution of Species**

Charles **Darwin** (1809–1882) – *Origin of Species* – develops the mechanism for evolution of species as natural selection (for more on the concept of natural selection see Chapter 4 – Classical Genetics and Evolution) followed by advances in understanding of inheritance through the work of Gregor **Mendel** (1822–1884) – then understanding of molecular genetics and DNA through work of James **Watson**, Francis **Crick**, and others (1950's)

9) *The Nature of Disease**

Louis **Pasteur** (1822–1895) – discovers connection of "germs" with fermentation and disease and develops pasteurization process (sanitation) – developments in miscroscope technology allow for viewing microorganisms directly in the 20th century

10) *The Industrial Revolution*

1800's brings technological advances of steam engine, manufacturing, sanitation, etc.

* The Praxis II Biology test may discuss any of these events from the standpoint of the History and Nature of Science; however, special attention should be given to the biological events noted with an asterisk.

MATHEMATICS, MEASUREMENT, AND DATA MANIPULATION

All branches of science rely heavily on the use of mathematics whether it is the use of statistics in understanding populations and their impact on ecological factors, ratios and proportions when dealing with genetics, or calculus when considering forces and elasticity in physics. Mathematics is used for *measuring* and collecting data, *interpreting* and *understanding* the physical world, and *comparing* and *presenting* information about the physical world.

Measurements and Accuracy

1. It is important to understand the difference between **precision** and **accuracy**. Accuracy represents how close a measurement is to the real or accepted value. Measurements are precise when repeated measurements show the same results. For example, you might make an inaccurate standard solution for an acid-base titration. If the standard solution has a lower concentration than thought, more of it would be required to neutralize the sample, and you will think that the sample has a higher concentration. If you attempt the neutralization several times and get the same answer each time, the results would be precise, but not accurate.

2. Measurements in science are always taken in units of the International System of Units (the Système Internationale) or **SI Units**. Standard measurements in SI for volume, length, mass, etc., are in metric units.

Table 2.1 Common International System of Units

UNIT	UNIT SYMBOL	QUANTITY TO MEASURE
meter	m	length
kilogram	kg	mass
second	s	time
degrees Celsius	°C	standard temperature
liter	l	volume
ampere	A	electric current
Kelvin	K	thermodynamic temperature
candela	cd	luminous intensity
mole	mol	amount of substance

Figure 2.2 Celsius (left)/Fahrenheit (right) thermometer showing freezing point of water at 1 ATM pressure (0 °C = 32 °F).

To manually convert Fahrenheit to Celsius . . .

1. Take the temperature in Fahrenheit subtract 32.
2. Divide by 1.8.
3. The result is degrees Celsius.

Example: To Convert 92°F to Celsius . . .

1. $92 - 32 = 60$
2. $60/1.8 = 33.3$
3. So . . . 92 °F = 33.3 °C

3. Be aware of **significant figures** in laboratory measurements. You are allowed one uncertain figure in your measurement. For example, in the following graduated cylinder measurement, the volume is delineated by tenths of a milliliter (mL).

   a. First, remember to read the bottom of the **meniscus** when measuring volume in glassware. The meniscus is the bottom (or top) of the curve of the liquid in a measuring container. In Figure 2.3 below, the liquid would measure 17.0 mL, not 18.0 mL.

Figure 2.3 Graduated cylinder showing meniscus.

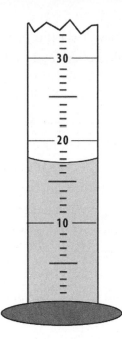

b. Since one uncertain digit is allowed, in the example (Figure 2.4) below you should record 11.45 mL. It might be 11.44 mL; you are uncertain about the +/– 0.01 mL amount, but you are certain that the +/– 0.1 mL aspect of the measurement is between 11.4 and 11.5 mL.

Figure 2.4 Graduated cylinder measurement.

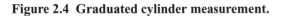

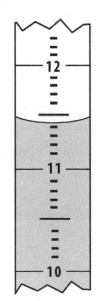

c. Also with regard to significant figures, remember that if they are multiplied or divided together to get some final answer, the number of significant figures in the answer should match the least number of significant figures in the numbers that lead to the answer.

Interpreting Results

1. Never expect quantitative measurements to exactly match the expected value. Be sure to calculate the **percent accuracy** (or conversely **percent error**) by dividing the difference between the measured and accepted/expected values, dividing by the accepted/expected value, and multiplying by 100. This figure should be a part of any laboratory report involving quantitative measurements.

$$\% \text{ Error} = |\text{Your Measured Result} - \text{Accepted Value}|/\text{Accepted Value}) \times 100$$

2. Analyze the **precision** of your measurements by making multiple measurements or comparing your value with your classmates.

3. Use tables or graphs to better summarize multiple data points.

4. As you examine the accuracy of your measurements, consider each step that you undertook to make the measurement. Consider how an inadvertent error in that step could have influenced the measurement, either by increasing or decreasing the value of the measurement relative to the expected value.

Reporting Results

1. When reporting data, use an appropriate form of notation for the discipline of the experiment. For example, certain chemistry experiments may require notation in chemical equations and molecular diagrams. Other experimental results, particularly those that are very large or small in scale should be reported in **scientific notation**. Scientific notation is accomplished by writing any number in the form . . . a $\times$ 10^b . . . where

the number is expressed as a power of ten such that a is equivalent to a number between 1 and 10.

Examples: $2,398 = 2.398 \times 10^3$ in scientific notation
$0.00000626 = 6.26 \times 10^{-6}$
$-42 = -4.2 \times 10^1$

2. Some data reports will need to be in the form of graphs, ratios, percentages, or some other form. Always be sure to check what form is required for any type of data display or report and be sure to include appropriate units of measure where applicable (gallons, Newtons, pounds, PSI, etc.).

When graphing a value as a function of another value (variable), the value that you measure should be on the y-axis; this is the **dependent variable**. It has changed as a result of changing the independent variable, which should be on the x-axis. In other words, the y-axis (the **dependent variable**) depends on x (the independent variable) which "just is"—it doesn't depend on anything within the experiment. In the following example we have used *Days 1–10* as the Independent variable (y) and *Temperature* measured on those days as the Dependent variable (x). The temperature "depended" on which day it was. We put the measurements first in a table, then graphed the results on an x, y coordinate graph.

Table 2.2 Day versus Temperature

FIRST COORDINATE, THE INDEPENDENT VARIABLE, IN THIS EXAMPLE: DAY	SECOND COORDINATE, THE DEPENDENT VARIABLE IN THIS EXAMPLE: TEMPERATURE IN DEGREES
1	-7.6
2	-2.0
3	-5.05
4	-1.0
5	-5.7
6	5.8
7	6.6
8	18.0
9	5.6
10	5.8

Figure 2.5 Graph of Day versus Temperature

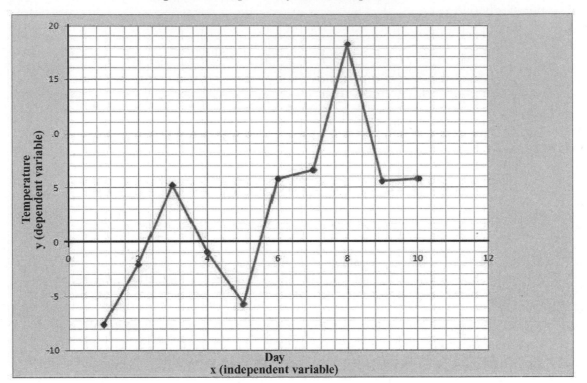

LABORATORY PROCEDURES AND SAFETY

One of the essential activities of teaching science is conducting safe and appropriate laboratory experiences. Giving students opportunities to conduct inquiries in a lab environment will be an important step in building their knowledge of the scientific enterprise. It is the teacher's role to insure the safe and appropriate use of all laboratory apparatus, models, and specimens for the safety and well-being of the students and for teaching responsible and effective scientific techniques. In fact, teachers have a legal obligation, a duty of care, recognized by law (NSTA, 2007) to protect students by holding them to a standard of conduct that will protect others against unreasonable risk. Teachers that do not tend to this duty place not only their students at risk, but also leave themselves and their school open to liability. It is therefore paramount for the science educator to provide the safest possible learning environment in the laboratory. The teacher is not alone in this duty, it is shared by the administration, school board, parents, and students, who all bear a responsibility in supporting the teacher in providing the safest laboratory experience possible.

In addition to all safety precautions posted in the classroom and/or laboratory and specified in a given activity or laboratory procedure, always insure that the following safety guidelines are implemented:

General

- Keep laboratory, classroom and storage areas neat and clean. Accidents are more likely to occur in a disorganized lab or with items improperly labeled or cared for.

- Be sure laboratory activities for students are age-appropriate and that students are aware of safety procedures for all activities, equipment, and chemicals.

Apparel

- Clothing should not be baggy or have loosely hanging items such as belts, scarves, or jewelry that could catch on fire or get caught in equipment.

- Sleeves should be rolled up and secured.

- Hair should be tied back.

- Wear goggles during all procedures involving moving objects, chemicals, biological materials, or anything else indicating need for goggles.

- Shoes must be close-toed to protect from spills or other hazards.

- Wear safety aprons during all procedures involving chemicals, biological materials, or anything else indicating need for clothing protection.

- Wear gloves when handling chemicals, live specimens, microbes, or in any other case where the laboratory instructions call for glove use.

Figure 2.6 Some standard laboratory equipment.

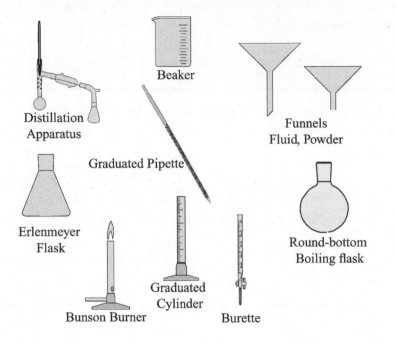

Substance Control

- When working with any substance in the science classroom or laboratory, be particularly aware of product labels and instructions – follow all safety and disposal guidelines. Keep all products in original containers or in an appropriately labeled container that is suitable for that product.

- Never eat or drink anything in a laboratory situation.

- Be aware of Material Safety Data Sheets (MSDS) for any and all substances used in a laboratory activity.

- Be familiar with safety equipment location and use (such as eye wash station, emergency cutoff valves, spill kits, etc.).

- Pay special attention to harmful and corrosive liquids and gases. Use venting appropriately. Always transfer acids or bases *into* water while stirring. Do not stir water into acid or base.

- Keep all poisonous, corrosive, flammable, and otherwise dangerous substances (check MSDS sheets) in locked cupboard when not in use.

- Dispose of substances and specimens according to supplier instructions and all state, local, and school policies.

Fire Control

- Know the location and proper use protocol of fire blanket, fire extinguishers, emergency cutoff buttons, etc.

- Instruct students in safe fire exit practices.

Accidents

- Report all accidents according to school policy.

- Clean up all spills and broken objects according to supplier's directions.

Handling Live and Preserved Organisms

- No investigations in the laboratory, classroom, or at home should inflict pain or harm on a mammal, bird, reptile, fish, or amphibian.

- Treat all living (and preserved) things, including plants and invertebrates with appropriate care and respect.

- It is the teacher's responsibility to know specific state laws regarding treatment of living and dead organism's in the laboratory environment. [See National Association of Biology Teachers' (www.nabt.org) *Statement of Position: The Use of Animals in Biology Education.* Adopted by the Board of Directors, August 2008]

- Dissection of certain preserved organisms is encouraged by organizations such as the National Association of Biology Teachers at appropriate ages – as left up to the teacher's discretion and as determined advantageous for the Biology classroom.

- Presence of appropriately cared-for live animals in the classroom is also encouraged as left to the teacher's discretion.

- Any experimentation on animals of any kind should be subject to IRB (Institutional Review Board) approval within the locale of the school.

- Use antiseptic procedures with all microbes as if all are dangerous.

Figure 2.7 Safety symbol notations.

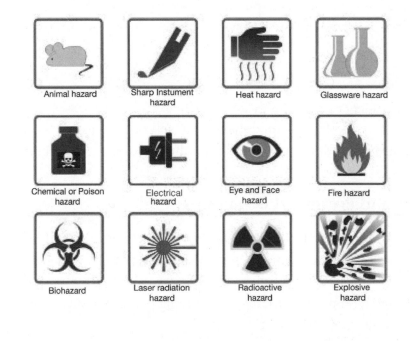

In addition to the basics of maintaining a safe laboratory environment, it is also science education professionals' responsibility to develop their own laboratory and classroom instructional guidelines, deal with professional development, communicate with colleagues, parents, etc. The NSTA (2007) identifies the following declarations as guidelines necessary to insure a safe and effective laboratory learning environment:

- Integrate laboratory investigations into science instruction so that all students—including students with academic, remedial, or physical needs; gifted and talented students; and English language learners—have the opportunity to participate in laboratory investigations in a safe environment (NSTA 2007).

- Be proactive in seeking professional development opportunities to learn and implement practices and procedures necessary to conduct safe laboratory science investigations, including storage, use, and disposal of materials and chemicals; use of personal protective equipment; engineering controls; and proper administrative procedures (Roy 2006).

- Request and encourage school and district leadership to provide necessary professional development opportunities for staff and take personal professional responsibility to learn and implement these safe practices and procedures into teaching.

- Exercise reasonable judgment when conducting laboratory investigations.

- Accept the duty of care to provide all students and staff with a safe environment while performing hands-on science investigations or demonstrations in the laboratory, classroom, or field setting; using, storing, disposing/recycling, or transporting chemicals; or engaging in other related activities.

- Modify or alter activities in a safe manner, or select alternative activities to perform, when in the exercise of their duty, they determine that the proposed activities cannot be performed safely or a safe environment cannot be maintained.

- Identify, document, and notify school and district officials about existing or potential safety issues that impact the learning environment, including hazards such as class-size overcrowding in violation of occupancy load codes (BOCA 1996, ICC 2003, NFPA 2006) or contrary to safety research (West et al., 2005), inadequate or defective equipment, inadequate number or size of labs, or improper facility design (Motz et al., 2007), and give necessary recommendations to correct the issue or rectify a particular situation. Overcrowding has two research-based safety concerns: sufficient supervision and adequate individual workspace. Classes containing more than 24 students engaged in science activities cannot safely be supervised by one teacher. Additionally, research data show that accidents rise dramatically as class enrollments exceed 24 students or when inadequate individual workspace is provided (West et al., 2005).

- Communicate fully and regularly (at least once quarterly) with administrators regarding issues impacting the provision of safe science instruction.

- Share the responsibility with school district officials in establishing and implementing written safety standards, policies, and procedures, and ensure their compliance.

- Understand the scope of the duty of care in acting as a reasonably prudent person in providing science instruction, and acknowledge the limitations of insurance in denying coverage for reckless and intentional acts, as well as the potential for individual liability for acts outside the course and scope of employment. [*See generally*, Restatement (Second) of Torts §202. 1965; Anderson et al. 1999, p. 398.]

REFERENCES

AAAS. (2009). Project 2061 Benchmarks: Science for all americans. New York: Oxford University Press.

Abd-El-Khalick, F., Bell, R. L., & Lederman, N. G. (1998). The nature of science and instructional practice: Making the unnatural natural. *Science Education, 82*(4), 417–436.

Belt, W., & Dunkleberger, G. (1985). Safety considerations for the biology teacher. *The American Biology Teacher, 47*(6), 340–345.

Hatton, J., Plouffe, P. B., & Cushing, J. T. (1999). Science and its ways of knowing. *American Journal of Physics, 67,* 360.

Lederman, N. G., & Zeidler, D. (1986). Science teachers. Paper presented at the 59th Annual Meeting of the National Association for Research in Science Teaching, San Francisco, CA.

McComas, W. F. (1998). *The nature of science in science education: Rationales and strategies.* Boston: Kluwer Academic Publishers.

National Research Council (USA). (1996). *National science education standards: Observe, interact, change, learn* National Academy Press.

National Science Teachers Association (NSTA). 2007. NSTA Position Statement: Liability of Science Educators for Laboratory Safety.

Smith, M. U., & Scharmann, L. C. (1999). Defining versus describing the nature of science: A pragmatic analysis for classroom teachers and science educators. *Science Education, 83*(4), 493–509.

Smith, M. U., & Siegel, H. (2004). Knowing, believing, and understanding: What goals for science education? *Science & Education, 13*(6), 553–582.

Strike, K. A., & Ternasky, P. L. (1993). Ethics for professionals in education: Perspectives for preparation and practice. New York: Teachers College Press.

Molecular and Cellular Biology

CHEMICAL BASIS OF LIFE

Matter—Atoms, Elements, Molecules

The study of matter is known as chemistry. In order to understand why cells behave the way they do, you must first understand some basic chemistry—the basic components of matter and how they interact. Matter is made up of basic substances called **elements**, which cannot be broken down into any other substance. The simplest unit of an element that retains the element's characteristics is known as an **atom**. All matter is made up of atoms. The properties of matter are a result of the structure of atoms and their interaction with each other.

Each atom of a given element has a **nucleus** containing a unique number of protons and about the same number of neutrons. The nucleus is surrounded by many electrons which have much less mass than protons and neutrons. Elements are listed by atomic number on the periodic table of the elements. The **atomic number** is the number of protons found in the nucleus of an atom of that element.

Protons, neutrons, and electrons also differ in their **charge**. In an uncharged atom, the number of protons is equal to the number of electrons. Electrons have much less mass than protons and neutrons. Electrons have a charge of –1, while protons have a charge of +1. Neutrons have no charge. The number of protons in the nucleus of an atom carries a positive charge equal to this number; that is, if an atom's nucleus contains 4 protons, the charge is + 4. Since positive and negative charges attract, the positive charges of the nucleus attract an equal number of negatively charged electrons. In an uncharged atom, the number of protons is equal to the number of electrons.

Electrons travel freely in a three-dimensional space that may be called an electron cloud, an electron shell, or an orbital. Current models of the atom follow the principles of quantum mechanics, which predict the probabilities of an electron being in a certain area at a certain time.

Figure 3.1 Periodic Table of the Elements

	1	2	3	4	5	6	7	8	9	10	11	12	13	14	15	16	17	18
1	1 H 1.01																	2 He 4.00
2	3 Li 6.94	4 Be 9.01											5 B 10.81	6 C 12.01	7 N 14.01	8 O 16.00	9 F 19.00	10 Ne 20.18
3	11 Na 22.99	12 Mg 24.30											13 Al 26.98	14 Si 28.09	15 P 30.97	16 S 32.07	17 Cl 35.45	18 Ar 39.95
4	19 K 39.10	20 Ca 40.08	21 Sc 44.96	22 Ti 47.87	23 V 50.94	24 Cr 52.00	25 Mn 54.94	26 Fe 55.84	27 Co 58.93	28 Ni 58.69	29 Cu 63.55	30 Zn 65.39	31 Ga 69.72	32 Ge 72.61	33 As 74.92	34 Se 78.96	35 Br 79.90	36 Kr 83.80
5	37 Rb 85.47	38 Sr 87.62	39 Y 88.91	40 Zr 91.22	41 Nb 92.91	42 Mo 95.94	43 Tc (98)	44 Ru 101.07	45 Rh 102.91	46 Pd 106.42	47 Ag 107.87	48 Cd 112.41	49 In 114.82	50 Sn 118.71	51 Sb 121.76	52 Te 127.60	53 I 126.90	54 Xe 131.29
6	55 Cs 132.91	56 Ba 137.33		72 Hf 178.49	73 Ta 180.95	74 W 183.84	75 Re 186.21	76 Os 190.23	77 Ir 192.22	78 Pt 195.08	79 Au 196.97	80 Hg 200.59	81 Tl 204.38	82 Pb 207.20	83 Bi 208.98	84 Po (209)	85 At (210)	86 Rn (222)
7	87 Fr (223)	88 Ra (226)		104 Rf (261)	105 Db (262)	106 Sg (263)	107 Bh (264)	108 Hs (265)	109 Mt (268)	110 Uun (269)	111 Uuu (272)	112 Uub (277)						

57 La 138.91	58 Ce 140.12	59 Pr 140.91	60 Nd 144.24	61 Pm (145)	62 Sm 150.36	63 Eu 151.96	64 Gd 157.25	65 Tb 158.93	66 Dy 162.50	67 Ho 164.93	68 Er 167.26	69 Tm 168.93	70 Yb 173.04	71 Lu 174.97
89 Ac (227)	90 Th 232.04	91 Pa 231.04	92 U 238.03	93 Np (237)	94 Pu (244)	95 Am (243)	96 Cm (247)	97 Bk (247)	98 Cf (251)	99 Es (252)	100 Fm (257)	101 Md (258)	102 No (259)	103 Lr (262)

Elements are listed by atomic number

Table 3.1 Common Names of Elements

ATOMIC NUMBER	SYMBOL	COMMON NAME
1	H	Hydrogen
2	He	Helium
6	C	Carbon
7	N	Nitrogen
8	O	Oxygen
11	Na	Sodium
12	Mg	Magnesium
14	Si	Silicon
15	P	Phosphorous
16	S	Sulphur
17	Cl	Chlorine
19	K	Potassium
20	Ca	Calcium
24	Cr	Chromium
26	Fe	Iron
29	Cu	Copper
30	Zn	Zinc
47	Ag	Silver
53	I	Iodine
79	Au	Gold
80	Hg	Mercury
82	Pb	Lead
86	Rn	Radon

Electrons travel freely in a three-dimensional space that may be called an electron cloud, an electron shell, or an orbital. Current models of the atom follow the principles of quantum mechanics, which predict the probabilities of an electron being in a certain area at a certain time. Although the term "orbital" is used, electrons do not orbit the nucleus like a planet orbiting a sun. The orbital (or electron cloud, or electron shell) represents a probability of finding an electron at a particular location.

Each shell has a particular amount of energy related to it, and is therefore also referred to as an **energy level**. Energy levels are designated by a number-letter combination (i.e., 1s, 2s, 2p. etc.). The quantum number of the energy level closest to the nucleus is 1, and progresses as the levels get farther from the nucleus (2, 3, etc.). The letter designation indicates the shape of that particular energy level. The energy level closest to the nucleus has the least energy related to it; the farthest has the most.

Each energy level has a limited capacity for holding electrons and each energy level requires a different number of electrons to fill it. Lower energy levels (closer to the nucleus) have less capacity for electrons than those farther from the nucleus. Since electrons are attracted to the nucleus, electrons fill the electron shells closest to the nucleus (lowest energy levels) first. Once a given level is full, electrons start filling the next level out. The outermost occupied energy level of an element is called the **valence shell**. The number of electrons in the valence shell determines the combinations that this atom will be likely to make with other atoms. Atoms are more stable when every electron is paired and are most stable when their valence shell is full. The tendency for an atom toward stability means that elements having unpaired or partially filled valence shells will easily gain or lose electrons in order to obtain a more stable configuration.

Chemical Bonds

The valence properties of atoms determine how they will bond with other atoms. Different types of bonds exist, and they form between the atoms that make up a molecule, between charged ions, or between different molecules with partial charges.

A **covalent bond** is formed between atoms when they share electrons. For instance, hydrogen has only one electron, which is unpaired, leaving the 1s valence shell one electron short of being full (2). Oxygen has 6 electrons in its valence shell; it needs 2 more electrons for its valence shell to be full (8). It is therefore easy for 2 hydrogen atoms to share their electrons with the oxygen, filling the effective valence shells of each.

Figure 3.2 Covalent Water Molecule

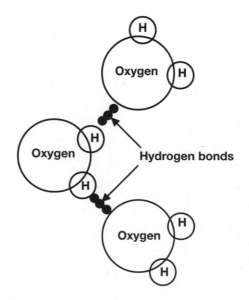

Covalent bonds are the strongest type of chemical bond. They result in a **molecule**, which is two or more atoms held together by covalently shared electrons. A **compound** is formed when two or more *different* atoms bond together chemically to form a unique substance (ex. H_2O, CH_4). (In contrast, two atoms of the *same* element covalently bonded, e.g., O_2, results in a molecular element.)

Another type of bond involves charged atoms, which are called **ions**. An uncharged atom may be more stable if its valence shell loses one or more electrons. It may lose one or more electrons to become a positively charged particle, or a positive ion. Similarly, an atom that gains one or more electrons to fill its valence shell becomes a negative ion. When such an exchange happens, the resulting oppositely-charged ions are attracted to each other and form an **ionic bond**. An example of a substance held together by ionic bonds is NaCl (sodium chloride or table salt). Ionic bonds are weaker than covalent bonds.

Some molecules have a weak, partial negative charge in one region of the molecule and a partial positive charge in another region. Molecules that have regions of partial charge are called **polar molecules**. For instance, water molecules (which have a net charge of 0) have a partial negative charge near the oxygen atom and a partial positive charge near each of the hydrogen atoms. Thus, when water molecules are close together, their positive regions are attracted to the negatively charged regions of nearby molecules; the negative regions are attracted to the positively charged regions of nearby molecules. The force of attraction between water molecules, shown above as a dotted line, is called a **hydrogen bond**. A hydrogen bond is a weak chemical bond that temporarily holds separate molecules together. For example, hydrogen bonds cause complementary strands of DNA to "zip" together to form a double strand.

Chemical Reactions

Chemical reactions occur when molecules interact with each other to form one or more molecules of another type. Chemical reactions that occur within cells provide energy, nutrients, and other products that allow the organism to function. Chemical reactions are symbolized by an equation where the reacting molecules (reactants) are shown on one side and the newly formed molecules (products) on the other, with an arrow indicating the direction of the reaction. There are several categories of chemical reactions. Some chemical reactions are simple, such as the breakdown of a compound into its components (a decomposition reaction).

A **simple combination reaction** is the reverse of decomposition. When one compound breaks apart and forms a new compound with a free reactant it is called a **replacement reaction**.

The Thermodynamics of Chemical Reactions

Chemical reactions may require an input of energy or they may release energy. Reactions that require energy are called **endothermic** reactions. Reactions that release energy are termed **exothermic**. Through endothermic reactions on the cellular level, living things are able to store chemical energy.

All chemical reactions are subject to the laws of thermodynamics. The first law of thermodynamics (also known as the law of conservation of matter and energy) states that matter and energy can neither be created nor destroyed. In other words, the sum of matter and energy of the reactants must equal that of the products. The second law of thermodynamics, or the law of increasing disorder (or entropy), asserts that all reactions spread energy, which tends to diminish its availability. So, although we know from the first law that the energy must be equal on both sides of a reaction equation, reaction processes also tend to degrade the potential energy into a form that cannot perform any cellular work. The energy available to perform the work of a reaction is known as **free energy**.

Properties of Water

Water has unique characteristics that are important to the processes of life. The transparent quality of water keeps it from disturbing processes within cells that require light (such as in photosynthetic and light-sensing cells).

The way water responds to temperature change is also unique. Most substances contract upon becoming a solid; however, water expands as it solidifies (freezes), forming a loose lattice structure (crystal). This crystalline form also makes frozen water (ice) less dense than liquid water. This accounts for lakes and other bodies of water freezing from the top first (the ice rises to the surface) insulating the water and organisms below from harsh temperature changes.

In addition, water has a high **specific heat**; it resists changes in temperature. The presence of water in an environment will tend to moderate otherwise harsh temperature changes. This is seen in the milder climates one experiences in regions near large bodies of water.

Hydrogen bonds between water molecules also give water a high **surface tension**, allowing small particles, and even some organisms (such as the water strider) to rest on the surface.

Because water is a **polar** molecule, it is able to dissolve many types of organic and inorganic substances. This property promotes several biological processes such as muscle contraction, nerve stimulation, and transport across membranes (permeability).

Because water molecules are polar, certain types of chemicals dissociate in water. Some chemicals yield protons and others accept protons when dissolved in water. An **acid** is a chemical that donates protons (H+ ions) when dissolved in water. A chemical that accepts protons (H+ ions) or donates hydronium ions (OH–) when dissolved in water is a **base**.

Because OH– and H+ ions combine to form water (H_2O), the presence of the base will lower the concentration of H+ ions. Acids and bases tend to neutralize each other when dissolved together in water. The neutralization of an acidic solution with a basic solution produces water and a salt (an ionic compound) from the original acid and base molecules.

Acidity, then, is a measure of the concentration of H+ ions in a solution, and is described by the **pH scale**. The pH of a substance can range from 0 (the highest possible concentration) to 14 (the lowest possible). A pH of 7 is neutral (as is pure water). A substance with pH below 7 is acidic and one with a pH above 7 is basic (or alkaline). The pH of biological substances, such as blood and extracellular fluid, and of the water surrounding living things, is important to the chemistry of life processes.

Buffers

A buffer is an aqueous combination of a weak acid and its conjugate base, or a weak base and its conjugate acid.

A buffer solution resists a change in pH when new H+ or OH– ions are added. The H+ ions react with the weak base to form water; the OH– ions react with the weak acid to form water.

Maximum buffer capacity occurs when pH = pKa for the weak acid. However, the buffering capacity will be exhausted if either the weak acid or the weak base are used up.

Chemical Structure of Organic Compounds

Organic compounds are the building blocks of all living things. The special properties exhibited by the various types of organic molecules allow for the specialized functions within the cells and tissue of living things. **Organic compounds** are defined as those that contain carbon. Organic molecules may also include hydrogen, oxygen, nitrogen, sulfur, phosphorous, and some metal ions. Organic substances include many types of molecules active in biological processes (or biomolecules), such as carbohydrates, lipids, proteins, and nucleic acids. Many biological molecules, including DNA and protein, are large **polymers** made up of many of the same or similar subunits, called **monomers**.

Carbohydrates are made up of only carbon, hydrogen, and oxygen atoms, in varying ratios. The ratio of hydrogen to oxygen in carbohydrates is always 2:1, just as in water (H_2O) – thus the name *carbo* (carbon) *hydrate* (plus water). Sugars and starches are both forms of carbohydrates.

All carbohydrates are made up of a basic sugar unit called a **monosaccharide**, which usually contains 3 to 7 carbon atoms along with oxygen and hydrogen. The most common monosaccharides are hexoses (six-carbon sugars); they usually have a ring-shaped (or cyclic) structure. Glucose is one of the most important monosaccharides in human metabolism, as cells prefer this as an energy source.

Figure 3.3 Structural formula of Cyclic Glucose (a common hexose).

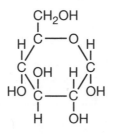

Two monosaccharide molecules may join together to form a **disaccharide** and liberate a molecule of water. Table sugar (sucrose) is a disaccharide of glucose and fructose (the most common monosaccharides). Glucose and fructose have the same chemical formula ($C_6H_{12}O_6$) but different arrangements of atoms; they are **isomers** of each other.

When three monosaccharides join together, the chain is then called a trisaccharide. When more than three merge the resultant molecule is known as a **polysaccharide**. Plant starches are the most familiar polysaccharides, and serve as energy storage within the plant's cells, to be broken down when energy is needed. Plants also synthesize starches that provide structure to their cells; the most common is a plant fiber known as **cellulose** (a long chain of water-insoluble polysaccharides).

Glycogen is a polysaccharide composed of many joined glucose units. Many animals use glycogen as a short-term storage molecule for energy. In mammals, glycogen is found in muscle and liver tissue.

Lipids

Lipids are organic compounds composed of carbon, hydrogen, and oxygen. Unlike carbohydrates, the ratio of hydrogen to oxygen in lipids is always greater than 2:1. Lipids include waxes, steroids, phospholipids, and fats.

Lipids are hydrophobic (literally, "water fearing") and will not dissolve in water. These various types of substances perform many functions within cells. Some form structural components of cell membranes (phospholipids), some provide moisture barriers (waxes), and others are primarily used to store energy (fats). Other lipids serve as vitamins or hormones.

Figure 3.4 Production of Fat.
The bonding of three fatty acids to a molecule of glycerol produces a
fat (triglyceride) molecule and releases 3 water molecules. The release of water allows for the compacting
of the high-energy fatty acids into a more concentrated form—the fat molecule.

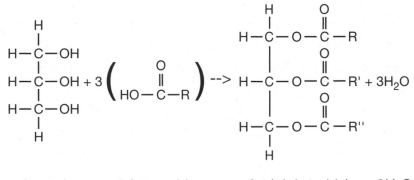

glycerol   +   3 fatty acids   =   fat (triglyceride) + 3H$_2$O

Fats are highly efficient lipid molecules used for long-term energy storage. When an organism takes in more carbohydrates than are necessary for its current energy use, the excess is stored as fat molecules. These molecules "store" a lot of energy in a dense amount of mass, making it available to be used later. In addition to storing energy, fats also function in organisms to provide a protective layer that insulates internal organs and maintains heat within the body.

Proteins

Present in every living cell, **proteins** are large un-branched polymers made up of amino acid monomers. **Amino acids** are cyclical molecules that contain carbon, hydrogen, oxygen, nitrogen, and sometimes sulfur and phosphorous. In plants and animals, there are twenty common amino acids that can combine in various sequences to form thousands of different proteins. Amino acids are connected into chains by a water-releasing (dehydration) reaction that forms **peptide bonds**. For this reason, proteins may also be called **polypeptides**.

Proteins found in living things may have dozens or hundreds of amino acids. The long, linear strings of amino acids form unique shapes by folding up in various ways. The three-dimensional shape of a protein molecule is the characteristic that allows it to perform its specific functions within cells.

Enzymes are special proteins that act as catalysts for reactions. A catalyst is a substance that changes the speed of a reaction without being affected itself. Enzyme names have the suffix -*ase* (such as polymerase, lactase).

Nucleic Acids

There are two groups of nucleic acids: **deoxyribonucleic acid (DNA)** and **ribonucleic acid (RNA)**. They are both polymers composed of chains of nucleotide monomers.

Each **nucleotide** has a five-carbon sugar (pentose) attached to a phosphate group and a **nitrogenous base**, which gives each nucleotide its unique chemical identity. Nucleotides join to form DNA or RNA, with alternating sugar and phosphate groups forming the backbone of the long molecule. In DNA, the sugar molecule is deoxyribose; in RNA it is ribose.

Figure 3.5 A DNA Molecule.
Each molecule of DNA consists of a chain of nucleotides
(each containing a phosphate group, a sugar, and a nitrogenous base).
1\110chains bond together with hydrogen bonds, forming a double-helix structure.

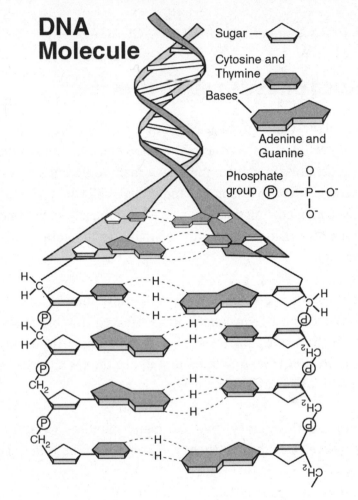

The **nitrogen bases** in DNA include **adenine**, **cytosine**, **guanine**, and **thymine** (A, C, G, and T). These parts of the nucleotides can hydrogen-bond to form complementary pairs. That is, cytosine (C) and guanine (G) form hydrogen bonds and therefore pair together, while thymine (T) hydrogen bonds with adenine (A). Via hydrogen bonding, two complimentary DNA strands pair up to form a shape like a twisted ladder. This double-helix structure of DNA was discovered and modeled by two scientists, James Watson and Francis Crick in the 1950s. It is therefore known as the Watson-Crick model of DNA.

In RNA, thymine is replaced by the base **uracil** (U). RNA chains are generally single strands, but can pair up with a complimentary DNA strand. **Complementary** strands have sequences of nucleotides that can **base-pair** (hydrogen bond) with each other.

DNA strand: CTAATGTCATGTAT

Complementary DNA strand: GATTAGAGTACATA

Complementary RNA strand: GAUUAGAGUACAUA

CELL STRUCTURE AND FUNCTION

The **cell** is the smallest and most basic unit of most living things (organisms). A single organism can be unicellular (consisting of just one cell), or multicellular (consisting of many cells). A multicellular organism may have many different types of cells that differ in structure to serve different functions. Individual cells may contain organelles that assist them with specialized functions. For example, muscle cells tend to contain more mitochondria (organelles that make energy available to the cells) since muscle requires the use of extra energy.

Scientists first began to describe cells after the invention of the light microscope in the mid-1600s. Antoine van Leeuwenhoek first observed tiny organisms (he called them "animalcules") with the use of microscopes. We now know these tiny organisms were one-celled bacteria. Robert Hooke was the first to use the term "cells" when he observed cell walls of dead cork under a light microscope.

In the mid-nineteenth century, two German scientists (Matthias Schleiden and Theodor Schwann) developed the **cell theory**. It consists of the following tenets:

1. All living things are made up of one or more cells.

2. Cells are the basic units of life.

3. All cells come from pre-existing cells.

These tenets of the cell theory developed by scientists over 150 years ago are still held today.

The light microscope is useful in examining most cells and some cell organelles (such as the nucleus). However, many cell organelles are very small and require the magnification and resolution power of an **electron microscope**.

There are two main types of cells: prokaryotic and eukaryotic. **Prokaryotes** are very simple; they have no nucleus or any other membrane-bound structures. The DNA in prokaryotic cells usually forms a single chromosome, which floats within the cytoplasm. Prokaryotic organisms are unicellular and include all bacteria.

Plant, fungi, and animal cells, as well as protozoa, are eukaryotic. **Eukaryotic cells** contain membrane-bound intracellular organelles (cell components that perform particular functions), including a nucleus. The DNA within eukaryotes is organized into chromosomes.

All cells are enclosed within the **cell membrane** (or plasma membrane). Near the center of each eukaryotic cell is the **nucleus**, which contains the chromosomes. Between the nucleus and the cell membrane, the cell is filled with **cytoplasm**. Since all of the organelles outside the nucleus but within the cell membrane exist within the cytoplasm, they are called **cytoplasmic organelles**.

The shape and size of cells can vary widely. The longest nerve cells (neurons) may extend over a meter in length with an approximate diameter of only 4-100 micrometers (1 millimeter = 1,000 micrometers, μm). A human egg cell may be 100 micrometers in diameter. The average size of a bacterium is 0.5 to 2.0 micrometers. However, most cells are between 0.5 and 100 micrometers in diameter. The size of a cell is limited by the ratio of its volume to its surface area. In the illustration below, note the variation of shape of cells within the human body:

Figure 3.6 Varying Cell Types.
The six sketches of human cell types show some of the diversity in shape and size among cells with varying functions. The sketches are not sized to scale.

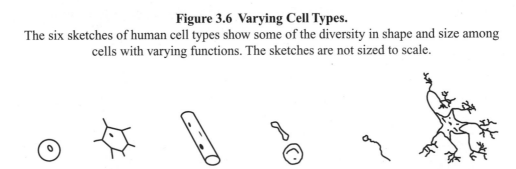

egg cell   epithelial cell   muscle cell   red blood cell   sperm cell   nerve cell
(ovum)   (cheek)   (no nucleus)   (neuron)

Animal cells differ in structure and function from cells of plants, fungi, and protists. For example, the photosynthetic cells have the added job of producing food, so they are equipped with specialized organelles. Plant cells also have a central vacuole and cell walls, structures not found in animal cells.

Figure 3.7 Viruses and Cells.
Viruses are much smaller than cells, ranging from approximately 0.05 – 0.1 micrometers.
The prokaryotic cell has no nucleus or other membrane-bound organelles and is approximately
1-10 micrometers in diameter. The eukaryotic cell has membrane-bound organelles,
including a nucleus containing the chromosomes. Eukaryotic cells are
approximately 10-100 micrometers in diameter.

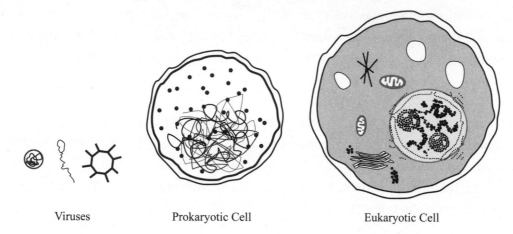

Viruses   Prokaryotic Cell   Eukaryotic Cell

Viruses are much smaller than even the smallest cells. Scientists do not agree as to whether viruses are actually alive. Although they can reproduce, they do not have the ability to conduct metabolic functions on their own. Virus structure consists of only a protein capsule, DNA, or RNA, and sometimes enzymes. Viruses survive and replicate by invading a living cell. The virus then utilizes the cell's mechanisms to reproduce itself, sometimes destroying the cell in the process.

The cell membrane is an especially important cell organelle with a unique structure that allows it to control movement of substances into and out of the cell. Made up of a fluid **phospholipid bilayer**, proteins, and carbohydrates, this extremely thin (approximately 80 angstroms) membrane can only be seen clearly with an electron microscope. The **selective permeability** of the cell membrane serves to manage the concentration of substances within the cell.

Figure 3.8 Cell Membrane.
A phospholipid bilayer with embedded globular proteins.

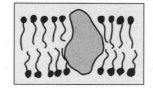

Substances can cross the cell membrane by passive transport, facilitated diffusion, or active transport. **Facilitated diffusion** does not require added energy, but it cannot occur without the help of specialized proteins. Transport requiring energy output from the cell is called **active transport**. During **passive transport**, substances freely pass across the membrane without the cell expending any energy.

Simple diffusion is one type of passive transport. **Diffusion** is the process whereby molecules and ions flow through the cell membrane from an area of higher concentration to an area of lower concentration (thus tending to equalize concentrations). Where the substance exists in higher concentration, collisions occur, which tend to propel them away toward lower concentrations. Diffusion generally is the means of transport for ions and molecules that can slip between the lipid molecules of the membrane. Diffusion requires no added energy to propel substances through a membrane.

Figure 3.9 Diffusion.
CO_2 diffuses out of the cell since its concentration is higher inside the cell.
O_2 diffuses into the cell because its concentration is higher outside. Molecules diffuse from areas of high concentration to areas of lower concentration.

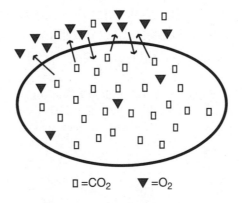

☐ = CO_2 ▼ = O_2

Another type of passive transport is **osmosis**, a special process of diffusion occurring only with water molecules. Osmosis does not require the addition of any energy, but occurs when the water concentration inside the cell differs from the concentration outside the cell. The water on the side of the membrane with the highest water concentration will move through the membrane until the concentration is equalized on both sides. When the water concentration is equal inside and outside the cell, it is called isomotic or isotonic. For instance, a cell placed in a salty solution will tend to lose water until the solution outside the cell has the same concentration of water molecules as the cytoplasm (the solution inside the cell).

Figure 3.10 Osmosis.
Water crosses the membrane into a cell that has a higher concentration of sugar molecules
than the surrounding solution. Water crosses the membrane to leave the cell
when there is a higher concentration of Na$^+$ ions outside the cell than inside the cell.

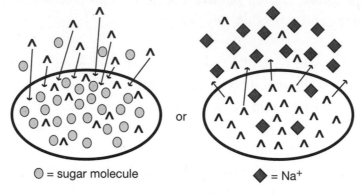

⬭ = sugar molecule   ◆ = Na$^+$

∧ = water molecule

Facilitated diffusion allows for transfer of substances across the cell membrane with the help of specialized proteins. These proteins, which are embedded in the cell membrane, are able to pick up specific molecules or ions and transport them through the membrane. The special protein molecules allow the diffusion of molecules and ions that cannot otherwise pass through the lipid bilayer.

Figure 3.11 Facilitated Diffusion.
Specialized proteins embedded in the cell membrane permit passage
of substances of a particular shape and size.

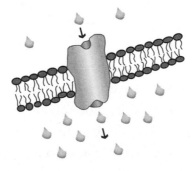

Active transport, like facilitated diffusion, requires membrane-bound proteins. Unlike facilitated diffusion, active transport uses energy to move molecules across a cell membrane against a concentration gradient (in the opposite direction than they would go under normal diffusion circumstances). With the addition of the energy obtained from ATP, a protein molecule embedded in the membrane changes shape and moves a molecule across the membrane against the concentration gradient.

Large molecules are not able to pass through the cell membrane, but may be engulfed by the cell membrane. **Endocytosis** is the process whereby large molecules (i.e., some sugars or proteins) are taken up into a pocket of membrane. The pocket pinches off, delivering the molecules, still inside a membrane sack, into the cytoplasm. This process, for instance, is used by white blood cells to engulf bacteria. **Exocytosis** is the reverse process, exporting substances from the cell.

Animal Cells

Figure 3.12 A Generalized Animal Cell (cross-section).

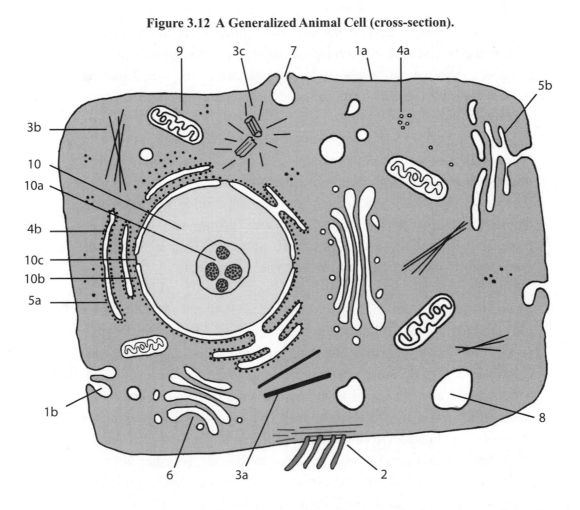

Since there are many types of animal cells, the diagram is generalized. In other words, some animal cells will have all of these organelles, others will not. However, this illustration will give you a composite picture of the organelles within the typical animal cell. It is also important to note the function of each organelle. Each labeled component is explained by the corresponding text in the section below.

1. The **cell membrane (1a)** encloses the cell and separates it from the environment. It may also be called a plasma membrane. This membrane is composed of a double layer (bilayer) of phospholipids with globular proteins embedded within the layers. The membrane is extremely thin (about 80 angstroms; 10 million angstroms = 1 millimeter) and elastic. The combination of the lipid bilayer and the proteins embedded within it allows the cell to determine what molecules and ions can pass, and regulate the rate at which they enter and leave.

   Endocytic vesicles (1b) form when the plasma membrane of a cell surrounds a particle outside the cell, then pinches off and releases a membrane-bound sack containing the particle into the cytoplasm. This process allows the cell to absorb larger molecules than would be able to pass through the cell membrane, or that need to remain packaged within the cell.

2. **Microvilli** are projections of the cell extending from the cell membrane. Microvilli are found in certain types of cells, for example, those involved in absorption (such as the cells lining the intestine). These filaments increase the surface area of the cell membrane, increasing the area available to absorb nutrients. They also contain enzymes involved in digesting certain types of nutrients.

3. The **cytoskeleton** provides structural support to a cell. **Microtubules (3a)** are long, hollow, cylindrical protein filaments, which give structure to the cell. These filaments are scattered around the edges of a cell and form a sort of loose skeleton or framework for the cytoplasm. Microtubules also are found at the base of cilia or flagella (organelles which allow some cells to move on their own) and give these organelles the ability to move. **Microfilaments (3b)** are double-stranded chains of proteins, which serve to give structure to the cell. Together with the larger microtubules, microfilaments form the cytoskeleton, providing stability and structure. **Centrioles (3c)** are structural components of many cells, and are particularly common in animal cells. Centrioles are tubes constructed of a geometrical arrangement of microtubules in a pinwheel shape. Their function includes the formation of new microtubules, but is primarily the formation of structural skeleton around which cells split during mitosis and meiosis.

Figure 3.13 Cross-section of a Centriole.
Centrioles are tubes constructed of a geometrical arrangement
of microtubules in a pinwheel shape.

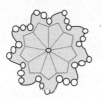

4. **Ribosomes** are the site of protein synthesis within cells. Ribosomes are composed of certain protein molecules and RNA molecules (ribosomal RNAs, or rRNAs). **Free ribosomes (4a)** float unattached within the cytoplasm. The proteins synthesized by free ribosomes are made for use in the cytoplasm, not within membrane-bound organelles. **Attached ribosomes (4b)** are attached to the ER (see No. 5). Proteins made at the site of attached ribosomes are destined for use within the membrane-bound organelles.

5. The **endoplasmic reticulum**, a large organization of folded membranes, is responsible for the delivery of lipids and proteins to certain areas within the cytoplasm (a sort of intra-cellular highway). **Rough endoplasmic reticulum** or **RER (5a)** has attached ribosomes. In addition to packaging and transport of materials within the cell, the RER is instrumental to protein synthesis. **Smooth endoplasmic reticulum** or **SER (5b)** is a network of membranous channels. Smooth endoplasmic reticulum does not have attached ribosomes. The endoplasmic reticulum is responsible for processing lipids, fats, and steroids, which are then packaged and dispersed by the Golgi apparatus.

6. The **Golgi apparatus** (also known as Golgi bodies or the Golgi complex) is instrumental in the storing, packaging, and shipping of proteins. The Golgi apparatus looks much like stacks of hollow pancakes and is constructed of folded membranes. Within these membranes, cellular products are stored, or packaged by closing off a bubble of membrane with the proteins or lipids inside. These packages are shipped (via the endoplasmic reticulum) to the part of the cell where they will be used, or to the cell membrane for secretion from the cell.

7. **Secretory vesicles** are packets of material packaged by either the Golgi apparatus or the endoplasmic reticulum. Secretory vesicles carry substances produced within the cell (a protein, for example) to the cell membrane. The vesicle membrane fuses with the cell membrane in a process called **exocytosis**, allowing the substance to escape the cell.

8. **Lysosomes** are membrane-bound organelles containing digestive enzymes. Lysosomes break down unused material within the cell, damaged organelles, or materials absorbed by the cell for use.

9. **Mitochondria** are centers of cellular respiration (the process of breaking up covalent bonds within sugar molecules with the intake of oxygen and release of ATP, adenosine tri-phosphate). Mitochondria (plural of mitochondrion) are more numerous in cells requiring more energy (muscle, etc.). Mitochondria are self-replicating, containing their own DNA, RNA, and ribosomes. They have a double membrane; the internal membrane is folded. Cellular respiration reactions occur along the folds of the internal membrane (called **cristae**). Mitochondria are thought to be an evolved form of primitive bacteria (prokaryotic cells) that lived in a symbiotic relationship with eukaryotic cells more than 2 billion years ago. This concept, known as the **endosymbiont hypothesis**, is a plausible explanation of how mitochondria, which have many of the necessary components for life on their own, became an integral part of eukaryotic cells.

10. The **nucleus** is an organelle surrounded by two lipid bilayer membranes. The nucleus contains chromosomes, nuclear pores, nucleoplasm, and a nucleolus. The **nucleolus (10a)** is a rounded area within the nucleus of the cell where ribosomal RNA is synthesized. This rRNA is incorporated into ribosomes after exiting the nucleus. Several nucleoli (plural of nucleolus) can exist within a nucleus. The **nuclear membrane (10b)** is the boundary between the nucleus and the cytoplasm. The nuclear membrane is actually a double membrane, which allows for the entrance and exit of certain molecules through the nuclear pores. **Nuclear pores (10c)** are points at which the double nuclear membrane fuses together, forming a passageway between the

inside of the nucleus and the cytoplasm outside the nucleus. Nuclear pores allow the cell to selectively move molecules in and out of the nucleus. There are many pores scattered about the surface of the nuclear membrane.

Plant Cells

Figure 3.14 A Typical Plant Cell.

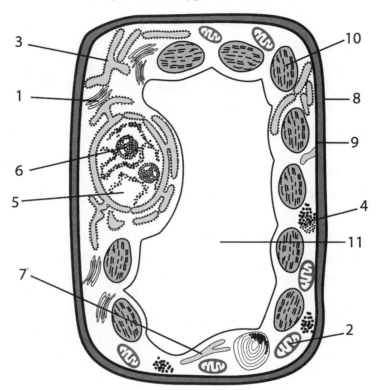

The structure of plant cells differs noticeably from animal cells with the addition of three organelles: the cell wall, the chloroplasts, and the central vacuole. In Figure 3.14, the organelles numbered 1 to 7 function the same way in plant cells as in animal cells (see above).

1. **Golgi apparatus**

2. **Mitochondria**

3. **Rough endoplasmic reticulum**

4. **Ribosome**

5. **Nucleus**

6. **Nucleolus**

7. **Smooth endoplasmic reticulum**

8. **Cell walls** surround plant cells. (Bacteria also have cell walls.) Cell walls are made of cellulose and lignin, making them strong and rigid (whereas the cell membrane is relatively weak and flexible). The cell wall encloses the cell membrane, providing strength and protection for the cell. The cell wall allows plant cells to store water under relatively high concentration. The combined strength of a plant's cell walls provides support for the whole organism. Dry wood and cork are essentially the cell walls of dead plants. The structure of the cell wall allows substances to pass through it readily, so transport in and out of the cell is still regulated by the cell membrane.

9. The **cell membrane** (or plasma membrane) functions in plant and animal cells in the same way. However, in some plant tissues, channels connect the cytoplasm of adjacent cells.

10. **Chloroplasts** are found in plant cells (and also in some protists). Chloroplasts are the site of photosynthesis within plant cells. **Chlorophyll** pigment molecules give the chloroplast their green color, although the chloroplasts also contain yellow and red carotenoid pigments. In the fall, as chloroplasts lose chlorophyll, these pigments are revealed, giving leaves their red and yellow colors. The body (or **stroma**) of the chloroplast contains embedded stacked, disk-like plates (called **grana**), which are the site of photosynthetic reactions.

11. The **central vacuole** takes up much of the volume of plant cells. It is a membrane-bound fluid-filled space, which stores water and soluble nutrients for the plant's use. The tendency of the central vacuole to absorb water provides for the rigid shape (turgidity) of some plant cells. (Animal cells may also contain vacuoles for varying purposes,

and these too are membrane-bound, fluid-filled spaces. For instance, contractile vacuoles perform the specific function of expelling waste and excess water from single-celled organisms.)

Enzymes are protein molecules that act as catalysts for organic reactions. (A catalyst is a substance that lowers the activation energy of a reaction. A catalyst is not consumed in the reaction.) Enzymes do not make reactions possible that would not otherwise occur under the right energy conditions, but they lower the activation energy, which increases the rate of the reaction.

Figure 3.15 Effect of Enzyme on a Reaction.
Adding an enzyme lowers the activation energy for a reaction.

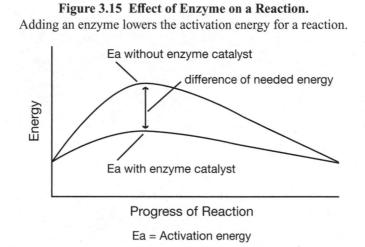

Enzymes are named ending with the letters -*ase*, and usually begin with a syllable describing the catalyzed reaction (i.e., hydrolase catalyzes hydrolysis reactions, lactase catalyzes the breakdown of the sugar lactose). Thousands of reactions occur within cells, each controlled by one or more enzymes. Enzymes are synthesized within the cell at the ribosomes, as all proteins are.

Enzymes are effective catalysts because of their unique shapes. Each enzyme has a uniquely shaped area, called its **active site**. For each enzyme, there is a particular substance known as its **substrate**, which fits within the active site (like a hand in a glove). When the substrate is seated in the active site, the combination of two molecules is called the **enzyme-substrate complex**. An enzyme can bind to two substrates and catalyze the formation of a new chemical bond, linking the two substrates. An enzyme may also bind to a single substrate and catalyze the breaking of a chemical bond, releasing two products. Once the reaction has taken place, the unchanged enzyme is released.

The operation of enzymes lowers the energy needed to initiate cellular reactions. However, the completion of the reaction may either require or release energy. Remember from earlier in this chapter that reactions requiring energy are called endothermic reactions. Reactions that release energy are called exothermic reactions. Endothermic reactions can take place in a cell by being coupled to the breakdown of ATP or a similar molecule. Exothermic reactions are coupled to the production of ATP or another molecule with high-energy chemical bonds.

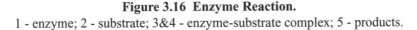

Figure 3.16 Enzyme Reaction.
1 - enzyme; 2 - substrate; 3&4 - enzyme-substrate complex; 5 - products.

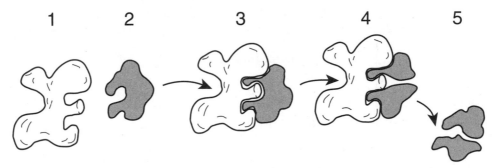

Some enzymatic reactions require a non-protein substance called a **cofactor**. The cofactor binds to the active site. This allows the substrate to fit into the active site. Some cofactors are inorganic. **Inorganic cofactors** include metal ions—for example, iron, copper, or zinc. Other cofactors are organic molecules. **Organic cofactors** are also called **coenzymes**. Some coenzymes are not made by cells but must be obtained in the diet. Most vitamins are coenzymes (or precursors of coenzymes). **Prosthetic groups** are similar to cofactors; they also facilitate the enzyme reaction. However, prosthetic groups are bound to the enzyme, rather than being separate atoms or molecules.

In some cases, other substances compete to attach to an enzyme's active site. If one of these substances, known as an **inhibitor**, attaches to the enzyme first, the cellular reaction will not take place. Environmental conditions within the cell, such as high temperature or acidity, may also inhibit an enzymatic reaction. These conditions may change the shape of the active site and render the enzyme ineffective.

Enzyme reactions may also be controlled by mechanisms within the cell. Enzyme control (or **regulation**) may occur when the product of the reaction is also an inhibitor to the reaction. This slows down the production rate as the concentration of the product increases. In other cases, a particular molecule serves as a regulator, by changing the structure of the active site and thus making the enzyme more or less effective.

Energy Transformations

All living things require energy. Ultimately, the source of most energy for life on Earth is the sun. Photosynthetic organisms (plants, some protists, and some bacteria) are able to harvest solar energy and transform it into chemical energy eventually stored within covalent bonds of molecules (such as carbohydrates, fats, and proteins). These organisms are called primary producers. Consumers eat producers and utilize the chemical energy stored in them to carry on the functions of life. Other organisms then consume the consumers. In each of these steps along the food chain, some energy is lost as heat (see discussion of thermodynamic laws earlier in this chapter).

Cellular metabolism is a general term, which includes all types of energy transformation processes, including photosynthesis, respiration, growth, movement, etc. Energy transformations occur as chemicals are broken apart or synthesized within the cell. The process whereby cells build molecules and store energy (in the form of chemical bonds) is called **anabolism**. **Catabolism** is the process of breaking down molecules and releasing stored energy.

ATP

ATP (adenosine triphosphate) is known as the energy currency of cellular activity. While energy is stored in the form of carbohydrates, fats, and proteins, the amount of energy contained within the bonds of any of these substances would overwhelm (and thus kill) a cell if released at once. In order for the energy to be released in small packets usable to a cell, large molecules need to be broken down in steps. ATP is an efficient storage molecule for the energy needed for cellular processes. ATP consists of a nitrogenous base (adenine), a simple sugar (ribose), and three phosphate groups. When a cellular process requires energy, a molecule of ATP can be broken down into ADP (adenosine diphosphate) plus a phosphate group. Even more energy is released when ATP is decomposed into AMP (adenosine monophosphate) plus two phosphate groups. Coupling these energy-releasing reactions with energy-absorbing reactions allows the cell to carry out its functions.

Photosynthesis

The process of **photosynthesis** includes a crucial set of reactions. These reactions convert the light energy of the sun into chemical energy usable by living things. Photosynthetic organisms use the converted energy for their own life processes, and also store energy that may be used by organisms that consume them.

Although the process of photosynthesis actually occurs through many small steps, the entire process can be summed up with the following equation:

$$6CO_2 + 6H_2O + \text{light energy} \rightarrow C_6H_{12}O_6 + 6O_2$$
$$(\text{carbon dioxide} + \text{water} \rightarrow \text{glucose} + \text{oxygen})$$

Chlorophyll is a green pigment (a pigment is a substance that absorbs light energy) which is able to absorb a photon of light, allowing photosynthesis to occur. Chlorophyll is contained in the grana of the chloroplast (see discussion of plant cells earlier in this chapter). It is not used up in the photosynthetic process, but must be present for the reactions to occur. There are two phases of the photosynthetic process, the light reaction, or photolysis, and the dark reaction, or CO_2 fixation. Energy from the sun is transformed by photosynthetic organisms into chemical energy in the form of ATP.

During the **light reaction (photolysis)**, the chlorophyll pigment absorbs a photon of light, leaving the chlorophyll in an excited (higher energy) state. The light reaction is a decomposition reaction, which separates water molecules into hydrogen and oxygen atoms utilizing the energy from the excited chlorophyll pigment. The oxygen atoms from the water combine to form O_2 (gas) and are released into the environment. The free hydrogen is grabbed and held by a particular molecule (called the hydrogen acceptor) until it is needed. The excited chlorophyll also supplies energy to a series of reactions that produce ATP from ADP and inorganic phosphate (Pi).

The **dark reaction (CO_2 fixation)** then occurs in the stroma of the chloroplast. This second phase of photosynthesis does not require light; however, it does require the use of the products (hydrogen and ATP) of photolysis. In a multi-step process, six CO_2 molecules are linked with hydrogen (produced in photolysis) forming glucose (a six-carbon sugar). Glucose molecules can then be linked to form polysaccharides (starch or sugars), which are then stored in the cell.

Cellular Respiration

Unlike photosynthesis (which only occurs in photosynthetic cells), respiration occurs in all cells. Respiration breaks down molecules and releases energy for use by the cell. There are several steps involved in cellular respiration. Some require oxygen (that is, they are **aerobic**) and some do not (they are **anaerobic** reactions).

Glycolysis is the breaking down of glucose into smaller carbon-containing molecules; these breakdown reactions yield ATP (glyco = sugar, lysis = breakdown). It is the first step in all respiration pathways and occurs in the cytoplasm of all living cells. Each molecule of glucose (six carbons) is broken down into two molecules of pyruvic acid (or pyruvate) with three carbons each, two ATP molecules, and two hydrogen atoms (attached to NADH, nicotinamide adenine dinucleotide). This is an **anaerobic reaction** (no oxygen is required). The process of glycolysis is summarized by the following chemical equation:

$$\text{glucose (6 C)} + 2ADP + 2\ Pi + 2NAD^+ \rightarrow 2\text{ pyruvic acid (3 C each)} + 2ATP + 2NADH + 2H^+$$

After glycolysis, respiration will continue on one of two pathways, depending upon whether oxygen is present.

Aerobic Pathways

Aerobic respiration (in the presence of oxygen) begins with glycolysis and proceeds through two major steps, the **Krebs cycle** (also known as the citric acid cycle) and **electron transport**. The first step, the Krebs cycle, occurs in the matrix of a cell's mitochondria and breaks down pyruvic acid molecules (three carbons each) into CO_2, H^+ (protons), and 2 ATP molecules. The Krebs cycle also liberates electrons, which then enter the next step.

The second step occurs along the **electron transport system**, or ETS, which captures the energy released by the Krebs cycle. The ETS is a series of **cytochromes** on the cristae of the mitochondria. Cytochromes are pigment molecules, which include a protein and a **heme** (iron-containing) group. The iron in heme groups may be either oxidized (loses electron to form Fe^{+3}) or reduced (gains electron to form Fe^{+2}) as electrons are passed along the ETS. As electrons pass from one cytochrome to another, energy is given off. Some of this energy is lost as heat; the rest is stored in molecules of ATP. This process can produce the most ATP per cycle, 32 ATP molecules per glucose molecule. The final step of the electron transport chain occurs when the last electron carrier transfers two electrons to an oxygen atom that simultaneously combines with two protons from the surrounding medium to produce water.

Anaerobic Pathways

If no oxygen is present within the cell, respiration will proceed anaerobically after glycolysis. Anaerobic respiration is also called **fermentation**. Anaerobic respiration breaks down the two pyruvic acid molecules (three carbons each) into end products (such as ethyl alcohol, C_2H_6O or lactic acid $C_3H_6O_3$), plus carbon dioxide (CO_2). The net gain from anaerobic respiration is two ATP molecules per glucose molecule. Fermentation is not as efficient as aerobic respiration; it uses only a small part of the energy available in a glucose molecule.

MOLECULAR BASIS OF HEREDITY

Earlier in this chapter, the Watson-Crick model of DNA was discussed. Watson and Crick were responsible for explaining the structure of the DNA molecule, which laid the foundation of our current understanding of the function of chromosomes and genes. Today, through the discoveries of these two scientists, and through the collaborative work of scientists worldwide, the study of chromosomes and genetic inheritance has proceeded to discover the intricacies of the **genomes** (sum total of genetic information) of many organisms, including humans. The study of genomes has developed further to include **genome mapping**, which allows fragments of DNA to be assigned to specific chromosomes. Maps are created for specific species based on results of studies of the genetic material found within that species.

A **gene** is a length of DNA that encodes a particular protein. Each protein the cell synthesizes performs a specific function in the cell. The function of one protein, or the function of a group of proteins, is called a **trait**.

DNA Replication

In order to replicate, a portion of a DNA molecule unwinds, separating the two halves of the double helix. (This separation is aided by the enzyme helicase.) Another enzyme (DNA polymerase) binds to each strand and moves along them as it connects nucleotides using the original DNA strands as templates. The new strand is complementary to the original template and forms a new double helix with one of the parent strands. If no errors occur during DNA synthesis, the result is two identical double helix molecules of DNA.

The process of DNA replication, however, is occasionally subject to a mistake known as a **mutation**. All the DNA of every cell of every organism is copied repeatedly to form new cells for growth, repair, and reproduction. A mutation can result from an error that randomly occurs during replication. Mutations can also result from damage to DNA caused by exposure to certain chemicals, such as some solvents or the chemicals in cigarette smoke, or by radiation, such as ultraviolet radiation in sunlight or x-rays. Cells have built-in mechanisms for finding and repairing most DNA errors, however, they do not fix them all. The result of a DNA error, a mutation, in most cases expresses itself in a change (small or large) in the cell structure and function.

DNA carries the information for making all the proteins a cell can make. The DNA information for making a particular protein can be called the gene for that protein. Genetic traits are expressed as a result of the combination of proteins encoded by the DNA of a cell. Protein synthesis occurs in two steps called transcription and translation.

Transcription refers to the formation of an RNA molecule, which corresponds to a gene. The DNA strand "unzips"; individual RNA nucleotides are strung together to match the DNA sequence by the enzyme RNA polymerase. The new RNA strand (known as messenger RNA or **mRNA**) migrates from the nucleus to the cytoplasm, where it is modified in a process known as **post-transcriptional processing**. This processing prepares the mRNA for protein synthesis by removing the non-coding sequences. In the processed RNA, each unit of three nucleotides or **codon** encodes a particular amino acid.

The next phase of protein synthesis is called **translation**. In order for the protein synthesis process to continue, a second type of RNA is required, transfer RNA or **tRNA**. Transfer RNA is the link between the "language" of nucleotides (codon and anticodon) and the "language" of amino acids (hence the word "translation"). Transfer RNA is a chain of about 80 nucleotides. At one point along the tRNA chain, there are three unattached bases, which are called the anticodon. This anticodon will line up with a corresponding codon during translation. Each tRNA molecule also has an attached, specific amino acid.

Translation occurs at the ribosomes. A ribosome is a structure composed of proteins and ribosomal RNA (rRNA). A ribosome attaches to the mRNA strand at a particular codon known as the start codon. This codon is only recognized by a particular initiator tRNA. The ribosome continues to add tRNA whose anticodons make complementary bonds with the next codon on the mRNA string, forming a peptide bond between amino acids as each amino acid is held in place by a tRNA. At the end of the translation process, a terminating codon stops the synthesis process and the protein is released.

Structural and Regulatory Genes

Genes encode proteins of two varieties. **Structural genes** code proteins that form organs and structural characteristics. **Regulatory genes** code proteins that determine functional or physiological events, such as growth. These proteins regulate when other genes start or stop encoding proteins, which in turn produce specific traits.

Transduction and Transformation

In most organisms, DNA replication preserves a continuity of traits throughout the organism's lifespan. However, the genetic makeup of bacteria can be changed through one of two processes, transduction or transformation. **Transduction** is the transfer of genetic material (portions of a bacterial chromosome) from one bacterial cell to another. The transfer is mediated by a bacteriophage (a virus that targets bacteria). Bacteria may also absorb and incorporate pieces of DNA from their environment (usually from dead bacterial cells), a process called **transformation**.

Cell Division

The process of cell reproduction is called **cell division**. The process of cell division centers on the replication and separation of strands of **DNA**.

Structure of Chromosomes

Chromosomes are long chains of subunits called **nucleosomes**. Each nucleosome is composed of a short length of DNA wrapped around a core of small proteins called **histones**. The combination of DNA with histones is called **chromatin**. Each nucleosome is about 11 nm in diameter (a nanometer is one billionth of a meter) and contains a central core of eight histones with the DNA double helix wrapped around them. Each gene spans dozens of nucleosomes. The DNA plus histone strings are then tightly packed and coiled, forming chromatin.

In a cell that is getting ready to divide, each strand of chromatin is duplicated. The two identical strands (called **chromatids**) remain attached to each other at a point called the **centromere**. During cell division, the chromatin strands become more tightly coiled and packed, forming a chromosome, which is visible in a light microscope. At this stage, a chromosome consists of two identical chromatids, held together at the centromere, giving each chromosome an **X** shape.

Figure 3.17 A Chromosome.

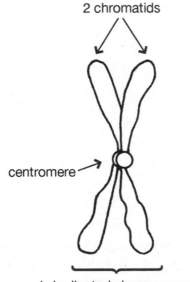

Within the nucleus, each chromosome pairs with another of similar size and shape. These pairs are called **homologs**. Each set of homologous chromosomes has a similar genetic constitution, but the genes are not necessarily identical. Different forms of corresponding genes are called **alleles**.

Figure 3.18 Paired Homologous Chromosomes.

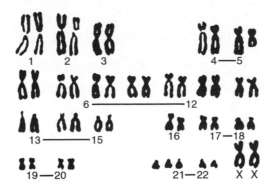

The Cell Cycle

A cell that is going to divide progresses through a particular sequence of events ending in cell division, which produces two daughter cells. This is known as the **cell cycle** (see Figure 3.19). The time taken to progress through the cell cycle differs with different types of cells, but the sequence is the same. Cells in many tissues never divide.

Figure 3.19 The Cell Cycle.
Interphase includes the G1, S, and G2 phases.
The cell division phase includes mitosis and cytokinesis.

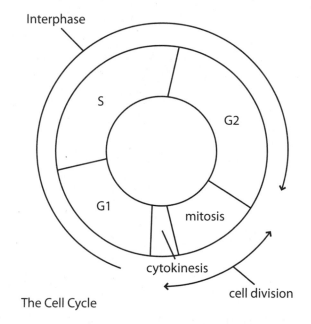

The Cell Cycle

There are two major periods within the cell cycle: interphase and mitosis (also called the M phase or cell division phase). **Interphase** is the period when the cell is active in carrying on its function. Interphase is divided into three phases. During the first phase, the **G_1 phase**, metabolism and protein synthesis are occurring at a high rate, and most of the growth of the cell occurs at this time. The cell organelles are produced (as necessary) and undergo growth during this phase. During the second phase, the **S phase**, the cell begins to prepare for cell division by replicating the DNA and proteins necessary to form a new set of chromosomes. In the final phase, the **G_2 phase**, more proteins are produced, which will be necessary for cell division, and the centrioles (which are integral to the division process) are replicated as well. Cell growth and function occur through all the stages of interphase.

Mitosis

Mitosis is the process by which a cell distributes its duplicated chromosomes so that each daughter cell has a full set of chromosomes. It is important to note that one chromosome in each daughter cell is from each parent (maternal and paternal). In other words, mitosis is set up so that you don't end up with two maternal chromosome 5's in a single cell. Mitosis progresses through four phases: prophase, metaphase, anaphase, and telophase (see Figure 3.20).

Figure 3.20 Mitosis.
See explanations of numbered steps below.

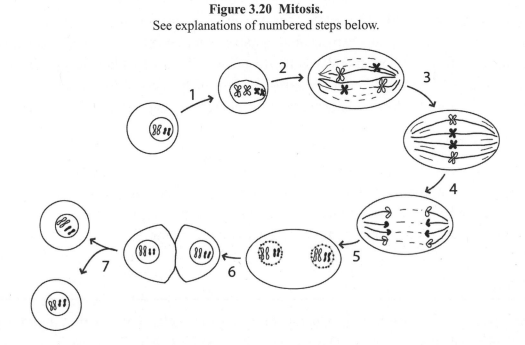

During **prophase (1, 2)**, the first stage of mitosis, the chromatin condenses into chromosomes within the nucleus and becomes visible through a light microscope. The centrioles move to opposite ends of the cell, and **spindle fibers** begin to extend from each centriole toward the center of the cell. At this point, although the chromosomes become visible, the nucleolus no longer is. During the second part of prophase, the nuclear membrane dissolves and the spindle fibers attach to the centromeres, forming a junction called a **kinetochore**. The chromosomes then are pulled to the center by attached spindle fibers in preparation for the next step, metaphase.

During **metaphase (3)**, the spindle fibers pull the chromosomes into alignment along the equatorial plane of the cell, creating the metaphase plate. This arrangement insures that one copy of each chromosome is distributed to each daughter cell.

During **anaphase (4)**, the chromatids are separated from each other when the centromere divides. Each former chromatid is now called a chromosome. Each pair of identical chromosomes move along the spindle fibers to opposite ends of the cell. **Telophase (5)** occurs as nuclear membranes form around the chromosomes. The chromosomes disperse through the new nucleoplasm, and are no longer visible as chromosomes under a standard microscope. The spindle fibers disappear. After telophase, the process of **cytokinesis (6)** produces two separate **cells (7)**.

Cytokinesis differs somewhat in plants and animals. In animal cells, a ring made-up of the protein actin surrounds the center of the cell and contracts. As the actin ring contracts, it pinches the cytoplasm into two separate compartments. Each cell's plasma membrane seals, making two distinct daughter cells. In plant cells, a cell plate forms across the center of the cell and extends out towards the edges of the cell. When this plate reaches the edges, a cell wall forms on either side of the plate, and the original cell then splits into two.

Mitosis, then, produces two nearly identical daughter cells. (Cells may differ in distribution of mitochondria or because of DNA replication errors, for example.) Only eukaryotic unicellular organisms (protists and some fungi) reproduce by mitosis. (Bacteria, which lack a nucelous, divide through **binary fission**.)

Meiosis

Meiosis is the process of producing four daughter cells, each with a **haploid** set of unduplicated chromosomes. The parent cell is **diploid**, that is, it has a normal set of paired chromosomes. Meiosis goes through a two-stage process resulting in four new cells, rather than two (as in mitosis). Each cell has half the chromosomes of the parent. Meiosis occurs in reproductive organs, and the resultant four haploid cells are called **gametes** (egg and sperm). When two haploid gametes fuse during the process of fertilization, the resultant cell has one chromosome set from each parent, and is diploid. This process allows for the huge genetic diversity available among species.

Figure 3.21 Meiosis.
See explanations of numbered steps below.

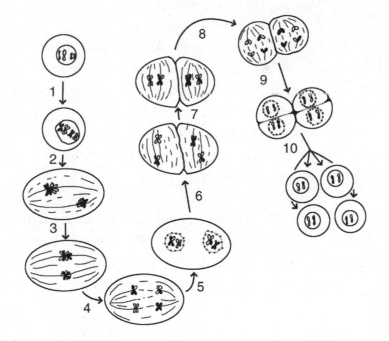

Two distinct nuclear divisions occur during meiosis, reduction (or meiosis 1, steps **1 to 5** in Figure 3.21), and division (or meiosis 2, steps **6 to 10**). **Reduction** affects the **ploidy** (referring to haploid or diploid) level, reducing it from 2n to n (i.e., diploid to haploid). **Division** then distributes the remaining set of chromosomes in a mitosis-like process.

The phases of meiosis 1 are similar to the phases of mitosis, with some notable differences. As in mitosis, chromosome replication **(1)** occurs before prophase; then during prophase 1 **(2)**, homologous chromosomes pair up and join at a point called a **synapse** (this happens only in meiosis). The attached chromosomes are now termed a tetrad, a dense four-stranded structure composed of the four chromatids from the original chromosomes. At this point, some portions of the chromatid may break off and reattach to another chromatid in the tetrad. This process, known as **crossing over**, results in an even wider array of final genetic possibilities. Genetic engineering, discussed further in Chapter 6, involves manipulation of the genes of an organism, usually to obtain a desired characteristic. Often this manipulation involves a sort of artificial "crossing over," where a specific protion of one chromatid is attached to a specific portion of another. The resulting DNA is is a combination of the maternal and paternal chromosomes.

The nuclear membrane disappears during late prophase (or prometaphase). Each chromosome (rather than each chromatid) develops a kinetochore, and as the spindle fibers attach to each chromosome, they begin to move.

In metaphase 1 **(3)**, the two chromosomes (a total of four chromatids per pair) align themselves along the equatorial plane of the cell. Each homologous pair of chromosomes contains one chromosome from the mother and one from the father from the original sexual production of that organism. When the homologous pairs orient at the cell's center in preparation for separating, the chromosomes randomly sort. The resulting cells from this meiotic division will have a mixture of chromosomes from each parent. This increases the possibilities for variety among descendent cells.

Anaphase 1 **(4)** occurs next as the chromosomes move to separate ends of the cell. This phase differs from the anaphase of mitosis where one of each chromosome pair (rather than one chromatid) separates. In telophase 1 **(5)**, the nuclear envelope may or may not form, depending on the type of organism. In either case, the cell then proceeds to meiosis 2.

The nuclear envelopes dissolve (if they have formed) during prophase 2 **(6)** and spindle fibers form again. All else proceeds as in mitosis, through metaphase 2 **(7)**, anaphase 2 **(8)**, and telophase 2 **(9)**. Again, as in mitosis, each chromosome splits into two chromatids. The process ends with cytokinesis **(10)**, forming four distinct gamete cells.

Restriction Enzymes

The study of DNA has been greatly aided by the discovery of restriction enzymes (restriction endonucleases). Restriction enzymes cut sections of DNA molecules by cleaving the sugar-phosphate backbone at a particular nucleotide sequence.

Scientists have isolated hundreds of different restriction endonucleases that act on a few hundred different DNA sequences. Restriction enzymes are made by bacteria and act to destroy foreign DNA (for example, viral DNA) that has entered the bacterial cell.

In the laboratory, restriction enzymes are used to cut DNA into small strands of DNA for study. Restriction enzymes are generally named after their host of origin, rather than the substrate upon which they act. For example, EcoRI is from the host *Escherichia coli*, Hind II and Hind III from *Haemophilus influenzae*, XhoI from *Xanthomonas holcicola*, etc.

Classical Genetics and Evolution

CLASSICAL GENETICS

The process by which characteristics pass from one generation to another is known as **inheritance**. The study of the principles of heredity (now called genetics) advanced greatly through the experimental work of **Gregor Mendel** (c. 1865). Mendel studied the relationships between traits expressed in parents and offspring, and the hereditary factors that caused expression of traits.

Mendel systematically bred pea plants to determine how certain hereditary traits passed from generation to generation. First, he established true-breeding plants, which produce offspring with the same traits as the parents. For example, the seeds of pea plants with yellow seeds would grow into plants that produced only yellow seeds. Green seeds grow into plants that produce only green seeds. Mendel named this first generation of true-breeding plants the parent or P_1 **generation**; he then bred the plant with yellow seeds and the plant with green seeds. Mendel called the first generation of offspring the F_1 **generation**. The F_1 generation of Mendel's yellow seed/green seed crosses contained only yellow seed offspring.

Mendel continued his experiment by crossing two individuals of the F_1 generation to produce an F_2 **generation**. In this generation, he found that some of the plants (one out of four) produced green seeds. Mendel performed hundreds of such crosses, studying some 10,000 pea plants, and was able to establish the rules of inheritance from them. The following are Mendel's main discoveries:

- Parents transmit hereditary factors (now called **genes**) to offspring. Genes then produce a characteristic, such as seed-coat color.

- Each individual carries two copies of a gene, and the copies may differ.

- The two genes an individual carries act independently, and the effect of one may mask the effect of the other. Mendel coined the terms geneticists still use: "dominant" and "recessive."

Modern Genetics

We now know that **chromosomes** carry all the genetic information in most organisms. Most sexually reproducing, eukaryotic organisms have corresponding pairs of chromosomes that carry genes for the same traits. These pairs are known as **homologous chromosomes**. Genes that produce a given trait exist at the same position (or **locus**) on homologous chromosomes. Each gene may have different forms, known as **alleles**. For instance, yellow seeds and green seeds arise from different alleles of the same gene. A gene can have two or more alleles, which differ in their nucleotide sequence. That difference can translate into proteins that function differently, resulting in variations of the trait.

Sexual reproduction (meiosis) produces gamete cells with ½ the genetic information of the parents (paired chromosomes are separated and sorted independently). Therefore, each gamete may receive one of any number of combinations of each parent's chromosomes.

In addition, a trait may arise from one or more genes. (However, because one-gene traits are easiest to understand, we will use them for most of our examples.) If a trait is produced from a gene or genes with varying alleles, several possibilities for traits exist. The combination of alleles that make a particular trait is the **genotype**, while the trait expressed is the **phenotype**.

An allele is considered **dominant** if it masks the effect of its partner allele. The allele that does not produce its trait when present with a dominant allele is **recessive**. That is, when a dominant allele pairs with a recessive allele, the expressed trait is that of the dominant allele.

A **Punnett square** is a notation that allows us to easily predict the results of a genetic cross. In a Punnett square, a letter is assigned to each gene. Uppercase letters represent dominant traits, while lowercase letters represent recessive traits (a convention begun by Mendel). The possible alleles from each parent are noted across the top and side of a box diagram; then the possible offspring are represented within the internal boxes. If we assign the allele that produces yellow seeds the letter **Y**, and the allele that produces green seeds **y**, we can represent Mendel's first cross between pea plants (**YY** × **yy**) by the following Punnett square:

	Y	Y
y	Yy	Yy
y	Yy	Yy

One parent pea plant had green seeds (green seeds is its phenotype), so it must not have had any of the dominant genes for yellow seeds (**Y**); therefore it must have the genotype **yy**. If the second parent had one allele for yellow and one for green then some of the offspring would have inherited two genes for green. Since Mendel started with true-breeding plants, we may deduce that one parent had two genes for green seeds (**yy**) and the other two genes for yellow seeds (**YY**).

When both alleles for a given gene are the same in an individual (such as **YY** or **yy**), that individual is **homozygous** for that trait. Furthermore, the individual's genotype can be called homozygous. Both of the above parents (**P₁**) were homozygous. The children in the **F₁** generation all have one dominant gene (**Y**) and one recessive gene (**y**), their phenotype is yellow, and their genotype is **Yy**. When the two alleles for a given gene are different in an individual (**Yy**), that individual's genotype is said to be **heterozygous** for that trait; its genotype is heterozygous.

Breeding two **F₁** offspring from the example above produces the following Punnett square of a double heterozygous (both parents **Yy**) cross:

	Y	y
Y	YY	Yy
y	Yy	yy

Through this Punnett square, we can determine that three-fourths of the offspring will produce yellow seeds. This is consistent with Mendel's findings. However, there are two different genotypes represented among the yellow seed offspring. One-half of the offspring were heterozygous yellow (**Yy**), while one-fourth is homozygous yellow (**YY**).

The example above shows a **monohybrid cross**—a cross between two individuals where only one trait is considered. Mendel also experimented with crossing two parents while considering two separate traits, a **dihybrid cross**.

The laws investigated by Mendel form the basis of modern genetics. However, Mendel's laws now incorporate modern terminology (i.e., "genes" rather than "hereditary factors," etc.).

The Law of Segregation

The first law of Mendelian genetics is the **law of segregation**. The law of segregation states that traits are expressed from a pair of genes in the individual (on homologous chromosomes). Each parent provides one chromosome of every pair of homologous chromosomes. Paired chromosomes (and thus corresponding genes) separate and randomly recombine during gamete formation.

The Law of Dominance

Mendel determined that one gene usually expressed itself over the other (was dominant). This is the **law of dominance**, Mendel's second law of inheritance. In Mendel's experiments, the first generation produced no plants with green seeds, leading him to recognize the existence of genetic dominance. The yellow-seed allele was clearly dominant.

The Law of Independent Assortment

Mendel also investigated whether genes for one trait always were linked to genes for another. In other words, Mendel experimented not only with pea seed-coat color, but also with pea-plant height (and a number of other traits in peas and other plants). He wanted to determine whether, if the parent plant had green seeds and was tall, all plants with green seeds would be tall. These dihybrid cross experiments demonstrated that most traits were independent of one another. That is, a pea plant could be green and tall or green and short, yellow and tall or yellow and short. In most cases, genes for traits randomly sort into pairs (although some genes lie close to others on a chromosome and can therefore be inherited together). Since homologous chromosomes separate and independently sort in gamete formation, alleles are also separated and independently sorted, an assertion known as the **law of independent assortment**.

The following Punnett square demonstrates independent assortment. **Y** stands for the allele for yellow color, **y** for the allele for green, **T** for the allele tall, and **t** for short:

	TY	Ty	tY	ty
TY	TTYY	TTYy	TtYY	TtYy
Ty	TTYy	TTyy	TtYy	Ttyy
tY	TtYY	TtYy	ttYY	ttYy
ty	TtYy	Ttyy	ttYy	ttyy

Incomplete Dominance

Some traits are determined by genes that are neither dominant nor recessive and instead produce offspring that are a mix of the two parents. For instance, in snapdragons a plant with red flowers crossed with a plant with white flowers produces offspring with pink flowers. This is known as **incomplete dominance** or **co-dominance**. Neither white nor red is dominant over the other. In incomplete dominance, the conventional way to symbolize the alleles is with a capital letter designating the trait (in this case C for color) and a superscript designating the allele choices (in this case ^{R} for red, ^{W} for white), making the possible alleles C^R and C^W. The following Punnett square represents the incomplete dominance of the allele for red flowers (C^R), the allele for white (C^W), and the combination resulting in pink ($C^R C^W$).

	C^R	C^R
C^W	$C^R C^W$	$C^R C^W$
C^W	$C^R C^W$	$C^R C^W$

In this case, two plants, one with white flowers, one with red, cross to form all pink flowers. If two of the heterozygous offspring of this cross are then bred, the outcome of this cross ($C^R C^W \times C^R C^W$) will be:

	C^R	C^W
C^R	$C^R C^R$	$C^R C^W$
C^W	$C^R C^W$	$C^W C^W$

One-fourth of the offspring will be red, one-half pink, and one-fourth white, a 1:2:1 ratio.

Multiple Alleles

In the instances above, two possible alleles exist in a species, so the genotype will be a combination of those two alleles. There are some instances where more than two choices of alleles are present. For instance, for human blood types there is a dominant allele for type A blood, another dominant allele for type B blood, as well as a recessive allele for neither A nor B, known as O blood. There are three different alleles and they may combine in any way. In multiple-allele crosses, it is conventional to denote the chromosome by a letter (in this case **I** for dominant, **i** for recessive), with a subscript letter representing the allele types (in this case **A**, **B**, or **O**). The alleles for A and B blood are co-dominant, while the allele for O blood is recessive. The possible genotypes and phenotypes then are as follows:

GENOTYPE	PHENOTYPE
IAIA	Type A blood
IBIB	Type B blood
IBiO	Type B blood
IAiO	Type A blood
IAIB	Type AB blood
iOiO	Type O blood

[Note: There is another gene responsible for the Rh factor that adds the + or − to the blood type.]

Linkage

While Mendel had established the law of independent assortment, later study of genetics by other scientists found that this law was not always true. In studying fruit flies, for instance, it was found that some traits are always inherited together; they were not independently sorted. Traits that are inherited together are said to be **linked**. Genes are portions of chromosomes, so most traits produced by genes on the same chromosome are inherited together. (The chromosomes are independently sorted, not the individual genes.)

However, an exception to this rule complicates the issue. During metaphase of meiosis I, when homologous chromosomes line up along the center of the dividing cell, some pieces of the chromosomes break off and move from one chromosome to another (change places). This random breaking and reforming of homologous chromosomes allows genes to change the chromosome they are linked to, thus changing the genome of that chromosome. This process, known as crossing over, adds even more variation of traits. It is more likely for crossing over to occur between genes that do not lie close together on a chromosome than between those that lie close together.

Gender is determined in an organism by a particular homologous pair of chromosomes. The symbols **X** and **Y** denote the sex chromosomes. In mammals and many insects, the male has an **X** and **Y** chromosome (**XY**), while the female has two **X**'s (**XX**).

Polygenic Inheritance

While the best-studied genetic traits arise from alleles of a single gene, most traits, such as height and skin color, are produced from the expression of more than one set of genes. Traits produced from interaction of multiple sets of genes are known as **polygenic traits**. Diseases such as diabetes and heart disease have multiple contributing factors involved in their development in a person. Besides genetic factors, these diseases can be all or partly caused by environmental or lifestyle factors.

Polygenic traits are difficult to map and difficult to predict because of the varied effects of the different genes and contributing factors on a specific trait or disease.

Human Genetic Disorders

Genetic disorders caused by chromosomal abnormalities may be the root of some forms of disabilities and illnesses. Some of these disorders arise as only a tendency to develop the illness (such as certain rare forms of cancer), being inherited from a parent's genetic makeup. For other genetic disorders, development of the disease is more concretely related to inherited genes. Most of these disorders are very rare, only affecting one in every few thousand or even million people. Genetic disorders, like other genetic traits, are mostly derived from abnormalities of a single gene. The patterns of inheritance for single gene disorders vary and are discussed below.

Diseases that can affect a person when only one mutated copy of the gene is present are called autosomal dominant disorders. Therefore, the majority of the time an affected person only has one affected parent, and each child of an affected person has a 50% chance of inheriting the mutated gene. Huntington's disease is the most common example of this type of disorder.

Autosomal recessive disorders, such as **Cystic Fibrosis** and **Sickle-Cell Anemia**, require two copies of the respective mutated gene to be inherited for a person to be affected. However, affected persons may receive one or both of the mutated genes from unaffected parents. Referred to as carriers, unaffected parents who possess one copy of the mutated gene may pass that gene on to their children. There is a 25% chance for each child of two unaffected parents to inherit the disorder itself.

Rett syndrome and a form of rickets are two examples of diseases that are caused by a dominant mutation in genes that are on the X chromosome. This type of condition is called an X-linked dominant disorder. Males and females may be affected by these types of disorders. However, symptoms of this type of disease in males are often much more severe and very commonly fatal early in life. This leads to more females exhibiting the diseases. Due to being associated with the X chromosome, the chances of a male passing the gene are different from those of a female. All sons of a male with an X-linked dominant disorder will be unaffected while all daughters will inherit the disorder. Women with these mutated genes, on the other hand, have a 50% chance with each pregnancy of passing the disorder to their child. However, with some of these types of disorders, including Rett syndrome, rarely are affected individuals able to reproduce.

Other disorders caused by mutation in genes on the X chromosome are known as X-linked recessive. These disorders more commonly affect males than females. The chances of the gene passing to decendents are different for males and females with these types of disorders also. A father with an X-linked recessive disorder will not pass this gene to any sons (since they receive his Y chromosome) while all of his daughters (who all receive his X chromosome) will be carriers (have one copy of the mutated gene). The sons of a woman who is a carrier of these disorders will have a 50% chance of being affected, and the daughters of a woman who is a carrier will have a 50% chance of being carriers themselves. Muscular dystrophy, color blindness, and hemophilia A are examples of this type of disorder.

Y-linked disorders, caused by Y chromosome mutations, only ever affect males and are passed to every son of an affected male. Mitochondrial disease, also known as maternal inheritance, are conditions that result from mitochondrial DNA abnormalities. Only cells of the egg contribute mitochondria to the developing embryo. Therefore, only mothers pass these types of conditions to their children.

Nature vs. Nurture

In the psychology realm of science, much is debated about the interaction between heredity and the environment. This is known as the **Nature versus Nurture Debate**. Involved in this issue is the study of the development of individuals' personality and whether the end result is caused from their inherited traits or the environment in which they were raised plus their personal experiences.

This debate has involved scientific studies on the affects of adoption as well as looking at differences and similarities among twins, raised together or in separate homes. Much of the modern thought on this topic is that both heredity and environment play extensive roles in a person's development. One psychologist, Donald Hebb, when asked, "Which, nature or nurture, contributes more to personality?" responded by asking, "Which contributes more to the area of a rectangle, its length or its width?"

DNA, on the molecular level, interacts with both other genes and the environment. Therefore, although we mentioned earlier in this chapter that there are many traits that are derived from single genes, modern biology identifies those complex traits that are more likely derived from other factors besides genes alone. In studies, development of many traits has been found to be related to a particular gene within the context of a specific environment. Therefore, the extent that a trait is affected by genes versus the environment will vary with different environments and genes, making consistent measurements difficult to obtain.

EVOLUTION

History of Evolutionary Concepts

Evolutionary concepts are the foundation of much of the current study in biology. The term **evolution** refers to the gradual change of characteristics within a population, producing a change in species over time. Evolution is driven by the process of **natural selection**, a feature of population genetics first articulated by Charles Darwin in his book

The Origin of Species by Means of Natural Selection, or The Preservation of Favoured Races in the Struggle for Life (published in 1859). Darwin was the first to explain natural selection as a driving force, and the first to lay out the full range of evidence for evolution. However, scientists before Darwin had already promoted some of the ideas inherent in evolutionary biology.

Carolus Linnaeus, the well known botanist (who is credited with developing the classification system for organisms still used widely today) speculated on the origin of and relationships between groups of species in the mid-1700s. The French scientist Lamarck proposed that organisms acquire traits

ORIGIN OF SPECIES.

INTRODUCTION.

WHEN on board H.M.S. 'Beagle,' as naturalist, I was much struck with certain facts in the distribution of the organic beings inhabiting South America, and in the geological relations of the present to the past inhabitants of that continent. These facts, as will be seen in the latter chapters of this volume, seemed to throw some light on the origin of species—that mystery of mysteries, as it has been called by one of our greatest philosophers. On my return home, it occurred to me, in 1837, that something might perhaps be made out on this question by patiently accumulating and reflecting on all sorts of facts which could possibly have any bearing on it. After five years' work I allowed myself to speculate on the subject, and drew up some short notes; these I enlarged in 1844 into a sketch of the conclusions, which then seemed to me probable: from that period to the present day I have steadily pursued the same object. I hope that I may be excused for entering on these personal details, as I give them to show that I have not been hasty in coming to a decision.

My work is now (1859) nearly finished; but as it will take me many more years to complete it, and as my health is far from strong, I have been urged to publish this Abstract. I have more especially been induced to do this, as Mr. Wallace, who is now studying the natural history of the Malay archipelago, has arrived at almost exactly the same general conclusions that I have on the origin of species. In 1858 he sent me a memoir on this subject, with a request that I would forward it to Sir Charles Lyell, who sent it to the Linnean Society, and it is published in the third volume of the Journal of that Society. Sir C. Lyell and Dr. Hooker, who both knew of my work—the latter having read my sketch of 1844—honoured me by thinking it advisable to publish, with Mr. Wallace's excellent memoir, some brief extracts from my manuscripts.

This Abstract, which I now publish, must necessarily be imperfect. I cannot here give references and authorities for my

over their life span that equip them to survive within their environment and pass those traits on to their offspring. He presented the idea that, for example, giraffes developed longer necks during their lifetime from their efforts to reach food high on tree branches. The children, born with longer necks would then further lengthen their necks reaching for high branches, passing these even longer necks on to their children. This Lamarckian theory of acquired characteristics has since been discredited.

Darwinian Concept of Natural Selection

Current theories of evolution have their basis in the work of Charles Darwin and one of his contemporaries, Alfred Russell Wallace. Darwin's book, however, served to catalyze the study of evolution across scientific disciplines. A synopsis of Darwin's ideas follows.

Population growth and maintenance of a species is dependent on limiting factors. (Populations will be studied further in Chapter 6.) Individuals within the species that are unable to acquire the minimum requirement of resources, are unable to reproduce. The ecosystem can support only a limited number of organisms—known as the carrying capacity (usually designated by the letter K).

Once the carrying capacity (K) is reached, a competition for resources ensues. Darwin considered this competition to be the basic *struggle for existence*. Some of the competitors will fail to survive. Within every population, there is variation among traits. Darwin proposed that those individuals who win the competition for resources pass those successful traits on to their children. Only the surviving competitors reproduce successfully generation after generation. Therefore, traits providing the competitive edge will be represented most often in succeeding generations.

Modern Concept of Natural Selection

Although the concepts of natural selection put forth by Darwin still form the basis of evolutionary theory today, Darwin had no real knowledge of genetics when he submitted his ideas. Several years after Darwin's writings, Mendel's work (on experimental genetics) was rediscovered independently by three scientists. The laws of genetics served to support the suppositions Darwin had made. Over the next 40 years, the study of genetics included not only individual organisms but also population genetics (how traits are preserved, changed, or introduced within a population of organisms). Progress in the studies of biogeography and paleontology of the early 1900s also served to reinforce Darwin's basic observations.

The modern concept of natural selection emerged from Darwin's original ideas, with additions and confirmations of genetics, population studies, and paleontology. This **modern synthesis** focused on the concept that evolution was a process of gradual (over thousands or hundreds of thousands of generations) adaptive change in traits among populations.

Mechanisms of Evolution

Modern understanding of the process of natural selection recognizes that there are some basic mechanisms that support evolutionary change. Modern theories focus on the change that occurs in entire *gene pools* of species, not among individual populations.

All evolution is dependent upon genetic change. The entire collection of genes within a given population is known as its **gene pool**. Individuals in the population will have only one pair of alleles for a particular single-gene trait. Yet, the gene pool may contain dozens or hundreds of alleles for this trait. Evolution (meaning a change in allele frequency over time) does not occur through changes from individual to individual, but rather as the gene pool changes through one of a number of possible mechanisms.

One mechanism that drives the changing of traits over time in a species is **differential reproduction**. Natural selection assumes some individuals within a population are more suited for survival, given environmental conditions. Differential reproduction takes this supposition one step further by proposing that those individuals within a population that are most adapted to the environment are also the most likely individuals to reproduce successfully. Therefore, the reproductive processes tend to strengthen the frequency of expression of heritable traits across the population. Differential reproduction increases the number of alleles for desirable traits in the gene pool. This trend will be established and strengthen gradually over time, eventually producing a gene pool where the heritable trait is more commonly expressed, if environmental conditions remain the same.

Another mechanism of genetic change is mutation. As discussed earlier in this chapter, a **mutation** is a change of the DNA sequence of a gene, resulting in a change of the trait. Although a mutation can cause a very swift change in the genotype (genetic code) and possibly phenotype (expressed trait) of the offspring, mutations do not necessarily produce a trait desirable for a particular environment. Mutation is a much more random occurrence than differential reproduction.

Although mutations occur quickly, the change in the gene pool is limited, so change in the population occurs very slowly (over multiple generations). Mutation does provide a vehicle for introducing new genetic possibilities. Genetic traits, which did not exist in the original gene pool, can be introduced through mutation.

Genetic Drift, or Neutral Selection

A third mechanism recognized to influence evolution is known as **genetic drift**. Over time, a gene pool (particularly in a small population) may experience a change in frequency of particular genes simply due to chance fluctuations. In a finite population, the gene pool may not reflect the entire number of genetic possibilities of the larger genetic pool of the species. Over time, the genetic pool within this finite population changes and evolution has occurred. Genetic drift has no particular tie to environmental conditions, and thus the random change in gene frequency is unpredictable. The change of gene frequency may produce a small or a large change, depending on what traits are affected. The process of genetic drift, as opposed to mutation, actually causes a reduction in genetic variety.

Genetic drift occurs within finite separated populations, allowing that population to develop its own distinct gene pool. However, occasionally an individual from an adjacent population of the same species may immigrate and breed with a member of the previously locally isolated group. The introduction of new genes from the immigrant results in a change of the gene pool, known as **gene migration**. Gene migration is also occasionally successful between members of different, but related, species. The resultant hybrids succeed in adding increased variability to the gene pool.

Hardy-Weinberg and Allele Frequencies

The study of genetics shows that in a situation where random mating is occurring within a population (which is in equilibrium with its environment), gene frequencies and genotype ratios will remain constant from generation to generation. This law is known as the **Hardy-Weinberg Law of Equilibrium**, named after the two men (G.H. Hardy and Wilhelm Weinberg, c. 1909) who first studied this principle in mathematical studies of genetics. The Hardy-Weinberg Law is a mathematical formula that shows why recessive genes do not disappear over time from a population.

According to the Hardy-Weinberg Law, the sum of the frequencies of all possible alleles for a particular trait is 1. That is, $p + q = 1$ where the frequency of one allele is represented by **p** and the frequency of another is **q**. It then follows mathematically that the frequency of *genotypes* within a population can be represented by the equation:

$$p^2 + 2pq + q^2 = 1$$

where the frequency of homozygous dominant genotypes is represented by p^2, the omozygous recessive by q^2, and the heterozygous genotype by $2pq$.

For instance, in humans the ability to taste the chemical phenylthio-carbamide (PTC) is a dominant inherited trait. If **T** represents the allele for tasting PTC and **t** represents the recessive trait (inability to taste PTC), then the possible genotypes in a population would be **TT**, **Tt**, and **tt**. If the frequency of non-tasters (tt) in a particular population is 4% or 0.04 (that is, $q^2 = .04$), then the frequency of the allele **t** equals the square root of 0.04, or 0.2. It is then possible to calculate the frequency of the dominant allele, **T**, in the population using the equation:

$$p + 0.2 = 1$$
$$\text{so, } p = 0.8$$

The frequency of the allele for tasting PTC is 0.8. The frequency of the various possible genotypes (**TT**, **Tt**, and **tt**) in the population can also be calculated since the frequency of the homozygous dominant genotype (TT) is p^2 or 0.64 or 64%. The frequency of the heterozygous genotype (Tt) is $2pq$, and can be calculated once p and q are known.

$$2pq = 2(0.8)(0.2) = 0.32 = 32\%.$$
Frequency of TT = 64%, Tt = 32%, tt = 4% . . . totaling 100% or $0.64 + 0.32 + 0.04 = 1$

In order for Hardy-Weinberg equilibrium to occur, the population in question must meet several conditions, viz., random mating (no differential reproduction) must be taking place and no migration, mutation, selection, or genetic drift can be occurring. When these conditions are met, Hardy-Weinberg equilibrium can occur, and there will be no changes in the gene pool over time. Hardy-Weinberg is important to the evolutionary process because it shows that alleles that have no current selective value will be retained in a population over time.

Speciation

A species is an interbreeding population that shares a common gene pool and produces viable offspring. Up to this point we have been considering mechanisms that produce variation within species. It is apparent that to explain evolution on a broad scale we must understand how genetic change produces new species. There are two mechanisms that produce separate species, allopatric speciation and sympatric speciation. In order for a new species to develop, substantial genetic changes must occur between populations, which prohibit them from interbreeding. These genetic changes may result from genetic drift or from mutation that takes place separately in the two populations. **Allopatric speciation** occurs when two populations are geographically isolated from each other. For instance, a population of squirrels may be geographically separated by a catastrophic event such as a volcanic eruption. Two populations (separated by the volcanic low) continue to reproduce and experience genetic drift and/or mutation over time. This limits each population's gene pool and produces changes in expressed traits. Later, the geographical separation may be eliminated as the volcanic low subsides; even so, the two populations have now experienced too much change to allow them to interbreed successfully again. The result is the production of two separate species.

Speciation may also occur without a geographic separation when a population develops members with a genetic difference, which prevents successful reproduction with the original species. The genetically different members reproduce with each other, producing a population, which is separate from the original species. This process is called **sympatric speciation**.

As populations of an organism in a given area grow, some will move into new geographic areas looking for new resources or to escape predators. (In this case, a natural event does not separate the population; instead, part of the population moves.) Some of these adventurers will discover new niches and advantageous conditions. Traits that allow this traveling population to use its resources more effectively and to produce more offspring will grow more common over several generations through the process of natural selection. Over time the species will specially adapt to live more effectively in the new environment. Through this process, known as **adaptive radiation**, a single species can develop into several diverse species over time.

All of the above examples describe evolutionary change over a relatively short period of time. While species were traditionally thought to have evolved at a slow, uniform pace over time, scientists have more recently proposed speciation events interspersed within periods of relative stasis. This model is called **punctuated equilibrium**. Punctuated equilibrium was first proposed as paleontologists studied the fossil record. The older model, **gradualism**, would predict smooth, continuous transitions in the fossil record. However, the fossil record seems to show that organisms in general survive many generations with very little change over long periods of geologic time. New species appear in the fossils suddenly, without transitional forms, though "sudden" in this context needs to be understood on a geologic time scale. Punctuated equilibrium does not propose "fast" evolutionary change; it would still operate on the scale of tens or hundreds of thousands years.

Genetic Diversity

As will be noted in the sections to follow, the diversity of species that have evolved on earth is vast. Not only is there great diversity between species, but there are also many distinguishable differences that exist between members of the same species. The genetic variation carried by members of a species for a given trait is known as a polymorphism. For example, gender is an example of dimorphism (two variations) in most mammalian species (male and female). Evolutionary mechanisms exist that tend toward a **balanced polymorphism** in order to keep any particular version within a species from dominating, unless that particular version is more suited for its ecological niche (aka being "fitter"). In the example of gender, it is favorable to the species to have an even mix of genders and the tendency of the gene pool is to favor that balance. If there becomes a shortage of males, the males become more highly sought after and thus "fitter" in the selection process.

Heterozygote advantage is one mechanism whereby polymorphism is maintained. Having two different alleles for a given phenotype is a positive trait for survival in many instances. For example, a well known situation exists with the gene inheritance of the blood trait for Sickle Cell. The allele HbS is an allele for production of a variant hemoglobin sensitive to oxygen deprival and causing misshapen red blood cells. The allele HbA is the allele for normal hemoglobin production. The HbS allele is found mainly in humans of African and Asian Indian descent. If a person has two HbA alleles, they have normal hemoglobin carrying red blood cells (most of the population). When two HbS alleles are inherited, the person has the disease known as Sickle Cell Anemia, with the accompanying debilitating symptoms and shortened life span. However, a person heterozygous for this trait, HbAHbS, is a carrier for Sickle Cell and has what is known as Sickle Cell Trait. While this trait carries some discomforting symptoms, they are far less debilitating and it also has a positive characteristic; those with Sickle Cell Trait also have a natural resistance to malaria, a deadly illness of the African/Asian regions. For this reason, while the homozygous trait is deadly, the heterozygous trait is advantageous, and therefore is favored, selected, and retained in the population.

A second mechanism of polymorphism is frequency-dependent selection, which occurs as the frequency of one phenotype increases relative to another.

PLANT AND ANIMAL EVOLUTION

Evolution of the First Cells

The modern theory of the evolution of life on Earth assumes the earliest forms of life began approximately four billion years ago. It is presumed that conditions on Earth were very different from conditions today. The pre-life Earth environment would have been rich in water, ammonia, and methane, all compounds rich in hydrogen. In order for life to arise on Earth, organic molecules such as amino acids (the building blocks of proteins), sugars, acids, and bases would need to have formed from the available chemicals.

Over the last century there has been much research into plausible mechanisms for the origin of life. The **Oparin Hypothesis** is one theory regarding origin of life, developed by a Russian scientist (A.I. Oparin) in 1924. Oparin proposed that the Earth was approximately 4.6 billion years old and that the early Earth had a reducing atmosphere, meaning there was very little free oxygen present. Instead, there was an abundance of ammonia, hydrogen, methane, and steam (H_2O), all escaping from volcanoes.

The Earth was in the process of cooling down, so there was a great deal of heat energy available, as well as a pattern of recurring violent lightning storms providing another source of energy. During this cooling of the Earth, much of the steam surrounding the Earth would condense, forming hot seas. In the presence of abundant energy, the synthesis of simple organic molecules from the available chemicals became possible. These organic substances then collected in the hot, turbulent seas (sometimes referred to as the "primordial soup").

As the concentration of organic molecules became very high, they began forming into larger, charged, complex molecules. Oparin called these highly absorptive molecules "coacervates." Coacervates were also able to divide.

Oparin's research involved finding experimental evidence to support his ideas that amino acids could combine to form proteins in early Earth conditions. Oparin knew proteins were catalysts so they could encourage further change and development of early cells.

Stanley Miller provided support for Oparin's hypotheses in experiments where he exposed simple inorganic molecules to electrical charges similar to lightning. Miller recreated conditions as they were supposed to exist in early Earth history, and was successful in his attempt to produce complex organic molecules including amino acids under these conditions. Miller's experiments served to support Oparin's hypotheses.

Sidney Fox, a major evolution researcher of the 1960s, conducted experiments that proved ultraviolet light may induce the formation of dipeptides from amino acids. Under conditions of moderate dry heat, Fox showed formation of proteinoids, polypeptides of up to 18 amino acids. He also showed that polyphosphoric acid could increase the yield of these polymers, a process that simulates the modern role of ATP in protein synthesis. These proteins formed small spheres known as microspheres; these showed similarities to living cells.

Further strides were made by researcher Cyril Ponnamperuma who demonstrated that small amounts of guanine formed from the thermal polymerization of amino acids. He also proved the synthesis of adenine and ribose from long-term treatment of reducing atmospheric gases with electrical current.

Once organic compounds had been synthesized, primitive cells most likely developed that contained genetic material in the form of RNA, and that used energy derived from ATP. These primitive cells were prokaryotic and similar to some bacteria now found on Earth.

The endosymbiont theory suggests that original prokaryotic cells took in other cells that performed various tasks. For instance, an original cell could absorb several symbiotic bacteria that then evolve into mitochondria. Several cells that lived in symbiosis would have combined and evolved to form a single eukaryotic cell.

Plant Evolution

The evolution of plant species is considered to have begun with heterotrophic prokaryotic cells. Since it is presumed that the early Earth's atmosphere was lacking in oxygen, early cells were anaerobic. Over time, some bacteria evolved the ability to carry on photosynthesis (cyanobacteria), thus becoming autotrophic, which in turn introduced significant amounts of oxygen into the atmosphere. As oxygen is poisonous to most anaerobic cells, a new niche opened up: cells able not only to survive in the presence of oxygen, but also to use it in metabolism.

Cyanobacteria were incorporated into larger aerobic cells, which then evolved into photosynthetic eukaryotic cells. Cellular organization increased, nuclei and membranes formed, and cell specialization occurred, leading to multicellular photosynthetic organisms, that is, plants.

The earliest plants were aquatic, but as niches filled in marine and freshwater environments, plants began to move onto land. Anatomical changes occurred over time, allowing plants to survive in a nonaqueous environment. Cell walls thickened, and tissues to carry water and nutrients developed. As plants continued to adapt to land conditions, differentiation of tissues continued, resulting in the evolution of stems, leaves, roots, and seeds. The development of the seed was a key factor in the survival of land plants. Asexual reproduction dominated in early species, but sexual reproduction developed over time, increasing the possibilities of diversity.

Processes of adaptive radiation, genetic drift, and natural selection continued over long periods of time to produce the incredible diversity seen in the plant world today.

Animal Evolution

The evolution of animals is thought to have begun with marine protists. Although there is no fossil record, going back to the protist level, animal cells bear the most similarity to marine protist cells. Fossilized burrows from multicellular organisms begin to appear in the geological record approximately 700 million years ago, during the Precambrian period. These multicellular animals had only soft parts—no hard parts, which could be fossilized.

During the Cambrian period (the first period of the Paleozoic Era), beginning about 570 million years ago, the fossil record begins to show multicellular organisms with hard parts, namely exoskeletons. The fossil record at this time includes fossil representations from all modern-day (and some extinct) phyla. This sudden appearance of multitudes of differentiated animal forms is known as the **Cambrian explosion**.

At the end of the Paleozoic Era, the fossil record attests to several mass extinction events. These combined events resulted in the extinction of about 95% of animal species developed to this point. Fossils indicate that many organisms, such as Trilobites, that were numerous in the Cambrian era, did not survive the end of the Paleozoic Era.

Approximately 505 million years ago was the beginning of the Ordovician period, which lasted until about 440 million years ago. The Ordovician period was marked by diversification among species that survived past the Cambrian extinctions. The Ordovician is also known for the development of land plants. Early forms of fish arose in the Cambrian, but developed during the Ordovician, these being the first vertebrates to be seen in the fossil record. Again, the end of the Ordovician is marked by vast extinctions, but these extinctions allowed the opening of ecological situations, which in turn encouraged adaptive radiation.

Adaptive radiation is the mechanism credited with the development of new species in the next period, the Silurian, from 440 to 410 million years ago. The Silurian period is marked by widespread colonization of landmasses by plants and animals. Large numbers of insect fossils are recognizable in Silurian geologic sediments, as well as fish and early amphibians. The mass movement onto land by formerly marine animals required adaptation in numerous areas including gas exchange, support (skeletal), water conservation, circulatory systems, and reproduction.

In the study of animal evolution, attention is paid to two concepts, homology and analogy. Structures that exist in two different species because they share a common ancestry are called **homologous**. For instance, the forelimbs of a salamander and an opossum are similar in structure because of common ancestry. **Analogous** structures are similar because of their common function, although they do not share a common ancestry. Analogous structures are the product of **convergent evolution**. For instance, birds and insects both have wings, although they are not relatives. Rather the wings evolved as a result of convergence. Convergence occurs when a particular characteristic evolves in two unrelated populations. Wings of insects and birds are analogous structures (they are similar in function regardless of the lack of common ancestors).

Figure 4.2 Geologic Time Scale

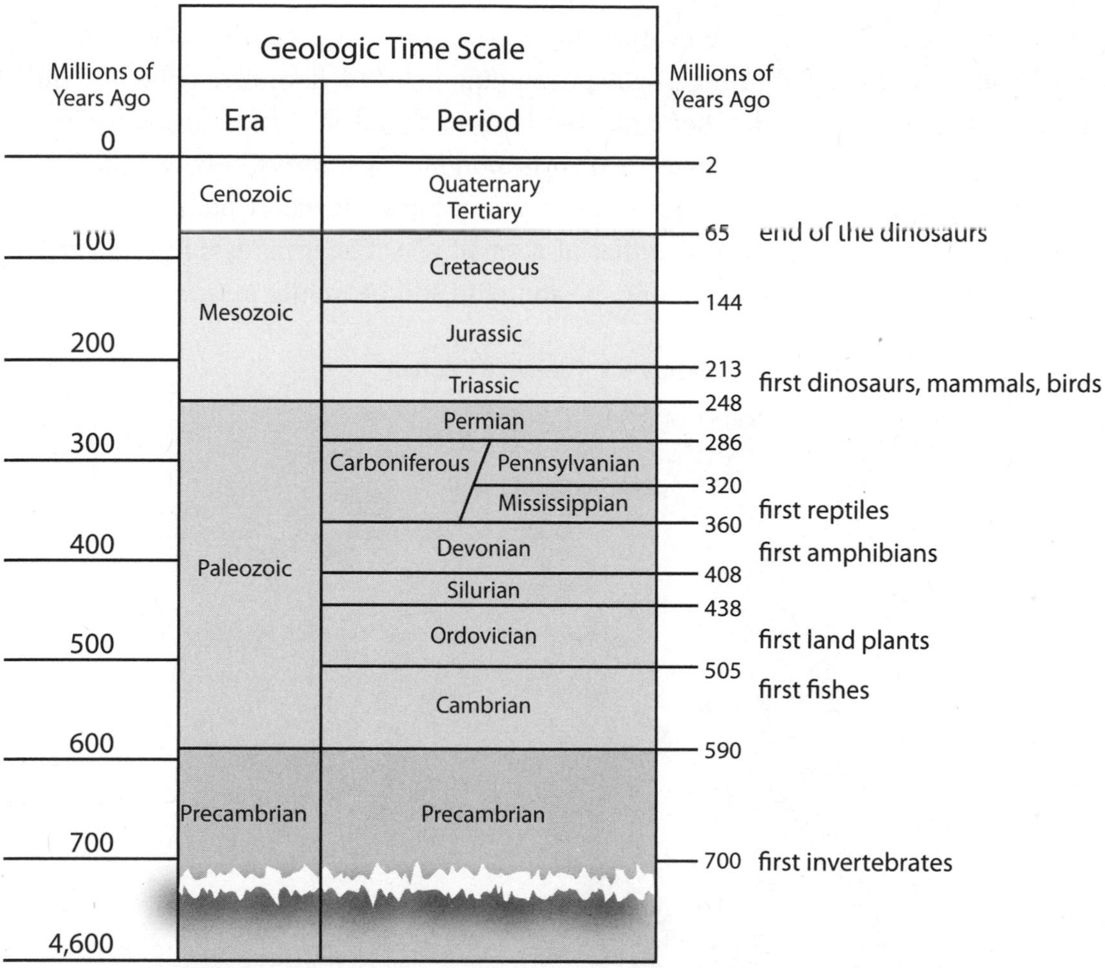

Geologic Time Scale			Millions of Years Ago	
Millions of Years Ago	Era	Period		
0			2	
	Cenozoic	Quaternary Tertiary		
100			65	end of the dinosaurs
	Mesozoic	Cretaceous	144	
200		Jurassic	213	
		Triassic	248	first dinosaurs, mammals, birds
300		Permian	286	
		Carboniferous / Pennsylvanian	320	
	Paleozoic	Mississippian	360	first reptiles
400		Devonian	408	first amphibians
		Silurian	438	
500		Ordovician	505	first land plants
		Cambrian		first fishes
600			590	
700	Precambrian	Precambrian	700	first invertebrates
4,600				

The process of **extinction** has played a large part in the direction evolution has taken. Extinctions occur at a generally low rate at all times. It is presumed that species that face extinction have not been able to adapt appropriately to environmental changes. However, there have also been several "extinction events" that have wiped out up to 95% of the species of their time. These events served to open up massive ecological niches, encouraging evolution of multitudes of new species. Approximately 400 million years ago, the first amphibians gave rise to early reptiles that then diversified into birds, then mammals. One branch of mammals developed into the tree dwelling primates, considered the ancestors of humans.

Human Evolution

Humans are thought to have evolved from primates who over time developed larger brains. A branch of bipedal primates gave rise to the first true hominids about 4.5 million years ago. The earliest known hominid fossils were found in Africa in the 1970s. The well-known "Lucy" skeleton was named *Australopithecus afarensis*. It was determined from the skeleton of *Australopithecus* that it was a biped. It had a human-like jaw and teeth, but a skull that was more like that of a small ape. The arms were proportionately longer than those of humans, indicating the ability to still be motile in trees.

Figure 4.3 Human Evolution

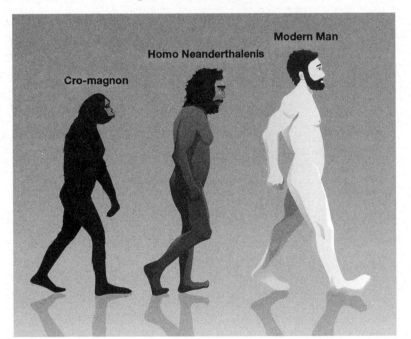

The fossilized skulls of *Homo erectus*, the oldest known fossil of the human genus, is thought to be about 1.8 million years old. The skull of *Homo erectus* was quite a lot larger than *Australopithecus*, about the size of a modern human brain (see Figure 4.4). *Homo erectus* was thought to walk upright and had facial features more closely resembling humans than apes. The oldest fossils to be designated *Homo sapiens* are also called Cro-Magnon man, with brain size and facial features essentially the same as modern humans.

Cro-Magnon *Homo sapiens* are thought to have evolved in Africa and migrated to Europe and Asia approximately 100,000 years ago.

Figure 4.4 Human Evolution by skull size and shape

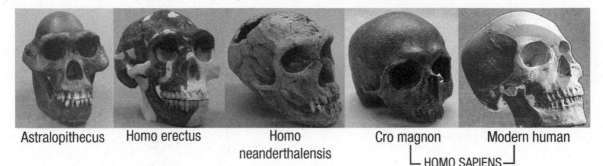

Astralopithecus   Homo erectus   Homo neanderthalensis   Cro magnon   Modern human

└ HOMO SAPIENS ┘

Evolutionary Ecology

Organisms evolve within ecosystems; therefore, the ecological circumstances affect (if not determine) the course of evolution of species in a particular area. Some organisms are better suited to develop in a new ecosystem. Others only thrive in an established equilibrium. The characteristics that differentiate these types of organisms are known collectively as **life history strategies**. There are two types of life history strategies: opportunistic and equilibreal.

Organisms with **opportunistic** life history strategies (also known as r-selected) tend to be pioneer species in a new or recently devastated community. In addition to traits that allow them to succeed in the long term, they also have traits that help make them succeed in a changing or new ecosystem. They tend to have short maturation times and short overall life spans. They tend to have high mortality rates. Often reproduction is asexual, with high numbers of offspring. They find it easy to disperse over large areas. They do not parent their young. These are rapidly reproducing species that are also easily wiped out by more sophisticated populations that follow. For example, dandelions are an opportunistic species. Species with **equilibreal** life strategies (also known as K-selected) are those organisms that overtake the opportunistic pioneer species. These tend to have long life spans with a long maturation time and a corresponding low mortality rate. They reproduce sexually and produce fewer (longer-living) offspring, which they tend to parent. They tend to stay within their established borders rather than dispersing. These characteristics form the basis for particular species to dominate in varying ecosystems. For example, an oak tree is an equilibreal species.

One of the most interesting ecological behaviors to explain through evolution is **altruism** (social behavior where organisms seem to place the needs of the community over their own needs). An altruistic trait may actually decrease the fitness of the individual with the trait (known as the cost of altruism), while it increases the fitness of the community (the benefit of altruism). When you look at altruism in terms of the individual, it would not have been an evolved trait since it decreases the individual's fitness. However, when looked at in terms of the community, an altruistic trait has value. In order for the traits of altruism to evolve, it would be necessary for some other factor to influence the preservation and proliferation of those traits. This is thought to occur in nature through a process known as **kin** selection.

Kin selection is the tendency of an individual to be altruistic toward a close relative, resulting in the preservation of its genetic traits. Close relatives have a greater likelihood of passing on identical traits to their offspring. For instance, kin selection for a gene that causes an animal to share food with its close relatives would result in this altruistic trait being spread throughout the gene pool and passed on to future generations. Thus, those relatives are more likely to survive, and their genes are passed on to the offspring, thus preserving the altruistic trait in future generations. Since the communities that have altruistic individuals are more likely to persevere, natural selection will work to maintain those communities, while the weaker communities die out. It is widely accepted that those communities containing altruistic individuals are made up of close relatives that have been able to preserve the altruism through kin selection.

Diversity of Life, Plants, and Animals

DIVERSITY OF LIFE

The world as we know it involves an array of organisms that some would consider immeasurable. In the field of biology, however, we seek to identify and understand our world and its inhabitants. It is out of this desire for knowledge that biologists from the past developed methods for categorizing and classifying all of the diverse living things that they found to exist.

Classification of Living Organisms

The study of **taxonomy** seeks to organize living things into groups based on morphology, or more recently, genetics. Scientists have sought to categorize the great diversity of life on Earth for hundreds of years.

Carolus Linnaeus, who published his book *Systema Naturae* in 1735, first developed our current methods of taxonomy. Linnaeus based his taxonomic keys on the **morphological** (outward anatomical) differences seen among species. Linnaeus designed a system of classification for all known and unknown organisms according to their anatomical similarities and differences. Although Linnaeus was a Biblical creationist who sought to show the great diversity of creation, and although he devised his system over 100 years before Darwin's *Origin of Species*, his system remains as the basis of our classification system today.

Linnaeus used two Latin-based categories—*genus* and *species*—to name each organism. Every genus name could include one or more types of species. We refer to this two-word naming of species as **binomial nomenclature** (literally meaning "two names" in Latin). For example, Linnaeus named humans *Homo sapiens* (literally "man who is wise"). *Homo* is the genus name and *sapiens* the species name. *Homo sapiens* is the only extant species left from the genus *Homo*.

Beyond genus and species, Linnaeus further categorized organisms in a total of seven levels. Every **species** also belongs to a **genus**, **family**, **order**, **class**, **phylum**, and **kingdom**. *Kingdom* is the most general category, *species* the most limited. Taxonomists now also add "sub" and "super" categories to give even more opportunity for grouping similar organisms, and have added categories even more general than kingdom (that is, **domains**).

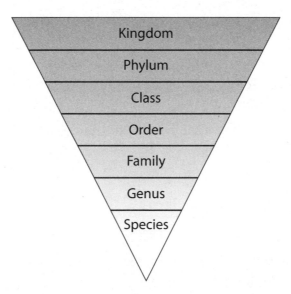

The most modern classification system contains three domains: the **Archaea**, the **Eubacteria**, and the **Eukaryota**. The organisms of the domain Archaea are prokaryotic, have unique RNA, and are able to live in the extreme ecosystems on Earth. The domain Archaea includes methane-producing organisms, and organisms able to withstand extreme temperatures and high salinity. The domain Eubacteria contains the prokaryotic organisms we call bacteria. [Note: Some taxonomists still use a system including five (or six)

kingdoms and no domains. In this case, the kingdom Monera would include organisms that are considered by other taxonomists to be included within the domains Archaea and Eubacteria.] The domain Eukaryota includes all organisms that possess eukaryotic cells. The domain Eukaryota includes the four kingdoms: **Kingdom Protista**, **Kingdom Fungi**, **Kingdom Animalia**, and **Kingdom Plantae**.

The following chart gives the major features of the four kingdoms of the Eukaryota:

KINGDOM	NO. OF KNOWN PHYLA/ SPECIES	NUTRITION	STRUCTURE	INCLUDED ORGANISMS
Protista	27/250,000 +	photosynthesis, some ingestion and absorption	large eukaryotic cells	algae & protozoa
Fungi	5/100,000 +	absorption	multicellular (eukaryotic) filaments	mold, mushrooms yeast, smuts, mildew
Animalia	33/1,000,000 +	ingestion	multicellular specialized eukaryotic motile cells	various worms, sponges, fish, insects, reptiles, amphibians, birds, and mammals
Plantae	10/250,000 +	photosynthesis	multicellular specialized eukaryotic nonmotile cells	ferns, mosses, woody and non-woody flowering plants

There are nine major phyla within the **Kingdom Animalia**. The phyla are as follows:

1. **Porifera** - the sponges

2. **Cnidaria** - jellyish, sea anemones, hydra, etc.

3. **Platyhelminthes** - flat worms

4. **Nematoda** - round worms

5. **Mollusca** - snails, clams, squid, etc.

6. **Annelida** - segmented worms (earthworms, leeches, etc.)

7. **Arthropoda** - crabs, spiders, lobster, millipedes, insects

8. **Echinodermata** - sea stars, sand dollars, etc.

9. **Chordata** - fish, amphibians, reptiles, birds, mammals, lampreys

Vertebrates are within the phylum Chordata, which is split into three subphyla, the **Urochordata** (animals with a tail cord such as tunicates), the **Cephalochordata** (animals with a head cord, such as lampreys), and **Vertebrata** (animals with a backbone).

The subphylum Vertebrata is divided into two **superclasses**, the **Aganatha** (animals with no jaws), and the **Gnathostomata** (animals with jaws). The Gnathostomata includes six classes with the following major characteristics:

a. **Chondrichthyes** - fish with a cartilaginous endoskeleton, two-chambered heart, 5-7 gill pairs, no swim bladder or lung, and internal fertilization (sharks, rays, etc.).

b. **Osteichthyes** - fish with a bony skeleton, numerous vertebrae, swim bladder (usually), two-chambered heart, gills with bony gill arches, and external fertilization (herring, carp, tuna).

c. **Amphibia** - animals with a bony skeleton, usually with four limbs having webbed feet with four toes, cold-blooded (ectothermic), large mouth with small teeth, three-chambered heart, separate sexes, internal or external fertilization, amniotic egg (salamanders, frogs, etc.).

d. **Reptilia** - horny epidermal scales, usually have paired limbs with five toes (except limbless snakes), bony skeleton, lungs, no gills, most have three-chambered heart, cold-blooded (ecothermic), internal fertilization, separate sexes, mostly egg-laying (oviparous), eggs contain extraembryonic membranes (snakes, lizards, alligators).

e. **Aves** - spindle shaped body (with head, neck, trunk, and tail), long neck, paired limbs, most have wings for lying, four-toed foot, feathers, leg scales, bony skeleton, bones with air cavities, beak, no teeth, four-chambered heart, warm blooded (endothermic), lungs with thin air sacs, separate sexes, egg-laying, eggs have hard calcified shell (birds - ducks, sparrows, etc.).

f. **Mammalia** - body covered with hair, glands (sweat, scent, sebaceous, mammary), teeth, fleshy external ears, usually four limbs, four-chambered heart, lungs, larynx, highly developed brain, warm-blooded, internal fertilization, live birth (except for the egg-laying monotremes), milk producing (cows, humans, platypus, apes, etc.).

PLANTS (BOTANY)

Most of us commonly recognize plants as organisms that produce their own food through the process of photosynthesis. (Some bacteria are also photosynthetic.) However, the plant kingdom is divided into several classifications according to physical characteristics.

Vascular plants (tracheophytes) have tissue organized in such a way as to conduct food and water throughout their structure. These plants include some that produce seeds (such as corn or roses) as well as those that do not produce any seeds (such as ferns). **Nonvascular** plants (bryophytes), such as mosses, lack special tissue for conducting water or food. They produce no seeds or flowers and are generally only a few centimeters in height.

Another method of classifying plants is according to their method of reproduction. **Angiosperms** are plants that produce flowers as reproductive organs. **Gymnosperms**, on the other hand, produce seeds without flowers. These include conifers (cone-bearers) and cycads.

Plants that survive only through a single growing season are known as **annuals**. Other plants are **biennial**; their life cycle spans two growing seasons. **Perennial** plants continue to grow year after year.

In Chapter 4 we discussed the process by which plants are said to have evolved. In this chapter we will discuss the structural and functional aspects of botany.

Plant Anatomy

Plants have structures with attributes that equip them to thrive in their environment. Angiosperms and Gymnosperms differ mostly in the structure of their stems and reproductive organs. Gymnosperms are mostly trees, with woody, instead of herbaceous stems. Gymnosperms do not produce flowers; instead they produce seeds in cones or cone-like structures.

Figure 5.1 A Typical Flowering Plant (angiosperm).
Note descriptions of numbered structures in text.

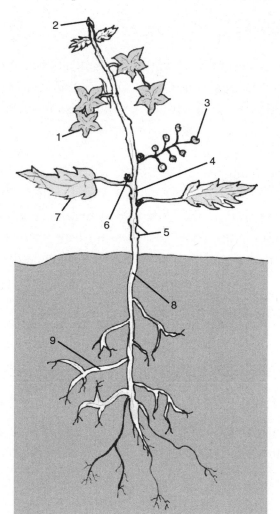

Angiosperms

The shoot system of angiosperms includes the stem, leaves, flowers, and fruit, as well as growth structures such as nodes and buds (see Figure 5.1:1-7). The signature structure of an angiosperm is the **flower (1)**, the primary reproductive organ. Before the flower blooms, it is enclosed within the **sepals (1-a)**, small, green, leaf-like structures, which fold back to reveal the flower **petals (1-b)**. The petals usually are brightly colored; their main function is to attract insects and birds, which may be necessary to the process of pollination. The short branch of stem, which supports the flower, is called the **pedicel (1-c)**.

Usually (but depending on the species), a single flower will have both male and female reproductive organs. The **pistil** is the female structure, and includes the stigma, style, ovary, and ovules. The **stigma (1-d)** is a sticky surface at the top of the pistil, which traps pollen grains. The stigma sits above a slender vase-like structure, the **style (1-e)**, which encloses the ovary. The **ovary (1-f)** is the hollow, bulb-shaped structure in the lower interior of the pistil. (After seeds have formed, the ovary will ripen and become fruit.) Within the ovary are the **ovules (1-g)**, small round cases each containing one or more egg cells. (If the egg is fertilized, the ovule will become a seed.) In the process of meiosis in the ovule, an egg cell is produced, along with smaller bodies known as polar nuclei. The polar nuclei will develop into the endosperm of the seed when fertilized by sperm cells.

Fig 5.2 Typical Flower.
Note numbered explanations in text.

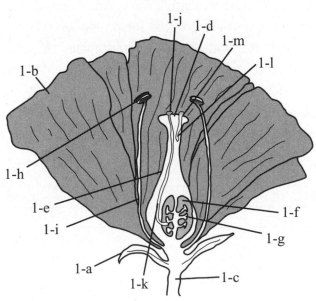

The male structure is the stamen, consisting of the **anther (1-h)** atop the long, hollow **filament (1-i)**. The anther has four lobes and contains cells (microspore mother cells) that become pollen. Some mature **pollen grains (1-j)** are conveyed (usually by wind, birds, or insects) to a flower of a compatible species, where they stick to the stigma. The stigma produces chemicals, which stimulate the pollen to burrow into the style, forming a hollow **pollen tube (1-k)**. This tube is produced by the tube **nucleus (1-l)**, which has developed from a portion of the pollen grain. The pollen tube extends down toward the ovary. Behind the tube nucleus are two **sperm nuclei (1-m)**. When the sperm nuclei reach the ovule, one will join with an egg cell, fertilizing it to become a zygote (the beginning cell of the embryo). The other sperm nucleus merges with the polar bodies forming the endosperm, which will feed the growing embryo.

The **shoot apex (2)** is composed of **meristem** tissue (consisting of undifferentiated cells capable of quick growth and specialization), and is the region where elongation of the stem occurs. The **terminal bud** (the beginning of a new set of leaves) is also located at the shoot apex. Each year, as the plant continues to grow taller, a new terminal bud and shoot apex are produced. The spot where the previous year's terminal bud was located is then called a **terminal bud scar**.

Fruit (3) is a matured ovary, which contains the seeds (mature fertilized ovules). The fruit provides protection for the seeds, as well as a method to disburse them. For instance, when ripened fruit is eaten by animals the seeds are discarded or excreted in the animal's waste, transferring the seed to a new location for germination. Each **seed** contains a tiny embryonic plant, stored food, and a seed coat for protection. When the seed is exposed to proper moisture, temperature, and oxygen, it germinates (begins to sprout and grow into a new plant). Stored food in a seed is found in the cotyledon. Angiosperms are also classified according to the structure of their cotyledons. Plants with two cotyledons in each seed are known as dicotyledons **(dicots)**; those with only one are known as monocotyledons **(monocots)**. The following chart outlines the major differences between monocots and dicots:

DICOTS	MONOCOTS
ex. oaks, flowers, vegetables	ex. grasses, lilies, palm trees
two cotyledons in seed	one cotyledon in seed
leaves have branched or networked veins	leaves have parallel veins
vascular bundles (collections of xylem and phloem tubes) arranged in rings	stems have random arrangement of are vascular bundles
taproot system with smaller secondary roots	fibrous roots
flowers with petals in multiples of four or five	flowers with petals in multiples of three

The **stem (4)** is the main support structure of the plant. The stem produces leaves and lateral (parallel with the ground) branches. **Nodes (5)** are the locations along the stem where new leaves sprout, and the space between nodes is the **internode**. New leaves begin as **lateral buds (6)**, which can be seen on growing plants.

The stem is also the main organ for transporting food and water to and from the leaves. In some cases the stem also stores food: for instance, a potato is a tuber (stem) that stores starch. The stem also contains meristem tissue.

Most of the stem tissue is made up of **vascular tissue**, including two varieties—**xylem** and **phloem**. Xylem tissue is composed of long tubular cells, which transport water up from the ground to the branches and leaves. Phloem tissue, made up of stacked cells connected by sieve plates (which allow nutrients to pass from cell to cell), transports food made in the leaves (by photosynthesis) to the rest of the plant.

The **leaf (7)** is the primary site of photosynthesis in most plants. Most leaves are thin, flat, and joined to a branch or stem by a petiole (a small stem-like extension). The petiole houses vascular tissue, which connects the veins in the leaf with those in the stem.

The **cuticle**, which maintains the leaf's moisture balance, covers most leaf surfaces. Considering a cross-section of a leaf, the outermost layer is the **epidermis (7-a, e)**. The epidermis is generally one cell thick. It secretes the waxy cuticle and protects the inner tissue of the leaf.

The mesophyll is composed of several layers of tissue between the upper and lower epidermis. The uppermost, the **palisade layer (7-b)**, contains vertically aligned cells with numerous chloroplasts. The arrangement of these cells maximizes the potential for exposure of the chloroplasts to needed sunlight. Most photosynthesis occurs in this layer.

The sugars produced by photosynthesis are transported throughout the plant via the **vascular bundles (7-c)** of xylem and phloem. The vascular bundles make up the veins in the leaf.

The next layer beneath the palisade cells is the **spongy layer (7-d)**, a layer of parenchyma cells separated by large air spaces. The air spaces allow for the exchange of gases (carbon dioxide and oxygen) for photosynthesis.

On the underside of the leaf there are openings ringed by **guard cells (7-f)**. The openings are called **stomata (7-g)** (or stomates). The stomata serve to allow moisture and gases (carbon dioxide and oxygen) to pass in and out of the leaf, thus facilitating photosynthesis.

Figure 5.3 Cross-section of a Leaf.

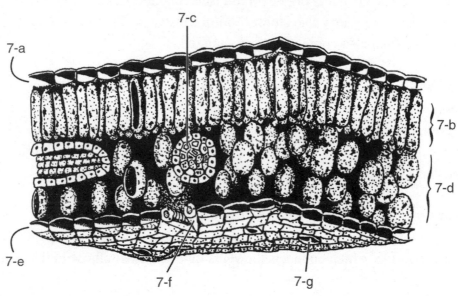

The root system of a typical angiosperm includes the **primary roots (8)**, which extend downward, and the **lateral roots (9)**, which develop secondarily and extend horizontally, parallel with the ground surface. Roots function to provide water and needed nutrients to the plant. Roots are structured to provide a large surface area for absorption. The network of the root system also anchors the plant.

Roots have four major structural regions, which run vertically from bottom to top. The **root cap** is composed of dead, thick-walled cells, and covers the tip of the root, protecting it as the root pushes through soil. The **meristematic region** is just above the root cap. It consists of undifferentiated cells, which carry on mitosis, producing cells that grow to form the **elongation region**. In the elongation region, cells differentiate, large vacuoles are formed, and cells grow. As the cells differentiate into various root tissues, they become part of the **maturation region**.

A cross-section of root tissue above the maturation region would reveal several types of **primary root tissue**. In the maturation region, the epidermis produces **root hairs**

(9-a), extensions of the cells, which reach between soil particles and retrieve water and minerals. The primary tissues include the outermost layer, the **epidermis (9-b)**. The epidermis is one cell layer thick and serves to protect the internal root tissue and absorb nutrients and water.

Figure 5.4 Root Cross-section.

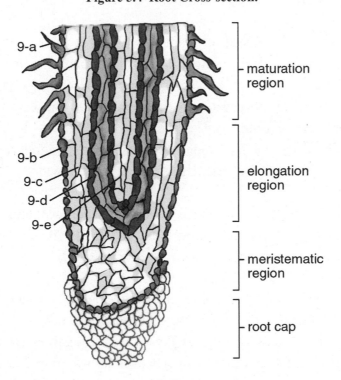

Inside the epidermis is a ring known as the **cortex (9-c)**, made up of large parenchyma cells. **Parenchyma** cells are present in many tissues of plants; they are thin-walled cells loosely packed to allow for flow of gases and uptake of minerals.

Inside the cortex is a ring of **endodermis (9-d)**, a single layer of cells, which are tightly connected so no substances can pass between cells. This feature allows the endodermis to act as a filter; all substances entering the vascular tissues from the root must pass through these cells. In the center of the root is the **vascular cylinder (9-e)**, including xylem and phloem tissue.

Plant Physiology

Water and Mineral Absorption and Transport

Although plants produce their own sugars and starches for food, they must obtain water, carbon dioxide, and minerals from their environment. Vascular plants have well-developed systems for absorption and transport of water and minerals.

Water is essential to all cells of all plants, so plants must have the ability to obtain water and transport water molecules throughout their structure. Most water is absorbed through the plant's root system, then makes its way in one of two pathways toward the xylem cells, which will transport water up the stem and to the leaves and flowers. The first pathway is for water to seep between the epidermal cells of the roots and between the parenchyma cells of the cortex. When water reaches the endodermal tissue, it enters the cells and is pushed through the vascular tissue toward the xylem.

A second pathway is for the water to pass through the cell wall and plasma membrane. Water travels along this intracellular route through channels in the cell membranes (plasmodesmata), until it reaches the xylem.

Once water reaches the xylem, hydrogen bonding between water molecules (known as **cohesion**) causes tension that pulls water through the water column up through the stem and on to the leaves (known as the **cohesion-tension process**). Some water that has traveled up through the plant to the leaves is evaporated, a process known as **transpiration**. As water is evaporated, it causes a siphoning effect (like sucking on a straw), which continues to pull water up from the root xylem, through the length of the plant and to the leaves.

Food Translocation and Storage

Food is manufactured by photosynthesis mostly in the leaves. The rest of the plant must have this food (carbohydrates) imported from the leaves. The leaves have source cells, which store the manufactured sugars. The food molecules are transferred from the source cells to phloem tissue through active transport (energy is expended to move molecules across the plasma membrane against the concentration gradient—from low concentration to high concentration). Once in the phloem, the sugars begin to build up, causing osmosis to occur (water enters the phloem lowering the sugar concentration). The entrance of water into the phloem causes pressure, which pushes the water-sugar solution through **sieve plates** that join the cells. This pressure thrusts the water-sugar solution to all areas of the plant, making food available to all cells in the plant.

C3 and C4 Plants

Refer to Chapter 3 for a more detailed review of photosynthesis. However, it is important to know that there are differences in the physiology of different plants. Accounting for over 95% of species of plants on the earth are C3 plants. In photosynthesis, these plants use the enzyme rubisco to make a three-carbon compound during the process of carbon fixation. The best climate for C3 plants would be cool, damp, and cloudy. Loss of carbon through photorespiration is high. However, the metabolic process for these plants is more energy efficient, and therefore, requires lower light levels.

C4 plants, which include many grasses such as sugar cane and maize, have an extremely low rate of carbon loss through photorespiration. The best habitat for these plants is hot and dry environments. C4 plants use water very efficiently.

Plant Reproduction and Development

The reproductive cycle of plants occurs through the alternation of haploid (n) and diploid (2n) phases. [Remember from Chapter 3 that the haploid cells have one complete set of chromosomes (n). Diploid cells have two sets of chromosomes (2n).] Diploid and haploid stages are both capable of undergoing mitosis in plants. The diploid generation is known as a **sporophyte**. The reproductive organs of the sporophyte produce **gametophytes** through the process of meiosis. Gametophytes may be male or female and are haploid. The male gametophyte produces **sperm (male gamete)**; the female produces an **egg cell (female gamete)**. When a sperm cell **fertilizes** an egg cell (haploid cells join to form a diploid cell) they produce a **zygote**. The zygote will grow into an **embryo**, which resides within the growing seed.

We are accustomed to identifying particular plants according to their adult phase, which is only one phase of the life cycle. Various phyla of plants have their own identifiable life cycles, which include an **alternation of generations**.

Figure 5.5 Alternation of Generations in Ferns.

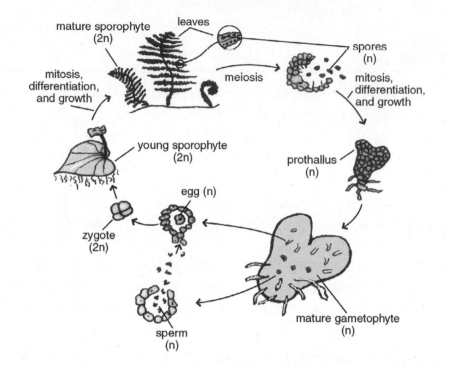

Mosses and ferns alternate haploid and diploid phases, developing two distinct generations of the plant, each with its own recognizable form. One generation is haploid, the other diploid. The haploid phase is most prominent in mosses, while in ferns the diploid stage is most prominent.

Figure 5.6 Pine Life Cycle.
The adult tree produces both male (pollen) and female (ovulate)
cones that form the pollen and ovules that combine to produce a seed.

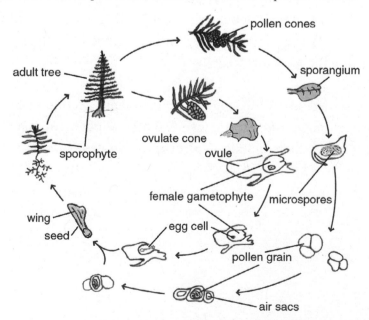

Figure 5.7 Angiosperm Life Cycle.
Pollen develops from the stamen; eggs develop from the pistil.
The pollen fertilizes the egg, resulting in an embryo within the seed.

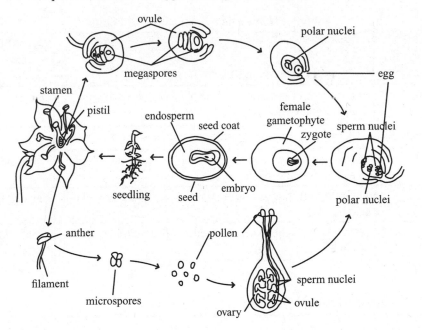

In conifers (such as pines), the sporophyte generation (diploid) is the familiar adult of the species. The process of meiosis produces the haploid gametophytes (male and female) from the male and female cone scales. The male gametophyte forms the male pollen grain and its attached air bladders, which assist it in being borne by the wind. The pollen contains sperm cells and tube cells, which will fertilize an egg cell of a female scale when they are brought into contact.

In angiosperms, the dominant adult generation is also the sporophyte—the flowering plant.

Asexual Plant Reproduction

Some plants may also reproduce through **vegetative propagation**—an asexual process. Asexual reproduction occurs through mitosis only (it does not involve gametes), and produces offspring genetically identical to the parent. While sexual reproduction leads to genetic variation and adaptation, asexual reproduction of a plant with a desirable set of genetic traits preserves these intact in successive generations. Many plants reproduce through a combination of sexual and asexual reproduction, reaping the advantages of each.

There are several types of plants that produce structures specifically designed to carry on vegetative propagation. These are described in the table below:

Table 5.1 Reproductive Structure of Plants

REPRODUCTIVE STRUCTURE	DESCRIPTION OF STRUCTURE	PLANTS WITH THESE STRUCTURES
tubers	underground storage stems which develop new shoots after dormant season	potatoes
rhizomes	underground runners that develop into new plant	irises
stolens	above-ground runners that grow roots of their own then develop into new plant	strawberries
bulbs	underground storage units that grow into many new plants via division	amaryllis
corms	resemble bulbs but with enlarged, solid stem for food storage	gladiolus, crocus

Plant Growth and Development

Hormones are chemicals that regulate the growth, development, and function of an organism. Plant cells produce hormones that bring about physiological changes within plant tissues. Each type of hormone affects changes in particular cells known as **target cells**. The traits regulated by hormones are many and varied, but there are some particularly important ones in plants. Note the most common hormones and their functions in the following table:

Table 5.2 Common Plant Hormones and their Functions

HORMONE	PROCESS REGULATED OR INFLUENCED
giberellins	cell division & cell elongation (65 hormones)
cytokinins	cell division & fruit development
abscisic acid	opening and closing of stomata (controlling water lost through transpiration and formation of winter buds that put plant in dormant state)
ethylene	ripening of fruit (spoiling releases ethylene which stimulates ripening of surrounding fruit); metabolic activity (i.e., producing female flowers to increase fertilization)
auxins	growth factors (i.e., tropisms)

A **tropism** is an involuntary response of an organism to an external stimulus such as light, water, gravity, or nutrients. For instance, plant stems are usually positively **phototropic** (they grow towards light), while plant roots are negatively phototropic (they grow away from light). Plant roots are positively **geotropic**; they grow toward the center of the earth, while stems are negatively geotropic, growing against gravity. Tropisms are thought to be caused by plant hormones, which react to the external stimulus causing some cells to grow quickly and others to grow slowly. Variations of auxin levels also influence the strength of petioles and stems, regulating when leaves or fruit drop.

There are other factors (besides hormones) that influence plant growth and development. For instance, plants respond to relative periods of light and darkness, a characteristic known as **photoperiodicity**. Light-sensitive chemicals in the leaves trigger a response in the plant, which encourages growth, flowering, or other reactions. Photoperiodicity causes flowering and growth of varying plants at different times of year.

ANIMALS (ZOOLOGY)

The animal kingdom includes a wide variety of phyla that have a range of body plans. This range includes certain invertebrates with relatively simple body plans as well as highly complex vertebrates (including humans). There are specific characteristics that differentiate animals from other living things. Organisms in the animal kingdom share the following traits:

1. Animal cells do not have cell walls or plastids.

2. Adult animals are multicellular with specialized tissues and organs.

3. Animals are heterotrophic (they do not produce their own food).

4. Animal species are capable of sexual reproduction, although some are also capable of asexual reproduction (ex. hydra).

5. Animals develop from embryonic stages.

In addition to the above traits, most adult animals have a symmetrical anatomy. Adult animals can have either radial symmetry (constituent parts are arranged radiating symmetrically about a center point) or bilateral symmetry (the body can be divided along a center plane into equal, mirror-image halves). There are a few exceptions to this rule, including the adult sponge whose body is not necessarily symmetrical. While there is wide variation in the physical structure of animals, the animal kingdom is usually divided into two broad categories—invertebrates and vertebrates. There are many more species of invertebrates than vertebrates.

Invertebrates are those species having no internal backbone structure; **vertebrates** have internal backbones. Invertebrates include sponges and worms, which have no skeletal structure at all, and arthropods, mollusks, crustaceans, etc., which have exoskeletons. In fact, there are many more phyla of invertebrates than vertebrates (about 950,000 phyla of invertebrates and only about 40,000 phyla of vertebrates).

Animal Anatomy

Tissues

Like all multicellular organisms, animal bodies contain several kinds of tissues, made up of different cell types. Differentiated cells may organize into specialized tissues performing particular functions. There are eight major types of animal tissue:

1) **Epithelial tissue** consists of thin layers of cells. Epithelial tissue makes up the layers of skin, lines ducts and the intestine, and covers the inside of the body cavity. Epithelial tissue forms the barrier between the environment and the interior of the body.

2) **Connective tissue** covers internal organs and composes ligaments and tendons. This tissue holds tissues and organs together, stabilizing the body structure.

3) **Muscle tissue** is divided into three types—smooth, skeletal, and cardiac. **Smooth** muscle makes up the walls of internal organs and functions in involuntary movement (breathing, digestion, etc.). **Skeletal** muscle attaches bones of the skeleton to each other and surrounding tissues. Skeletal muscles' function is to enable voluntary movement. **Cardiac** muscle is the tissue forming the walls of the heart. Its strength and electrical properties are vital to the heart's ability to pump blood.

4) **Bone tissue** is found in the skeleton and provides support, protection for internal organs, and ability to move as muscles pull against bones.

5) **Cartilage tissue** reduces friction between bones, and supports and connects them. For example, it is found at the ends of bones and in the ears and nose.

6) **Adipose tissue** is found beneath the skin and around organs, providing cushioning, insulation, and fat storage.

7) **Nerve tissue** is found in the brain, spinal cord, nerves, and ganglion. It carries electrical and chemical impulses to and from organs and limbs to the brain. Nerve tissue in the brain receives these impulses and sustains mental activity.

8) **Blood tissue** consists of several cell types in a fluid called plasma. It flows through the blood vessels and heart, and is essential for carrying oxygen to cells, fighting infection, and carrying nutrients and wastes to and from cells. Blood also has clotting capabilities, which preserve the body's functions in case of injury.

Tissues are organized into organs, and organs function together to form systems, which support the life of an organism. Studying these systems allows us to understand how organisms thrive within their ecosystem.

Systems

Many different body plans exist amongst animals, and each type of body plan includes systems necessary for the organism to live. Our discussion of systems here focuses on those found in most vertebrates. Vertebrates are highly complex organisms with several systems working together to perform the functions necessary to life. These include the digestive, gas exchange, skeletal, nervous, circulatory, excretory, and immune systems.

Digestive System

The **digestive system** (see Figure 5.8) serves as a processing plant for ingested food. The digestive system in animals generally encompasses the processes of **ingestion** (food intake), **digestion** (breaking down of ingested particles into molecules that can be absorbed by the body), and **egestion** (the elimination of indigestible materials). In most vertebrates, the digestive organs are divided into two categories, the **alimentary canal** and the **accessory organs**. The alimentary canal is also known as the **gastrointestinal** (or GI) **tract** and includes the mouth, pharynx, esophagus, stomach, small intestine, large intestine, rectum, and anus. The accessory organs include the teeth, tongue, salivary glands, liver, gallbladder, and pancreas.

The **mouth** (oral cavity, **1**) is the organ of ingestion and the first organ of digestion in the GI tract. The first step in digestion in many vertebrates occurs as food is chewed. Chewing is the initial step in breaking down food into particles of manageable size. Chewing also increases the surface area of the food and mixes it with saliva, which contains the starch-digesting enzyme **amylase**. Saliva is secreted by the **salivary glands (2)**. Chewed food is then swallowed and moved toward the **stomach (3)** by peristalsis (muscle contraction) of the **esophagus (4)**. The stomach is a muscular organ that stores incompletely digested food. The stomach continues the mechanical and chemical breakdown of food particles begun by the chewing process. The lining of the stomach secretes mucous to protect it from the strong digestive chemicals necessary in the digestive process. The stomach also secretes digestive enzymes and hydrochloric acid, which continue the digestive process to the point of producing a watery soup of nutrients, which then proceeds through the pyloric sphincter into the small intestine (the duodenum). The **pancreas (5)** and **gall bladder (6)** release more enzymes into the small intestine, the site where the final steps of digestion and most absorption occurs. The cells lining the **small intestine (7)** have protrusions out into the lumen of the intestine called **villi**. Villi provide a large surface area for absorption of nutrients. Nutrients move into the capillaries through or between the cells making up the villi. The enriched blood travels to the **liver (8)**, where some sugars are removed and stored. The undigestible food proceeds from the small intestine to the **large intestine (9)** where water is absorbed back into the body. The waste **(feces)** is then passed through the **rectum (10)** and excreted from the **anus (11)**.

Figure 5.8 Human Digestive System

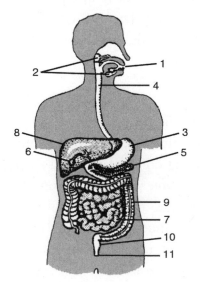

There are, of course, variations in the digestive system among animals of various classifications. Some vertebrates such as cows and deer are **ruminants**; they consume large amounts of vegetation. These animals have several chambers in their stomachs. Chewed vegetation is regurgitated from the first two stomach chambers as **cud**, and is chewed again, allowing much of their food to be broken down mechanically. Bacteria in the digestive track then break down cellulose, the main constituent of a ruminant's diet.

Many invertebrates, such as insects and earthworms, have digestive systems resembling those of vertebrates, including a mouth, esophagus, stomach, and intestines. Many of these species also have a **crop**, an organ that stores food until it is processed for absorption. Other animals have only a sac-like digestive cavity that performs the necessary functions of digestion.

Figure 5.9 Human Respiratory System

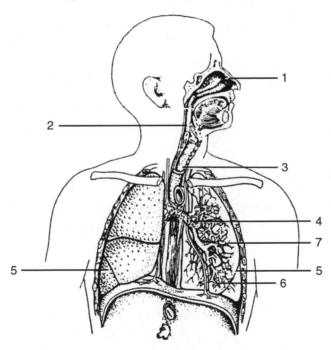

Respiratory or Gas Exchange System

Also known as the **respiratory system** (see Figure 5.9), the **gas exchange system** is responsible for the intake and processing of gases required by an organism, and for expelling gases produced as waste products. In humans, air is taken in primarily through the **nose** (although gases may be inhaled through the mouth, the nose is better at filtering out pollutants in the air). The **nasal passages (1)** have a mucous lining to capture foreign particles. This lining is surrounded by epithelial tissue with embedded capillaries, which serve to warm the entering air. Air then passes through the **pharynx (2)** and into the **trachea (3)**. The trachea includes the windpipe or **larynx** in its upper portion, and the **glottis**, an opening allowing gases to pass into the two branches known as the bronchi. The glottis is guarded by a flap of tissue, the **epiglottis**, which prevents food particles from entering the bronchial tubes. The **bronchi (4)** lead to the two **lungs (5)** where they branch out in all directions into smaller tubules known as **bronchioles (6)**. The bronchioles end in **alveoli (7)**, thin-walled air sacs, which are the site of gas exchange. The bronchioles are surrounded by capillaries, which bring blood with a high density of carbon dioxide and a low concentration of oxygen from the pulmonary arteries. At the alveoli, the carbon dioxide diffuses from the blood into the alveoli and oxygen diffuses from the alveoli into the blood. The oxygenated blood is carried away to tissues throughout the body.

All living organisms require the ability to exchange gases, and there are several variations to the means and organs utilized for this life process. Invertebrates such as the earthworm are able to absorb gases through their skin. Insects rely on the diffusion of gases through holes in the exoskeleton known as spiracles. In single-celled organisms such as the amoeba, diffusion of gases occurs directly through the plasma membrane.

Musculoskeletal System

The **musculoskeletal system** provides the body with structure, stability, and the ability to move. The musculoskeletal system is unique to vertebrates, although some invertebrates (such as mollusks and insects) have external support structures (exoskeletons) and muscle.

In humans, the musculoskeletal system is composed of joints, ligaments, cartilage, muscle groups, and 206 bones. The skeleton provides protection for the soft internal organs, as well as structure and stability, allowing for an upright stature and movement. Bones also perform the important function of storing calcium and phosphates, and producing red blood cells within the bone marrow. The 206 bones forming the human skeleton are linked with movable joints, and joined by muscle systems controlling movement.

Skeletal muscles are voluntary—they are activated by command from the nervous system. **Smooth muscle** lines most internal organs, protecting their contents and function, and generally contracting without conscious intent. For instance, the involuntary (automatic) contraction of smooth muscle in the esophagus and lungs facilitates digestion and respiration. **Cardiac muscle** is unique to the heart. It is involuntary muscle (like smooth muscle), but cardiac muscle also has unique features, which cause it to "beat" rhythmically. Cardiac muscle cells have branched endings that interlock with each other, keeping the muscle fibers from ripping apart during their strong contractions. In addition, electrical impulses travel in waves from cell to cell in cardiac muscle, causing the muscle to contract in a coordinated way with a rhythmic pace.

Nervous System

The **nervous system** is a communication network that connects the entire body of an organism, and provides control over bodily functions and actions. Nerve tissue is composed of nerve cells known as **neurons and glial cells**. Neurons carry impulses via electrochemical responses through their **cell body** and **axon** (long root-like appendage of the cell). Nerve cells exist in networks, with axons of neighbor neurons interacting across small spaces **(synapses)**. Chemical neurotransmitters send messages along the nerve network causing responses specific to varying types of nerve tissue. The nervous system allows the body to sense stimuli and conditions in the environment and respond with necessary reactions. **Sensory organs**—skin, eyes, nose, ears, etc.—transmit signals in response to environmental stimuli to the **brain**, which then conveys messages via nerves to glands and muscles, which produce the necessary response.

Figure 5.10 A typical neuron.

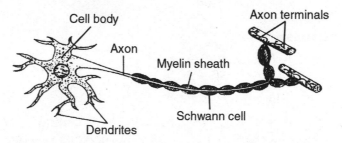

The human nervous system (and that of many mammals) is anatomically divided into two systems, the central nervous system and the peripheral nervous system. The following outline shows the components of each portion of the nervous system.

I. **Central Nervous System** (CNS) - two main components, the **brain** and the **spinal cord**. These organs control all other organs and systems of the body. The spinal cord is a continuation of the brain stem, and acts as a conduit of nerve messages.

II. **Peripheral Nervous System** (PNS) - a network of nerves throughout the body.
   A) **Sensory Division**
       1. **visceral sensory nerves** - carry impulses from body organs to CNS
       2. **somatic sensory nerves** - carry impulses from body surface to CNS
   B) **Motor Division**
       1. **somatic motor nerves** - carries impulses to skeletal muscle from CNS
       2. **autonomic**
           a.) **sympathetic** nervous system - carries impulses that stimulate organs
           b.) **parasympathetic** nervous system - carries impulses back from organs

Figure 5.11 Human Nervous System.

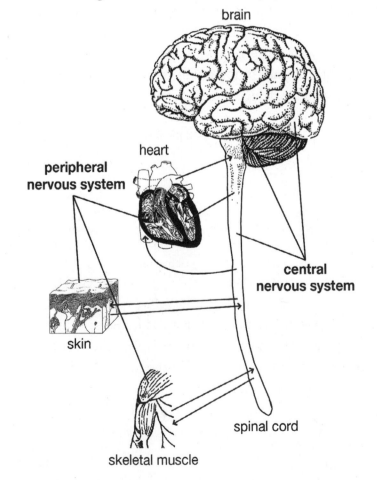

The brain of vertebrates has three major divisions, the forebrain, midbrain, and hindbrain. The **forebrain** is located most anterior, and contains the **olfactory lobes** (sense of smell), **cerebrum** (controls sensory and motor responses, memory, speech, and most factors of intelligence), as well as the **thalamus** (integrates senses), **hypothalamus** (is involved in hunger, thirst, blood pressure, body temperature, hostility, pain, pleasure, etc.), and **pituitary gland** (releases various hormones). The **midbrain** is between the forebrain and hindbrain and contains the **optic lobes** (visual center connected to the eyes by the optic nerves). The **hindbrain** consists of the **cerebellum** (controls balance, equilibrium, and muscle coordination) and the **medulla oblongata** (controls involuntary response such as breathing and heartbeat).

Within the brain, nerve tissue is grayish in color and is called **gray matter**. The nerve cells, which exist in the spinal cord and throughout the body, have insulation covering their axons. This insulation (called the **myelin sheath**) speeds electrochemical conduction within the axon of the nerve cell. Since the myelin sheath gives this tissue a white color, it is called **white matter**. The myelin sheath is made up of individual cells called Schwann cells.

The nervous systems of vertebrates and some invertebrates are highly sophisticated, providing conscious response and unconscious controls. However, the nervous systems of some species of invertebrates (such as jellyfish) are relatively simple networks of neurons that control only some aspects of their body functions.

Circulatory System

The process of cellular metabolism is a fundamental process of life and cannot proceed without a continuous supply of oxygen to every living cell within the body. The **circulatory system** is the conduit for delivering nutrients and gases to all cells and for removing waste products from them.

In invertebrates, the circulatory system may consist entirely of diffusion in the gastrovascular cavity, or it may be an **open circulatory system** (where blood directly bathes the internal organs), or a **closed circulatory system** (where blood is confined to vessels).

Closed circulatory systems are more typical of vertebrates. In vertebrates, **blood** flows throughout the circulatory system within **vessels**. Vessels include **arteries**, **veins**, and **capillaries**. The pumping action of the **heart** (a hollow, muscular organ) forces blood in one direction throughout the system. In large animals, valves within the heart, and some of the vessels in limbs, keep blood from flowing backwards (being pulled downward by gravity).

Blood carries many products to cells throughout the body, including minerals, infection-fighting white blood cells, nutrients, proteins, hormones, and metabolites. Blood also carries dissolved gases (particularly oxygen) to cells and waste gases (mainly carbon dioxide) away from cells.

Capillaries (tiny vessels) surround all tissues of the body and exchange carbon dioxide for oxygen. Oxygen is carried by **hemoglobin** (containing iron) in red blood cells. Oxygen enters the blood in the lungs and travels to the heart, then through **arteries** (larger vessels that carry blood away from the heart), **arterioles** (small arteries), to capillaries. The blood picks up carbon dioxide waste from the cells and carries it through capillaries, then **venules** (small veins), and **veins** (vessels that carry blood toward the heart), back to the heart and on to the lungs. Thus, blood is continually cycled.

Figure 5.12 Human Circulatory System
Blood flows from the heart through arteries to the capillaries
throughout the body and returns via the veins.

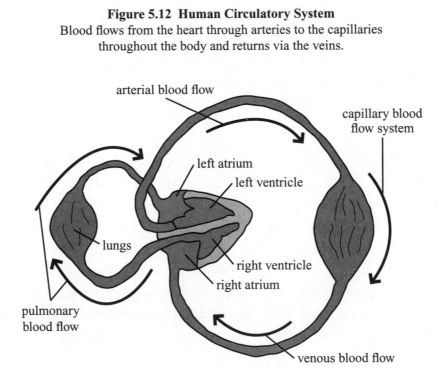

Excretory System

The **excretory system** is responsible for collecting waste materials, filtering waste out of body fluids, and transporting them to organs that expel them from the body. There are many types of waste that must be expelled from the body, and there are many organs involved in this process.

The primary excretory organs of most vertebrates are the kidneys. The **kidneys** filter metabolic wastes from the blood and excrete them as **urine** into the urinary tract. The urinary tract carries the fluid that is eventually expelled from the body. Urine is typically 95% water, and may contain urea (formed from breakdown of proteins), uric acid (formed from breaking down nucleic acids), creatinine (a byproduct of muscle contraction), and various minerals and hormones.

The **skin** is an accessory excretory organ; salts, urea, and other wastes are secreted with water from sweat glands in the skin.

The **liver** produces **bile** which aids in digesting fats and also carries away broken down pigments and chemicals (often from pollutants and medications) and secretes them into the small intestine, where they proceed to the large intestine and are expelled in the feces. The liver also breaks down some nitrogenous molecules (including some proteins), excreting them as urea.

The **lungs** are the sites of excretion for carbon dioxide.

Immune System

The **immune system** functions to defend the body from infection by bacteria and viruses. The **lymphatic system** is the principal infection-fighting component of the immune system. The organs of the lymphatic system in humans and other higher invertebrates include the lymph, lymph nodes, spleen, thymus, and tonsils. **Lymph** is a collection of excess fluid that is absorbed from between cells into a special system of vessels; it circulates through the lymphatic system and finally dumps into the bloodstream. Lymph also collects plasma proteins that have leaked into interstitial fluids.

Lymph nodes are small masses of lymph tissue whose function is to filter lymph and produce lymphocytes. **Lymphocytes** and other cells are involved in the immune system. Lymphocytes begin in bone marrow as stem cells and are collected and distributed via the lymph nodes. There are two classes of lymphocytes, B cells and T cells. **B cells** emerge from the bone marrow mature, and produce **antibodies**, which enter the bloodstream. These antibodies find and attach themselves to foreign **antigens** (toxins, bacteria, foreign cells, etc.). The attachment of an antibody to an antigen marks the pair for destruction.

The **spleen** contains some lymphatic tissue, and is located in the abdomen. It filters larger volumes of lymph than nodes can handle. The **tonsils** are a group of lymph cells connected together and located in the throat.

The **thymus** is another mass of lymph tissue, which is active only through the teen years, fighting infection and producing T cells. **T cells** mature in the thymus gland. Some T cells (like B cells) patrol the blood for antigens, but T cells are also equipped to destroy antigens themselves. T cells also regulate the body's immune responses.

Homeostatic Mechanisms

All living cells, tissues, organs, and organisms must maintain a tight range of physical and chemical conditions in order for them to live. Conditions such as temperature, pH, water balance, sugar levels, etc., must be monitored and controlled in order to keep them within the accepted ranges that will not inhibit life. When the conditions of an organism are within acceptable ranges, it is said to be in **homeostasis**. Organisms have a special set of mechanisms that serve to keep them in homeostasis. Homeostasis is a state of dynamic equilibrium, which balances forces tending toward change and forces acceptable for life functions.

There are many instances of feedback control. These take effect when any situation arises that may drive levels out of the normal acceptable range. In other words, the homeostatic mechanism is a reaction to a stimulus. This reaction, called a **feedback response**, is the production of some counterforce that levels the system.

Homeostasis is achieved mostly by actions of the sympathetic and parasympathetic nervous systems by a process known as **feedback control**. For instance, when the body undergoes physical activity, muscle action causes a rise in temperature. If not checked, rising temperature could destroy cells. In this instance, the nervous system detects rising temperature and reacts with a response that causes sweat glands to produce sweat. The evaporation of sweat cools the body.

Hormonal Control in Homeostasis and Reproduction

Hormones are chemicals produced in the endocrine glands of an organism, which generally travel through the circulatory system and are taken up by specific targeted organs or tissues, where they modify metabolic activities.

A hormone is manufactured in response to a particular **stimulus**. The hormone (for instance a **steroid**) enters the bloodstream from one of the ductless endocrine glands that manufacture hormones. The steroid passes through the cell membrane of the targeted cell and enters the cytoplasm. The hormone combines with a particular protein known as a receptor, creating the **hormone-receptor complex**. This complex enters the nucleus and binds to a DNA molecule, causing a gene to be transcribed. The mRNA molecule leaves the nucleus for the endoplasmic reticulum, where it encodes a particular protein. The protein migrates to the site of the stimulus and counteracts the source of the stimulus.

The second process targets receptors on a cell's membrane. A particular **receptor** exists on the membrane when the cell is in a particular condition (for instance, containing an excess of glucose). When the hormone binds with the receptor on the membrane, the receptor changes its form. This triggers a chain of events within the cytoplasm resulting in the production or destruction of proteins, thus moderating the conditions.

Hormones control many physiological functions, from digestion, to conscious responses and thinking, to reproduction. In humans, for instance, women of childbearing age have a continuous cycle of hormones. The hormone cycle causes the release of eggs at specific times. If the egg is fertilized, a different combination of hormones stimulates a chain of events that promotes the development of the embryo.

Animal Reproduction and Development

Reproduction in multicellular animals is a complex process that generally proceeds through the steps of **gametogenesis** (gamete formation) and then **fertilization**.

Gametes are the sex cells formed in the reproductive organs—sperm and eggs. When a sperm of one individual combines with the egg cell of another, the resulting cell is known as a **zygote**. A **zygote** then develops into a new individual. In the case of **spermatogenesis** (sperm formation), diploid **primary spermatocytes** are formed from special cells **(spermatogonia)** in the testes. The primary spermatocytes then undergo meiosis I, forming haploid **secondary spermatocytes** with a single chromosome set. (Please see the section on meiosis in Chapter 3.) The secondary spermatocytes go through meiosis II, forming **spermatids**, which are haploid. These spermatids then develop into the **sperm cells**.

In human female reproductive organs, egg cells are formed through a similar process known as **oogenesis**. **Primary oocytes** are typically present in great number in the female's ovaries at birth. Primary oocytes undergo meiosis I, forming one **secondary oocyte** and one smaller **polar body**. Both the secondary oocyte and the polar body undergo meiosis II; the polar body producing two polar bodies (not functional cells), and the oocyte producing one more polar body and one haploid **egg cell**. The egg cell is now ready for fertilization, and if there are sperm cells present, the egg may be fertilized, forming a diploid cell with a new combination of chromosomes, the zygote.

All multicellular organisms that reproduce sexually begin life as a zygote. The zygote then undergoes a series of cell divisions known as **cleavage**. After the first few divisions, the cluster of cells is called a morula. The **morula** then continues cell division, and the cluster begins to take shape as a thin layer of cells surrounding an internal cavity, the **blastula**. As cell division continues, the cells migrate and rearrange themselves, transforming the blastula into a two-layered cup shape, called the **gastrula** (a process known as **gastrulation**). As the gastrula develops, the cup shape reforms itself into a double-layered tube. The ectoderm, mesoderm, and endoderm form through the process of gastrulation and are collectively called the **germ layers**. As the germ layers develop, the embryo becomes recognizable, and differentiation continues until the organ systems are fully developed.

The outer layer of the gastrula tube will become the **ectoderm**, which later will develop into the skin, some endocrine glands, and the nervous system. The inner layer of the tube will become the **endoderm**, the precursor of the gut lining and various accessory structures. With further development, a third layer, between the ectoderm and endoderm arises—the **mesoderm**. The mesoderm layer will eventually form muscles, and organs of the skeletal, circulatory, respiratory, reproductive, and excretory systems.

Figure 5.13 Human Extraembryonic Membranes

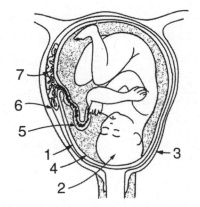

In addition to forming the tissues and organ systems of vertebrates, the germ layers also develop into **extraembryonic membranes** (i.e., membranes not part of the embryos themselves, see Figure 5.13). The first of these membranes is the **chorion (1)**. In egg-laying vertebrates, the chorion lies in contact with the innermost surface of the shell, while in other vertebrates it is the outermost membrane surrounding the **embryo (2)** and in contact with the **uterus (3)**. In both cases, the chorion functions in regulating the passage of gases and water from the embryo to its surrounding environment. In embryos without shells, the chorion also controls passage of nutrients and wastes between the embryo and the mother.

Within the chorion is the **amnion (4)**, a fluid-filled **(amniotic fluid)** sac enclosing the embryo. The amniotic fluid cushions the embryo and helps keep temperatures constant. The fluid also keeps the amnionic membrane from sticking to the developing embryo.

The third membrane is the **allantois (5)**. It arises from the developing digestive tract. In humans and other vertebrates that bear live young, the allantois appears in the third week of development and becomes part of the **umbilical cord**. It contains blood vessels, which function to exchange gases and nutrients between the embryo and the mother. In egg-laying reptiles, the allantois is a reservoir for wastes. It fuses with the chorion, forming the **chorioallantoic membrane**, which regulates gas exchanges through the shell.

The **yolk sac membrane (6)**, enclosing the **yolk sac (7)**, also forms from the developing digestive tract and also becomes part of the umbilical cord. The yolk sac stores nutrients for use by the embryo. The yolk sac is larger and contains more material in egg-laying species, since there is no continuing contact with the mother. The yolk sac cells also give rise to gametes, which develop in reproductive organs of the embryo.

In mammals, the outer cells of the embryo and the inner cells of the uterus combine to form the **placenta**. The placenta is the connection between the mother and embryo; it is the site of transfer for nutrients, water, and wastes between them. The embryo synthesizes its own blood that is kept separate from the mother's blood. In the placenta, the vessels (that connect the circulatory system of the embryo through the umbilical cord to the placenta) pass right next to the mother's blood vessels. Nutrients, water, and oxygen diffuse from the mother's blood to the embryo's, while wastes and carbon dioxide diffuse into the mother's blood supply.

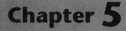

Parthenogenesis

A type of asexual reproduction that occurs in animals is **parthenogenesis**. This reproduction does not require fertilization by males of the species in order for an embryo to form and develop. Examples of animals that reproduce by parthenogenesis (though exceedingly rare) include fish, sharks and some reptiles.

CHAPTER 6

Ecology

Ecology is the study of how organisms interact with other organisms, and how they influence or are influenced by their physical **environment**. The word "ecology" is derived from the Greek term *oikos* (meaning "home" or "place to live") and *ology* (meaning "the study of"), so ecology is a study of organisms in their home. This study has revealed a number of patterns and principles that help us understand how organisms relate to their environment and how different organisms affect each other. First, however, it is important to grasp some basic vocabulary used in ecology.

The part of the Earth that includes all living things is called the **biosphere**. The Earth also includes the **atmosphere** (air), the **lithosphere** (ground), and the **hydrosphere** (water).

The study of ecology centers on the ecosystem. An **ecosystem** is a group of populations found within a given locality, plus the inanimate environment around those populations. An ecosystem can refer to a setting of any size. A **population** is the total number of a single species of organism found in a given ecosystem. Typically, there are many populations of different species within a particular ecosystem. The term **organism** refers to an individual of a particular species. Each species is a distinct group of individuals that are able to interbreed (mate), producing viable offspring. Although species are defined by their ability to reproduce, they are usually described by their morphology (their anatomical features).

Populations that interact with each other in a particular ecosystem are collectively termed a **community**. For instance, a temperate forest community includes pine trees, oaks, shrubs, lichen, mosses, ferns, squirrels, deer, insects, owls, bacteria, fungi, etc.

A **habitat** refers to the physical place where a species lives. A species' habitat must include all the factors that will support its life and reproduction. These factors may be **biotic** (i.e., living - food source, predators, etc.) and **abiotic** (i.e., nonliving - weather, temperature, soil features, etc.).

A species' **niche** is the role it plays within the ecosystem. It includes its physical requirements (such as light and water) and its biological activities (how it reproduces, how it acquires food, etc.). One important aspect of a species' niche is its place in the food chain.

ECOLOGICAL CYCLES

Every species within an ecosystem requires resources and energy in varying forms. The interaction of organisms and the environment can be described as cycles of energy and resources that allow the community to flourish. Although each ecosystem has its own energy and nutrient cycles, these cycles also interact with each other to form bioregional and planetary biological cycles.

The **energy cycle** supports life throughout the environment. There are also several **biogeochemical cycles** (the water cycle, the carbon cycle, the nitrogen cycle, the phosphorous cycle, etc.), which are also important to the health of ecosystems. A biogeochemical cycle is the system whereby the substances needed for life are recycled and transported throughout the environment.

Carbon, hydrogen, oxygen, phosphorous, and nitrogen are called macronutrients; they are used in large quantities by living things. Micronutrients, those elements utilized in trace quantities in organisms, include iodine, iron, zinc, and copper.

Energy Cycle (Food Chain)

Since all life requires the input of energy, the **energy cycles** within the ecosystem are central to its well-being. On Earth, the Sun provides the energy that is the basis of life in most ecosystems. (An exception is the hydrothermal vent communities that derive their energy from the heat of the Earth's core.) Without the constant influx of solar energy into our planetary ecosystem, most life would cease to exist. Energy generally flows through the entire ecosystem in one direction—from producers to consumers and on to decomposers (consumers may also consume decomposers) through the **food chain**.

Photosynthetic organisms—such as plants, some protists, and some bacteria—are the first link in most food chains; they use the energy of sunlight to combine carbon dioxide and water into sugars, releasing oxygen gas (O_2). Photosynthetic organisms are called producers, since they synthesize sugar and starch molecules using the Sun's energy to link the carbons in carbon dioxide. Primary consumers (also known as herbivores) are species that eat photosynthetic organisms. Consumers utilize sugars and starches stored in other organisms for energy. Secondary consumers feed on primary consumers, and on the chain goes, through tertiary, quaternary (etc.) consumers. Finally, decomposers (bacteria, fungi, some animals) are species that recycle the organic material found in dead plants and animals back into the food chain.

Figure 6.1 A Food Chain

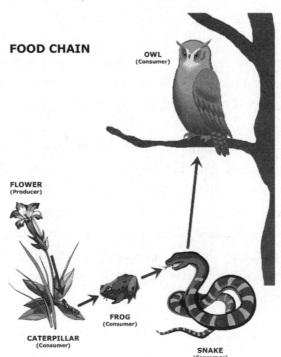

FOOD CHAIN

OWL
(Consumer)

FLOWER
(Producer)

FROG
(Consumer)

CATERPILLAR
(Consumer)

SNAKE
(Consumer)

Animals that feed only on other animals are called **carnivores** (meat-eaters), whereas those that consume both photosynthetic organisms and other animals are known as **omnivores**.

The energy cycle of the food chain is subject to the laws of thermodynamics. Energy can neither be created nor destroyed. However, every use of energy is less than 100% efficient; about 10% is lost as heat. When we call photosynthetic organisms producers, we mean that they produce food, using the Sun's energy to form chemical bonds in sugars and other biomolecules. Other organisms can use the energy stored in the bonds of these biomolecules.

The steps in the food chain are also known as **trophic levels**. Consider the food chain diagram (Figure 6.1) as one example of a food chain with many trophic levels. Plants are on the bottom in this example of the chain; they are the producers, the first trophic level. Producers are also known as **autotrophs**, as they produce their own food. Each trophic level is greater in **biomass** (total mass of organisms) than the level above it.

The caterpillar represents the **second trophic level**, or primary consumers, in this example of a food chain. Caterpillars consume plants and are consumed (in this example) by a frog, the secondary consumers, which represent the **third trophic level**. Snakes consume frogs, and are in turn consumed by an owl—making these the **fourth and fifth trophic levels**. In this example, bacteria are the decomposers that recycle some of the nutrients from dead owls (and other levels) to be reused by the first trophic level.

The illustration of a food chain, however, in nature is never actually as simple as shown. Owls consume snakes, but they may also consume toads (a lower level in the pyramid) and fish (from an entirely different pyramid). Thus, within every ecosystem there may be numerous food chains interacting in varying ways to form a **food web**. Furthermore, all organisms produce waste products that feed decomposers. The food web represents the cycling and recycling of both energy and nutrients within the ecosystem. The productivity of the entire web is dependent upon the amount of photosynthesis carried out by photosynthesizers.

Water Cycle

The availability of water is crucial to the survival of all living things. Water vapor circulates through the biosphere in a process called the **hydrologic cycle**. Water is evaporated via solar radiation from the ocean and other bodies of water into clouds. Water is also released into the atmosphere from vegetation (leaves) by transpiration. Some water is also evaporated directly from soil, but most water in the ground flows into underground aquifers, which eventually empty into the oceans. Water above ground flows into waterways, which also eventually flow into the ocean (a process known as runoff). Water vapor is then redistributed over land (and back into oceans as well) via clouds, which release water as precipitation.

Figure 6.2 The Water Cycle

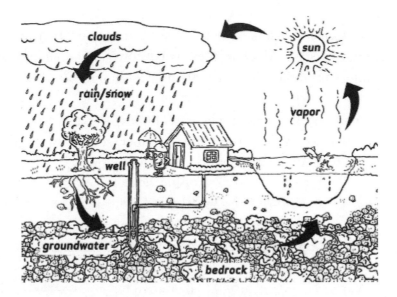

The water cycle also has a profound effect on Earth's climate. Clouds reflect the Sun's radiation away from the Earth, causing cool weather. Water vapor in the air also acts as a **greenhouse gas**, reflecting radiation from the Earth's surface back toward the Earth, and therefore trapping heat. The water cycle also intersects with nearly all the other cycles of elements and nutrients.

Nitrogen Cycle

Nitrogen is another substance essential to life processes, since it is a key component of amino acids (components of proteins) and nucleic acids. The nitrogen cycle recycles nitrogen. Nitrogen is the most plentiful gas in the atmosphere, making up 78% of the air. However, neither photosynthetic organisms nor animals are able to use nitrogen gas (N_2), which does not readily react with other compounds, directly from the air. Instead, a process known as **nitrogen-fixing** makes nitrogen available for absorption by the roots of plants. **Nitrogen fixing** is the process of combining gaseous (N_2) nitrogen with either hydrogen or oxygen to form a non-gas compound that can be utilized directly by plants.

Nitrogen-fixing bacteria live in the soil and perform the task of nitrogen fixation by combining nitrogen and hydrogen from the atmosphere, forming ammonium ($NH4^+$ ions). (Some cyanobacteria, also called blue-green bacteria, are also active in this process.) Ammonium ions are then absorbed and used by plants. Some types of nitrogen-fixing bacteria live in symbiosis on the nodules of the roots of legumes (beans, peas, clover, etc.), supplying the roots with a direct source of ammonia.

Some plants are unable to use ammonia, instead, they use **nitrates**. Some bacteria perform **nitrification**, a process, which further breaks down ammonia into nitrites (NO_2^-), and yet again by another bacteria, which converts nitrites into nitrates (NO_3^-).

Nitrogen compounds (such as ammonia and nitrates) are also produced by natural, physical processes such as volcanic activity. Another source of usable nitrogen is lightning, which reacts with atmospheric nitrogen to form nitrates.

Figure 6.3 The Nitrogen Cycle

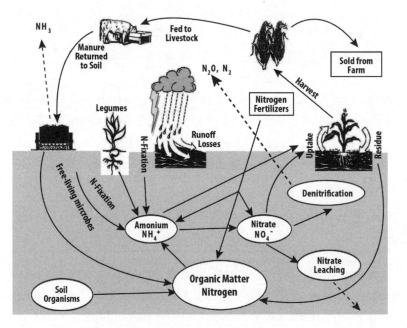

In addition, nitrogen passes along through the food chain, and is recycled through decomposition processes. When plants are consumed, the amino acids are recombined and used, a process that passes the nitrogen-containing molecules on through the food chain or web. Animal waste products, such as urine, release nitrogen compounds (primarily ammonia) back into the environment, yet another source of nitrogen. Finally, large amounts of nitrogen are returned to the Earth by bacteria and fungi, which decompose dead plant and animal matter into ammonia (and other substances), a process known as **ammonification**.

Various species of bacteria and fungi are also responsible for breaking down excess nitrates, a process known as **denitrification**, which releases nitrogen gas back into the air. The nitrogen cycle involves cycling nitrogen through both living and non-living entities.

Carbon Cycle

The carbon cycle is the route by which carbon is obtained, used, and recycled by living things. Carbon is an important element contained in the cells of all species. The study of organic chemistry is the study of carbon-based molecules.

Figure 6.4 The Carbon Cycle

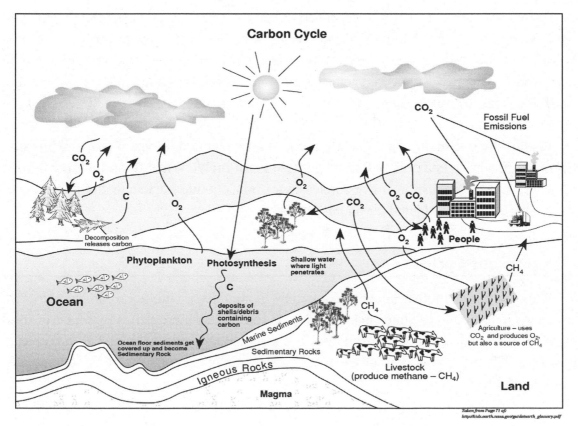

Earth's atmosphere contains large amounts of carbon in the form of carbon dioxide (CO_2). Photosynthetic organisms require the intake of carbon dioxide for the process of photosynthesis, which is the foundation of the food chain. Nearly all of the carbon within organisms is derived from the production of carbohydrates in photosynthetic organisms through photosynthesis. The process of photosynthesis also releases oxygen molecules (O_2), which are necessary to animal respiration. Animal respiration releases carbon dioxide back into the atmosphere in large quantities.

Since plant cells consist of molecules containing carbon, animals that consume photosynthetic organisms are consuming and using carbon from the photosynthetic organisms. Carbon is passed along the food chain as these animals are then consumed. Animal respiration releases carbon dioxide back into the atmosphere in large quantities. When animals and photosynthetic organisms die, decomposers, including the detritus feeders, bacteria, and fungi, break down the organic matter. Detritus feeders include worms, mites, insects, and crustaceans, which feed on dead organic matter, returning carbon to the cycle through chemical breakdown and respiration.

Carbon dioxide (CO_2) is also dissolved directly into the oceans, where it is combined with calcium to form calcium carbonate, which is used by mollusks to form their shells. When mollusks die, the shells break down and often form limestone. Limestone is then dissolved by water over time and some carbon may be released back into the atmosphere as CO_2, or used by new ocean species.

Finally, organic matter that is left to decay, may, under conditions of heat and pressure be transformed into coal, oil, or natural gas (the **fossil fuels**). When fossil fuels are burned for energy, the combustion process releases carbon dioxide back into the atmosphere, where it is available to plants for photosynthesis.

Phosphorous Cycle

Phosphorous is another mineral required by living things. Unlike carbon and nitrogen, which cycle through the atmosphere in gaseous form, phosphorous is only found in solid form, within rocks and soil. Phosphorous is a key component in ATP, NADP (a molecule that, like ATP, stores energy in its chemical bonds), and many other molecular compounds essential to life.

Phosphorous is found within rocks and is released by the process of erosion. Water dissolves phosphorous from rocks, and carries it into rivers and streams. Here phosphorous and oxygen react to form phosphates that end up in bodies of water. Phosphates are absorbed by photosynthetic organisms in and near the water and are used in the synthesis of organic molecules. As in the carbon and nitrogen cycles, phosphorous is then passed up the food chain and returned through animal wastes and organic decay.

New phosphorous enters the cycle as undersea sedimentary rocks are thrust up during the shifting of the Earth's tectonic plates. New rock containing phosphorous is then exposed to erosion and enters the cycling process.

POPULATION GROWTH AND REGULATION

The population growth of a species is regulated by limiting factors that exist within the species' environment. Population growth maintains equilibrium in all species under normal conditions because of these limiting factors. A population's overall growth rate is affected by the birth rate **(natality)** and death rate **(mortality)** of the population. The rate of increase within a population is represented by the birth rate minus the death rate. When the birth rate within a population equals the death rate, the population remains at a constant level.

Figure 6.5 Two Models of Population Growth

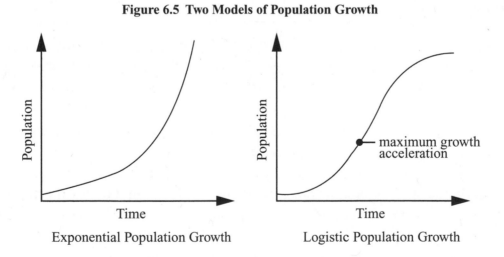

Exponential Population Growth   Logistic Population Growth

There are two models of population growth, the exponential curve (or J-curve) and the logistic curve (or the S-curve). The exponential curve represents populations in which there is no environmental or social limit on population size, so the rate of growth accelerates over time. Exponential population growth exists only during the initial population growth in a particular ecosystem, since as the population increases the limiting factors become more influential. In other words, a fish population introduced into a pond would experience exponential population growth until food and space supplies began to limit the population.

The logistic curve reflects the effects of limiting factors on population size, where growth accelerates to a point, then slows down. The logistic curve shows population growth over a longer period of time, and represents population growth under normal conditions.

Population growth is directly related to the life characteristics of the population such as the age at which an individual begins to reproduce, the age of death, the rate of growth, etc. For instance, species that grow quickly, mature sexually at an early age, and live a long life would have a population growth rate that exceeds that of species with a short life span and short reproductive span.

In general, most populations have an incredible ability to increase in numbers. A population without limiting factors could overpopulate the world in several generations. It is the limits existing within each ecosystem that keep this from happening.

Limiting Factors

Many factors affect the life of an ecosystem, which may be permanent or temporary. Populations within an ecosystem will be affected by changes in the environment from **abiotic factors** (physical, non-living factors such as fire, pollution, sunlight, soil, light, precipitation, availability of oxygen, water conditions, and temperature) and **biotic factors** (biological factors, including availability of food, competition, predator-prey relationships, symbiosis, and overpopulation).

These biotic and abiotic factors are known as **limiting factors** since they will determine how much a particular population within a community will be able to grow. For instance, the resource in shortest supply in an ecosystem may limit population growth. As an example, we know that photosynthetic organisms require phosphorous in order to thrive, so the population growth will be limited by the amount of phosphorous readily available in the environment. Conversely, growth may be limited by having more of a factor (such as heat or water) than it can tolerate. For example, plants need carbon dioxide to grow; however, a large concentration of carbon dioxide in the atmosphere is toxic.

Ecologists now commonly combine these two ideas to provide a more comprehensive understanding of how conditions limit growth of populations. It may be stated that the establishment and survival of a particular organism in an area is dependent upon both 1) the availability of necessary elements in at least the minimum quantity, and 2) the controlled supply of those elements to keep it within the limits of tolerance.

Limiting factors interact with each other and generally produce a situation within the ecosystem that supports homeostasis (a steady-state condition). **Homeostasis** is a dynamic balance achieved within an ecosystem functioning at its optimum level. Homeostasis is the tendency of the ecological community to stay the same. However, the balance of the ecosystem can be disturbed by the removal, or decrease, of a single factor or by the addition, or increase, of a factor.

Populations are rarely governed by the effect of a single limiting factor; instead, many factors interact to control population size. Changes in limiting factors have a domino effect in an ecosystem, as the change in population size of one species will change the dynamics of the entire community. The number of individuals of a particular species living in a particular area is called the population **density** (number of organisms per area).

Both abiotic and biotic limiting factors exist in a single community; however, one may be dominant over the other. Abiotic limiting factors are also known as **density-independent factors**. That is, they are independent of population density. For instance, the populations around Mount St. Helens were greatly affected by its eruption in 1980, and this effect had nothing to do with the population levels of the area before the eruption. In this situation, the density-independent physical factors dominated the population changes that took place.

Pollution is a major density-independent factor in the health of ecosystems. Pollution is usually a byproduct of human endeavors and affects the air or water quality of an ecosystem with secondary effects. In addition to producing pollution, humans may deliberately utilize chemicals such as pesticides or herbicides to limit growth of particular species. Such chemicals can damage the homeostatic mechanisms within a community, causing a long term upset in the balance of an ecosystem.

In other situations, biotic factors, called **density-dependent factors** may be the dominant influence on population in a given area. Density-dependent factors include population growth issues and interactions between species within a community.

Within a given area, there is a maximum level the population may reach at which it will continue to thrive. This is known as the **carrying capacity** of the environment. When an organism has reached the carrying capacity of the ecosystem, the population growth rate will level off and show no net growth. Populations also occupy a particular geographic area with suitable conditions. This total area occupied by a species is known as the **range**. Typically, populations will have the greatest density in the center of their range, and lower density at the edges. The area outside the range is known as the area of intolerance for that species, since it is not able to survive there. Environmental changes will affect the size and location of the range, making it a dynamic characteristic.

Over time, species may move in or out of a particular area, a process known as **dispersion**. Dispersion occurs in one of three ways—through **emigration** (permanent one way movement out of the original range), **immigration** (permanent one way movement into a new range), and **migration** (temporary movement out of one range into another, and back). Migration is an important process to many species and communities, since it allows animals that might not survive year-round in a particular ecosystem to temporarily relocate for a portion of the year. Therefore, migration gives the opportunity for greater diversity of species in an ecosystem.

Two or more species living within the same area and that overlap niches (their function in the food chain) are said to be in **competition** if the resource they both require is in limited supply. If the niche overlap is minimal (other sources of food are available) then both species may survive. In some cases, one of the species may be wiped out in an area due to competition, a situation called **competitive exclusion**. This is a rare but plausible occurrence.

A **predator** is an organism that captures and feeds on another for sustenance. The animal that is eaten is known as the **prey**. The **predator/prey** relationship is one of the most important features of an ecosystem. As seen in our study of the energy cycle, energy is passed from lower trophic levels to higher trophic levels, as one animal is consumed by another. This relationship not only provides transfer of energy up the food chain, it also is a population control factor for the prey species. In situations where natural predators are removed from a region, the overpopulation occurring amongst the prey species can cause problems in the population and community. For instance, the hunting and trapping of wolves in the United States has led to an overpopulation of deer (the prey of wolves), which in turn has caused a shortage of food for deer in some areas, causing these deer populations to starve.

When two species interact with each other within the same range it is known as **symbiosis**. **Amensalism** is one type of symbiosis where one species is neither helped nor harmed while it inhibits the growth of another species. **Mutualism** is a form of symbiosis where both species benefit. **Parasitism** is symbiosis in which one species benefits, but the other is harmed. (Parasites are not predators, since the parasitic action takes a long period of time and may not actually kill the host.)

When the entire population of a particular species is eliminated, it is known as **extinction**. Extinction may be a local phenomenon, the elimination of a population of one species from one area. However, species extinction is a worldwide phenomenon, where all members of all populations of a species die.

The extinction of a single species may also cause a chain reaction of secondary extinctions if other species depend on the extinct species. Conversely, the introduction of a new species into an area can also have a profound effect on other populations within that area. This new species may compete for the niche of native population or upset a predator/prey balance. For example, the brown tree snake (native to Australia) was introduced into islands in the Pacific years ago. (They probably migrated on ships.) The brown snake has caused the extinction of several species of birds on those Pacific islands. The bird populations could not withstand the introduction of this new predator.

Ultimately, the survival of a particular population is dependent on maintaining a **minimal viable population** size. When a population is significantly diminished in size, it becomes highly susceptible to breeding problems and environmental changes that may result in extinction.

Community Structure

Community structure refers to the characteristics of a specified community, including the types of species that dominate, major climatic trends of the region and, whether the community is open or closed. A **closed community** is one whose populations occupy essentially the same range with very similar distributions of density. These types of communities have boundaries called **ecotones** (such as a pond aquatic ecosystem that ends at the shore). An **open community** has indefinite boundaries, and its populations have varying ranges and densities (such as a forest). In an open community, the species are more widely distributed and animals may actually travel in and out of the area.

An open community is often more able to respond to calamity and may be therefore more resilient. Since the boundaries are subtler, the populations of a forest, for instance, may be able to move as necessary to avoid a fire. If, however, a closed community is affected by a traumatic event (for example, a pond being polluted over a short period of time) it may be completely wiped out.

Communities do grow and change over time. Some communities are able to maintain their basic structure with only minor variations for very long periods of time. Others are much more dynamic, changing significantly over time from one type of ecosystem to another. When one community completely replaces another over time in a given area, it is called **succession**. Succession occurs both in terrestrial and aquatic biomes.

Succession may occur because of small changes over time in climate or conditions, the immigration of a new species, disease, or other slow-acting factors. It may also occur in direct response to cataclysmic events such as fire, flood, or human intervention (for example, clearing a forest for farmland). The first populations that move back into a disturbed ecosystem tend to be hardy species that can survive in bleak conditions. These are known as **pioneer communities**.

An example of terrestrial succession occurs when a fire wipes out a forest community. The first new colonization will come from quick-growing species such as grasses, which will produce over time a grassland ecosystem. The decay of grasses will enrich the soil, providing fertile ground for germination of seeds for shrubs brought in by wind or animals. The shrubs will further prepare the soil for germination of larger species of trees, which over time will take over the shrub-land and produce a forest community once again. Each successive community changes the ecosystem in such a way as to favor a different community, which then replaces it.

When succession ends in a stable community, the community is known as the **climax community**. The climax community is the one best suited to the climate and soil conditions, and one that achieves a homeostasis. Generally, the climax community will remain in an area until a catastrophic event (fire, flood, etc.) destroys it.

BIOMES

A **biome** is an ecosystem that is generally defined by its climate characteristics. Each biome includes many types of community interacting within the climatic region. There are several major biomes that have been identified by ecologists. There are two basic types of biome—terrestrial and aquatic. **Terrestrial biomes** are those that exist on land, **aquatic biomes** are within large bodies of water. The following table gives the name of the major biomes with their major characteristics:

Table 6.1 Characteristics of Major Biomes

BIOME	TEMPERATURE	PRECIPITATION LEVEL	FEATURES
Tropical Rain Forest	warm	high	dense forest, heavy rainfall, abundant vegetation, relatively poor soil
Savanna	warm	moderate seasonal rains	grassland, light
Chaparral	hot summer, temperate winter	low in summer, high in winter	trees, shrubs, small animals, prolonged summer
Temperate Grassland	moderate and seasonal	low for most of year	large land tracts of grassland, shrubs and annuals, rodents, and some larger carnivores
Desert	extreme hot or cold	very low	sandy or rocky terrain, sparse vegetation, mainly succulents, small animals, rodents, reptiles
Tundra	extreme cold	low	modified grassland, perma-frost, short growing season with some plants and animals
Taiga	cold	moderate	snow most of year, thick coniferous forests, wide variety of animal life
Temperate Deciduous Forest	moderate, seasonal	moderate	many trees (that lose leaves in cold season), mosses, grasses, shrubs, abundant animal life
Marine Aquatic	varied	not applicable	large amounts of dissolved minerals (particularly salts) in the water, huge array of aquatic animal and plant life
Freshwater Aquatic	varied	not applicable	still or running water with little dissolved minerals, large array of aquatic plant and animal life

Island Biogeography

Biogeography is the study of how photosynthetic organisms and animals are distributed in a particular location, plus the history of their distribution in the past. Island biogeography is a subdiscipline that investigates the distribution of species in an island habitat. The study of island biogeography is of particular interest to ecologists, since islands are closer to being a closed system (that is, they have less interaction with other ecosystems) than other environments.

Since islands are by nature separated from other land ecosystems, species of both photosynthetic organisms and animals found on a particular island usually have arrived there by natural **dispersal** processes (by air or sea). For instance, there are many plant species with adapted seeds, which will float in water or be carried long distances by air and remain viable. Birds are adapted for dispersion, as are many species of insect, and many sea animals (tortoises, snails, etc.). Dispersal to an island is dependent on geographic as well as historical factors. Distance from other land masses is an important geographic factor. Obviously, the closer the island is to other land, the easier dispersal of species to that island will be. Conversely, islands separated by long stretches of water will have less dispersion. Prevailing winds and ocean currents are also geographic factors that will affect species introduction. Historical factors such as climate shifts (for instance, the shift to an ice age), drought, volcanic action, plate shifting (where the continental plates of the Earth's crust move slowly), etc., will also affect which species are able to travel to a given island. In recent history, dispersion has also occurred through human intervention. Species that inhabit a given ecosystem because humans transported them there are known as **introduced** species.

In some cases, new species develop from parents that were dispersed to the island. These new species are **native** to that island. Arrival of a species on an island, however, does not insure that it will survive and thrive there. In order to become an established part of the island ecosystem, a species must find a suitable habitat and niche. Ultimately, the species must be able to reproduce for many generations in its new setting, or it will not remain a part of the ecosystem. If the island contains a habitat suitable for the newly arrived species, then that species has a chance of survival in its new environment. Islands may contain several habitats; consequently, islands that support numerous habitats will be more likely to have a wider diversity of species.

Islands may also develop new habitats over time as the climate and geology change, and depending on the size and age of the island. In general, the larger the island and the older the island, the more species it will support. The one exception to this is an old island whose soil has eroded and lost its nutrients. In this case, its habitats may not be able to support life. Also, the harsher the climate (high or low temperature or water conditions) of the island, the fewer species it will have. The geology of the island (whether it is volcanic in origin, for instance) determines the characteristics of the soil, and thus has a direct effect on habitability as well.

PRINCIPLES OF BEHAVIOR

The study of **ethology** involves studying how animals act and react within their environments. Behavior simply is what an organism does and how it does it. Some behavioral characteristics are learned; others are instinctive (inherited).

Behavioral characteristics of animals may include how they acquire food, how they seek out and relate to a mate, how they respond to danger, or how they care for young. Behavior may be as simple as a reflex or may involve responses and interactions between the endocrine, nervous, and musculoskeletal systems.

Some behaviors are extremely simple in nature, such as a response to an environmental stimulus. These basic behaviors are innate; they exist from birth and are genetic in origin (they are inherited). **Innate behaviors** are the actions in animals we call **instincts**. Innate behaviors are highly stereotyped; all individuals of a species perform these behaviors in the same way. **Stereotyped behaviors** are of four basic varieties:

- **taxes** (plural of taxis) are directional responses either toward or away from a stimulus,

- **kineses** are changes in speed of movement in response to stimuli,

- **reflexes** are an automatic movement of a body part in response to a stimulus, and

- **fixed action patterns** (FAP) are complex but stereotyped behaviors in response to a stimulus.

The fixed action pattern is the most complex of stereotyped behaviors. It is a pre-programmed response to a particular stimulus known as a **releaser** or a **sign stimulus**. FAPs include courtship behaviors, circadian rhythms, and feeding of young. Organisms automatically perform FAPs without any prior experience (FAPs are not learned).

Some animal behaviors are learned. **Learned behaviors** may have some basis in genetics, but they also require learning. Generally, there are three types of learned behavior in animals: conditioning, habituation, and imprinting.

Conditioning involves learning to apply an old response to a new stimulus. The classic example of conditioning is that of Pavlov's dogs. Ivan Pavlov was a scientist who studied animal behavior. Dogs have an innate behavior to begin salivating when they see food. Pavlov was able to train dogs to salivate when they heard a bell ring. He trained, or conditioned, them by ringing the bell every time he fed the dogs. The dogs were conditioned to produce an instinctive behavior (salivating) in response to a new stimulus (bell).

B.F. Skinner was another scientist who studied conditioning. Skinner started with the thesis that learning happens through changes in overt behavior. Skinner believed that when a particular behavior is rewarded, the individual is being conditioned to repeat that behavior. Reinforcement of good behaviors results in repeating that behavior.

Habituation is a learned behavior where the organism produces less and less response as a stimulus is repeated, without a subsequent negative or positive action. For instance, a cat might innately respond to a dog's approach by hissing and raising its hair. However, if the dog regularly approaches, but never attacks, the cat eventually learns that the dog is not a threat and ceases to exhibit the fear behavior. Habituation safeguards species from wasting energy on irrelevant stimuli.

Imprinting is a learned behavior that develops in a critical or sensitive period of the animal's lifespan. Konrad Lorenz (a behavioral scientist) was able to show that baby geese responded to their mother's physical appearance shortly after birth. During the critical period after birth, the gosling learns to recognize his mother. However, if another object is exposed to the gosling during that critical period (immediately following hatching) the gosling would interpret the substituted object to be its mother. Imprinting generally involves learning a new releaser for an established FAP.

Social Behavior

Some animal species demonstrate **social behavior**—behavior patterns that take into account other individuals. One aspect of animal behavior regards the physical land area that an individual lives in. Animals will develop a **home range** (an area in which they spend most of their time). Animals may also develop an area of land as their **territory**, which lies within the home range, but is the area the individual will defend as his own. The establishment of a territory implies the recognition by one individual that other individuals exist, thus it is a simple social behavior.

Sexual and mating behaviors often rely on complex interactions of the endocrine, nervous, and musculoskeletal systems. In many cases, an individual will compete with another for a particular mate. There are often complex rituals, which are performed before the actual mating experience, involving many instinctive responses to stimuli and learned behaviors. The sexual and parenting behaviors of animals are social traits that are extremely diverse between species.

In some species, social interactions are highly complex, for instance an entire population may function as a hierarchy (or society), where individuals have specified roles and status. Insects such as ants and bees, some species of birds, and many primates are among the groups that form societies.

A **society** is an organization of individuals in a population in which tasks are divided, in order for the group to work together. For instance, bees are social insects with a hierarchy (including a queen bee and worker bees). Some individuals are responsible for caring for the queen, others work within the nest, and others gather nectar from outside sources to be brought to the nest. Most of the population is female; the males are called drones and their only responsibility is mating. This division of labor allows the society to perform a higher function than if each individual acted on it own. Within a society, the individuals may be constantly growing, changing, and adapting, while the functions of the community remain the same over time.

While the social behavior of insects is more a question of division of labor, societies of primates are built around the idea of **dominance**. Older, more established individuals, compete for status within the community. A hierarchy is formed through actual competitions among individuals. The community member(s) at the top of the hierarchy enjoy privileges related to their selection of food and mates. This hierarchy is challenged as individuals mature, causing a succession of leaders.

Social behavior is highly dependent on communication within the population, and the ability of individuals to adapt behavior according to the needs of the society as a whole. Social animals exhibit a characteristic known as **altruism**, that is, having traits that tend to serve the needs of the society as a whole in addition to its own individual needs.

SOCIAL BIOLOGY

Human Population Growth

As with the study of population growth among other species, human population growth is a direct function of human birth and death rates (natality and mortality). People are able to reason around many of the limiting factors (for example, problems of food shortage or disease), making human population growth a much more complex situation. Furthermore, reproductive behaviors of humans are also subject to the reasoning process, unlike the instinctual mating behaviors of most animals.

The development of vaccines and antibiotics has greatly increased the life-span of people in recent history, decreasing the mortality rate. Infant mortality rates have steeply declined in the last 150 years, as safer birthing processes and infant care have been developed. On the other hand, the development of contraceptives has reduced the natality rate in many countries.

Thomas Malthus is one of the most famous human population scientists. In the 1780s Malthus recognized the exponential properties of population growth and calculated that the Earth's food supply would eventually be exhausted by human overpopulation. However, Malthus's calculations did not take into account new technologies allowing for higher yield of food production. So, while the Earth's population has indeed increased exponentially (passing the six billion mark in 2000), and the doubling time (the amount of time it takes for a population to double in size) is decreasing significantly, the Earth has so far been able to support its population for the most part. (The Earth has an adequate food supply at present, yet people may currently starve because they are unable to produce food in their region and/or may be politically unable to import food.)

A theory known as **demographic transition** proposes that there are progressive demographic time periods of human population growth. In the first period, birth and death rates are approximately equal, allowing the population to be in equilibrium with the environment. Social evolution (ability to fight disease, mass produce food, etc.) causes the birth rate to overtake the death rate, in turn causing rapid population growth throughout another period. Agrarian lifestyles (where families have numerous children to "work the farm") become less common and children become a liability in urban society. However, **biomedical progress** of urban society causes a lowering of the infant mortality rate. Society then faces a period of dramatic population growth, most of it within cities. The final stage occurs as developed industrialized nations work to lower birth rates through contraceptive practices.

As the human population proceeds through demographic transition, the **age composition** (the relative numbers of individuals of specific ages within the population) changes. As birth rates increase, the population tends to shift toward youth, whereas medical advancements may increase the average age of the population. For instance, in 1900 approximately 40% of Americans were under 18, in 1960, 36% and in 1996, only 26% of Americans were under 18. Demographic transition also has an effect on the population growth rate.

Meanwhile, the introduction of **genetic engineering** in recent history has produced a complex array of implications. Genetic engineering is the intentional alteration of genetic material of a living organism. Genetic engineering of plant species has produced species able to resist drought, disease, or other threats—providing for more abundant food production. Genetic engineering is also responsible for disease-fighting breakthroughs such as the production of human insulin to fight diabetes. (Insulin is produced industrially using genetically engineered bacteria that produce human insulin.) The future of genetic engineering, however, is uncertain as we confront the ethical questions regarding the possibility of choosing characteristics of children, or cloning humans.

The growth of human population has also had a profound effect on the biosphere. **Environmental pollution** (the addition of contaminants to the air and water by human intervention and industry) has profoundly affected the ecosystems of the Earth. Most pollution has occurred in recent decades as industrialization has increased.

Progress has been made in the **management of resources** in the recent past. In our discussion of energy and biochemical cycles (early in this chapter), we noted that our biosphere has natural mechanisms that allow for the recycling of energy and nutrients. Careful resource management, including the active human intervention of recycling energy, water, nutrients, and chemicals, will encourage the natural cyclic processes within the biosphere to maintain a viable balance.

CHAPTER

Science, Technology, and Society

7

DISCOVERY, CHANGE, AND RISK MANAGEMENT

Scientific discovery is exciting and awe-inspiring. However, scientists make mistakes, and when scientists are allowed to make governing decisions that go unchecked by the greater public, these mistakes may become particularly obvious and harmful to society-at-large. For instance, there are examples of cases from the past hundred years where ignorance of greater ecological principles led to misguided environmental practices. This happened with the obsessive prevention of forest fires in the mid-20th century, which led to the unfortunate overgrowth of forests and contributed to the modern rise of persistent and harmful super wildfires. Ecologists are now aware of the ecological importance of so-called maintenance wildfires that contribute to a healthy ecosystem balance. This realization led to altered practices that allow for natural or prescribed burns.

Other advances are not easy calls. The development of DDT as a pesticide, for instance, was a huge advance against the worldwide epidemic of malaria and typhus in the mid-1900's. However, it later became evident, through studies of multiple ecological impacts on birds and other species, that DDT had far-reaching and powerful harmful effects on the larger global ecosystem. DDT was banned from use—eventually worldwide. This eased problems with extinction of species such as the Bald Eagle, but some still posit that the deleterious widespread problems of malaria in Africa have been prolonged because of the discontinuation of using DDT.

Figure 7.1 DDT Poster Circa 1947

Another example of scientific advance versus risk management comes from the world of medicine in the mid-1900's. Researchers thought they had found a drug that was highly effective in treating multiple problems, including morning sickness and insomnia during pregnancy. However, the regrettable error of prescribing thalidomide—a drug that had not been fully tested in pregnant women—resulted in tragic, and often fatal, birth defects. Because of the thalidomide problem, laws were passed in 1962 requiring tests for safety during pregnancy before a drug could be prescribed or used in the U.S. This experience significantly changed how drugs were tested and prescribed worldwide.

IMPACT OF SCIENCE AND TECHNOLOGY ON THE ENVIRONMENT AND HUMAN AFFAIRS

There are some issues of science and technology that uniquely impact our environment and human affairs, and are issues to biology education. Consider the following major scientific and technological issues that have uniquely impacted our environment and human affairs in the past 50 years . . .

Data Availability – Before computers were widely used to store large amounts of personal, medical, and research data, it was easier to safeguard access to personal information. However, the proliferation of computerized databases and the linking of databases has made it increasingly difficult to keep personal information secure. This has implications for human affairs as employers are now able to know whether an individual's habits may impact the workplace by accessing information regarding habits, such as smoking or drinking, and even more subtle information, such as genetic disposition. On the positive side, however, data availability can help in solving crimes and finding lost individuals and even pets. However, the widespread availability of and access to data raises many questions that must be assessed by a whole new field of ethicists.

Supercomputing – Supercomputing has had a huge impact on human affairs, making things possible that were never even imagined before this century. For example, supercomputers made mapping the human genome possible. Scientists are now testing applications that will go far beyond simply mapping genomes. Supercomputing in medical technology is almost capable of linking the human genome with individual medical records and in turn with pharmaceutical records and then with individualized prescription needs.

Supercomputers have allowed the military to streamline and make missions more effective, thus lowering casualties and expenses. Supercomputers allow scientists to model large systems, such as ecosystems, and study scenarios such as climate change, weather systems, catastrophic hazards (droughts, earthquakes, etc.) and learn about possible solutions to such problems. Many concepts regarding climate change, evolution, and other biological and human social system theory have been better understood through supercomputer simulations. In addition, modeling ecosystems, the universe, and the physical world by supercomputers has allowed for forecasting and modeling of both real and imagined scenarios.

Manufacturing – Advances in manufacturing have added comfort to most people's lives. However, it has also affected our environment significantly by adding to pollution, taking up valuable real estate for large processing plants, and changing our way of life. The students we teach are living in a very different world than the world their great grandparents inhabited. It is up to us to prepare them to care for this very different world.

Transportation – At this time, in some parts of the world there are more cars than there are people. It is possible to travel to any part of the world by air, train, bus, car, or boat and people do this much more readily than at any time in the past. While this makes it easy to go on vacation, travel for business and even visit relatives in distant places, it also can pose some unique challenges. For example, the possibilities of spreading viruses such as H1N1 are exacerbated by the ease of world travel. Global terrorism has become an increased concern as people are able to travel easily from country to country. Of course, cars and other means of transportation produce a huge amount of the world's pollution, contributing to concerns about pollution and global climate change.

While these major areas of scientific and technological advances have brought great opportunity for increased wealth, comfort, and health to human life and affairs, they have also brought an increased need for monitoring the ethics of decisions related to how technology is used. These are only a few of the changes that have impacted society. The following sections include additional examples.

Human- and Nature-induced Hazards

As we all know, the world is full of hazards—those that are nature-induced (or natural) and those that are human-induced (or man-made). In either case, such hazards are usually most detrimental when they are catastrophic—that is, when they have a sudden and unpredictable onset. Earthquakes and wildfires are usually unpredictable and are an example of natural hazards. Atomic bombs, such as those used in Japan in the 1940's, are examples of man-made hazards. In either case, man-made or natural, while these hazards are not in themselves biological—they have long-lasting biological and ecological impacts.

As science educators, it is important to help students understand human and nature-induced hazards for several purposes, including potential prediction and/or prevention and mitigation after the fact. Some natural hazards, such as earthquakes, are difficult to predict. Other natural hazards, such as hurricanes and volcanos, may give some warning before the occurrence. As educators it is important that we impart scientific reasoning skills to our students so that they can understand pertinent information regarding impending hazards and act in an appropriate manner. In addition, it is appropriate to encourage students to pursue careers in science, technology, engineering, and mathematics (STEM) fields, as this may aid in future prediction and mitigation of hazards. Further, students who understand the dangers of technologies, such as chemical and nuclear warfare, on the ecological systems of the world are more likely to make informed choices as citizens at the polls.

In recent years, the world has suffered notably and publicly from massive earthquakes, tsunamis (byproducts of undersea earthquakes), hurricanes, widespread wildfires, tornadoes, volcanoes, and widespread floods and droughts. These weather- and earth-related issues lead to secondary human issues such as famine and outbreak of disease. Some of these events are weather-related (hurricanes, tornadoes, droughts, wildfires due to lightening, floods) and some are not (earthquakes, volcanoes, tsunamis).

The disasters that have been weather-related, along with research that has noted changing weather patterns over the past one hundred years, has sparked debate regarding potential worldwide climate change. Many scientists posit that there is an overall change in our world climate that is occurring with the destruction of our atmospheric layering and the slight rise in global temperatures over time. This hazard is posited to impact our globe with catastrophic effects of melting glacial ice, flooding continental areas, and causing long-range change in global weather patterns. While scientists are still investigating and debating the details regarding these concepts, it is imperative that students be prepared to understand and make wise decisions relating to global climate change because this will be an issue their generation will deal with, regardless of what scientists ultimately discover.

Another issue of global impact that is crucial for students to understand and teachers to address is that of nuclear war. In a biology class it is not appropriate to discuss the details of the physics of nuclear capacity, but it is appropriate to discuss the impact of a nuclear attack on ecosystems. This is one of the greatest hazards that we face as a global society.

Issues and applications: production, storage, use, management, and disposal of consumer products and energy, and management of natural resources

In the past 50 years there has been a monumental escalation in the use of consumer products, and in particular electronics, including computers, communications, and entertainment devices. While these products increase the standard of living for people significantly by providing communication, productivity, and ready entertainment of all sorts, they also use unique resources of plastics and heavy metals. In addition, the technology has a quick turnover rate, resulting in many of these devices ending up in landfills after a short lifespan, since the recycling rate is sadly low. (Meskell, D., 2008)

In the years to come, as our supplies of natural resources such as wood, coal, natural gas, and fossil fuels for energy and manufacturing become more limited, it will be up to the students we are teaching to develop new techniques for their use, storage, and management. Today, there are clean-coal processes being developed and used that cause less pollution. New ways of thinking about resources have already made some changes and more are necessary. New research in the area of biofuels and nuclear energy are desperately needed.

Research and development in renewable energy from natural resources such as sunlight, wind, rain, tides, and geothermal heat are on the agenda for many institutions and industry leaders.

The idea of sustainability is becoming more popular and more necessary. Sustainable living is defined as living in such a way that one does not compromise life in the future in any way by using up resources or space that will be needed by self or others in the future.

Since carbon emissions from current use of fossil fuels as energy sources is considered to be the major contributor to global climate change and pollution contamination, carbon capture and storage has become an area of increased interest for research. There are many options for carbon capture and storage being considered, from capturing it in structural concrete to storing it in deep geological or ocean formations. Again, more research in these areas is needed.

Figure 7.2 Carbon Emissions

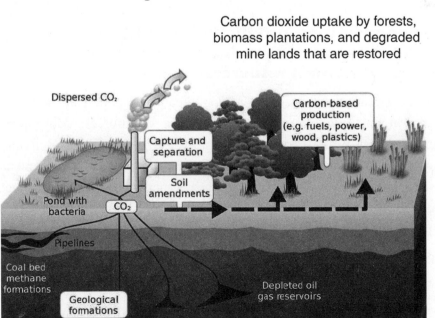

Ultimately, it is clear that our society is in need of mitigating its hunger for goods and technology with an understanding of how to manage its resources and store and handle its wastes. These issues will become increasingly prominent as our current students enter the world as engaged citizens.

Social, Political, Ethical, and Economic Issues in Biology

It is very important for educators to impart to their students a sense of ethics as it applies to the field of science and, specifically, biology. There are several issues that are important to consider in biology from an ethical standpoint—some fall under the medical purview discussed below. One ethical issue that impacts biology from a social and political viewpoint is human research. Before the 1970's, there was no regulation on how research was to be conducted on human subjects. However, some notable problems began to crop up in the mid-1900's. As previously mentioned, in the late 1950's the drug thalidomide was prescribed—without adequate testing—to ease nausea and insomnia in pregnant women. The drug caused serious debilitating birth defects and death in some infants. In another case, the U.S. Public Health Service conducted a study of antibiotic effectiveness in treating syphilis in Tuskeegee, Alabama, between 1932 and 1972. However, the health service withheld treatment from African-American sharecroppers— some of whom died. These unfortunate cases led to the establishment in 1974, and adoption in 1991 by 16 more federal agencies of 45 CFR 46, now known as the "Common Rule." The cornerstone of the "Common Rule" is the idea of informed consent—and that the rights and care of the subject be the primary concern, no matter the importance of the research. The Common Rule established the idea that all research on human subjects be overseen by an Institutional Review Board (IRB) to ensure that the rights of the subject are not impinged upon. It is crucial that science educators understand and stress to students the importance of human subject research ethics, as well as the ethical treatment of animals in research.

As we have seen in recent years, biology has played a central part in political debates. Issues such as abortion, stem-cell research, pharmaceutical research and development, medical privacy, pandemic disease prevention and management, aging research and management, agricultural issues, bio-energy issues, among others, impact the social and economic lives of our country and world. It is essential that students have a foundation in biology to make informed decisions regarding their futures and the futures of their families at the polls and in their homes.

Societal Issues with Health and Medical Advances

Since Watson and Crick modeled the DNA molecule as a double-helix in 1953, medicine has benefited greatly from advances in genetics (i.e., the human genome project, genetic engineering, stem-cell research, and other similar technologies). But along with the wonderful positive impacts come ethical questions. Should fetal tissue be used for stem cell research? Should human cloning—even if it is just body parts—be allowed? Should cloning of any sort be allowed? (It has been done, of course with the sheep Dolly and other examples.) What about genetic engineering? Is it safe? Is eating genetically engineered corn safe? Is genetically engineering a child appropriate? The questions are endless. Who will decide the answers to these questions and the millions more that become pertinent in the future? The students of today will answer them. For this reason it is essential for our biology students to be prepared with an understanding of genetics, cloning, technology, the human genome, evolution, phylogeny, and the interconnectedness of these topics.

Medical advances have increased the average life span. In addition, many common diseases can now be treated with inexpensive drugs. Yet, these advances bring problems of their own as people living longer means a burgeoning population and an aging population exists on earth. Who will take care of this aging population and how will they do it?

Technology has advanced to a place where machines can do a lot to keep people alive, but can they keep these people happy? Computers can store and manage immense amounts of data, but can they keep this data private?

The issues that biologists face today are not the straightforward issues of the last decade or the last century. Day by day, the world of biology and science education as a whole becomes more complex. As a science educator it is essential to communicate the overall concepts of our biological world through effective means to create a new generation of responsible, informed, and creative citizens of the future.

REFERENCES

McDonald, S. Human cloning. *Genesis, 1*, 26–28.

Meskell, D. (2008). "Green IT is essential to green government." GSA Office of Citizen Services and Communications. Intergovernmental Solutions Newsletter. *Green IT.* Issue 21, Fall 2008.

Schulte, P. A., & Salamanca-Buentello, F. (2007). Ethical and scientific issues of nanotechnology in the workplace. *Ciência & Saúde Coletiva, 12*(5), 1319–1332.

Williams, E. D. (2005). Federal protection for human research subjects: An analysis of the common rule and its interactions with FDA regulations and the HIPAA privacy rule. CRS Report for Congress. Available from: www.fas.org/sgp/crs/misc/RL32909.pdf. Accessed March 15, 2012.

Practice Test 1

Praxis II: Biology
Core Content Knowledge (0235)

This test is also on CD-ROM in our special interactive TestWare® for the PRAXIS II: Biology Core Content Knowledge. It is highly recommended that you first take this exam on computer. You will then have the additional study features and benefits of enforced time conditions and instantaneous, accurate scoring. See page 4 for instructions on how to get the most out of REA's TestWare®.

ANSWER SHEET FOR PRACTICE TEST 1

1. (A) (B) (C) (D)
2. (A) (B) (C) (D)
3. (A) (B) (C) (D)
4. (A) (B) (C) (D)
5. (A) (B) (C) (D)
6. (A) (B) (C) (D)
7. (A) (B) (C) (D)
8. (A) (B) (C) (D)
9. (A) (B) (C) (D)
10. (A) (B) (C) (D)
11. (A) (B) (C) (D)
12. (A) (B) (C) (D)
13. (A) (B) (C) (D)
14. (A) (B) (C) (D)
15. (A) (B) (C) (D)
16. (A) (B) (C) (D)
17. (A) (B) (C) (D)
18. (A) (B) (C) (D)
19. (A) (B) (C) (D)
20. (A) (B) (C) (D)
21. (A) (B) (C) (D)
22. (A) (B) (C) (D)
23. (A) (B) (C) (D)
24. (A) (B) (C) (D)
25. (A) (B) (C) (D)
26. (A) (B) (C) (D)
27. (A) (B) (C) (D)
28. (A) (B) (C) (D)
29. (A) (B) (C) (D)
30. (A) (B) (C) (D)
31. (A) (B) (C) (D)
32. (A) (B) (C) (D)
33. (A) (B) (C) (D)
34. (A) (B) (C) (D)
35. (A) (B) (C) (D)
36. (A) (B) (C) (D)
37. (A) (B) (C) (D)
38. (A) (B) (C) (D)

39. (A) (B) (C) (D)
40. (A) (B) (C) (D)
41. (A) (B) (C) (D)
42. (A) (B) (C) (D)
43. (A) (B) (C) (D)
44. (A) (B) (C) (D)
45. (A) (B) (C) (D)
46. (A) (B) (C) (D)
47. (A) (B) (C) (D)
48. (A) (B) (C) (D)
49. (A) (B) (C) (D)
50. (A) (B) (C) (D)
51. (A) (B) (C) (D)
52. (A) (B) (C) (D)
53. (A) (B) (C) (D)
54. (A) (B) (C) (D)
55. (A) (B) (C) (D)
56. (A) (B) (C) (D)
57. (A) (B) (C) (D)
58. (A) (B) (C) (D)
59. (A) (B) (C) (D)
60. (A) (B) (C) (D)
61. (A) (B) (C) (D)
62. (A) (B) (C) (D)
63. (A) (B) (C) (D)
64. (A) (B) (C) (D)
65. (A) (B) (C) (D)
66. (A) (B) (C) (D)
67. (A) (B) (C) (D)
68. (A) (B) (C) (D)
69. (A) (B) (C) (D)
70. (A) (B) (C) (D)
71. (A) (B) (C) (D)
72. (A) (B) (C) (D)
73. (A) (B) (C) (D)
74. (A) (B) (C) (D)
75. (A) (B) (C) (D)
76. (A) (B) (C) (D)

77. (A) (B) (C) (D)
78. (A) (B) (C) (D)
79. (A) (B) (C) (D)
80. (A) (B) (C) (D)
81. (A) (B) (C) (D)
82. (A) (B) (C) (D)
83. (A) (B) (C) (D)
84. (A) (B) (C) (D)
85. (A) (B) (C) (D)
86. (A) (B) (C) (D)
87. (A) (B) (C) (D)
88. (A) (B) (C) (D)
89. (A) (B) (C) (D)
90. (A) (B) (C) (D)
91. (A) (B) (C) (D)
92. (A) (B) (C) (D)
93. (A) (B) (C) (D)
94. (A) (B) (C) (D)
95. (A) (B) (C) (D)
96. (A) (B) (C) (D)
97. (A) (B) (C) (D)
98. (A) (B) (C) (D)
99. (A) (B) (C) (D)
100. (A) (B) (C) (D)
101. (A) (B) (C) (D)
102. (A) (B) (C) (D)
103. (A) (B) (C) (D)
104. (A) (B) (C) (D)
105. (A) (B) (C) (D)
106. (A) (B) (C) (D)
107. (A) (B) (C) (D)
108. (A) (B) (C) (D)
109. (A) (B) (C) (D)
110. (A) (B) (C) (D)
111. (A) (B) (C) (D)
112. (A) (B) (C) (D)
113. (A) (B) (C) (D)
114. (A) (B) (C) (D)

115. (A) (B) (C) (D)
116. (A) (B) (C) (D)
117. (A) (B) (C) (D)
118. (A) (B) (C) (D)
119. (A) (B) (C) (D)
120. (A) (B) (C) (D)
121. (A) (B) (C) (D)
122. (A) (B) (C) (D)
123. (A) (B) (C) (D)
124. (A) (B) (C) (D)
125. (A) (B) (C) (D)
126. (A) (B) (C) (D)
127. (A) (B) (C) (D)
128. (A) (B) (C) (D)
129. (A) (B) (C) (D)
130. (A) (B) (C) (D)
131. (A) (B) (C) (D)
132. (A) (B) (C) (D)
133. (A) (B) (C) (D)
134. (A) (B) (C) (D)
135. (A) (B) (C) (D)
136. (A) (B) (C) (D)
137. (A) (B) (C) (D)
138. (A) (B) (C) (D)
139. (A) (B) (C) (D)
140. (A) (B) (C) (D)
141. (A) (B) (C) (D)
142. (A) (B) (C) (D)
143. (A) (B) (C) (D)
144. (A) (B) (C) (D)
145. (A) (B) (C) (D)
146. (A) (B) (C) (D)
147. (A) (B) (C) (D)
148. (A) (B) (C) (D)
149. (A) (B) (C) (D)
150. (A) (B) (C) (D)

Directions: Each of the questions or incomplete statements below is followed by four possible answer choices or completions. Select the best choice in each case and fill in the corresponding oval on the answer sheet.

1. A small non-protein substance such as iron that works with enzymes to promote catalysis is known as

   (A) a mineral.
   (B) an inorganic cofactor.
   (C) a coenzyme.
   (D) a hormone.

2. A particular plant has individuals that are either male or female. A male individual of this plant may have

   I.   a filament.
   II. a stigma.
   III. an anther.

   (A) I only
   (B) I and II
   (C) I and III
   (D) I, II and III

3. The cells of which of the following organisms are prokaryotic?

   (A) Mold
   (B) Seaweed
   (C) Blue-green bacteria
   (D) Hydra

4. Which of the following represents a plausible progression in the evolution of plants?

   (A) autotrophic eukaryotic cells → aerobic prokaryotic cells → photosynthetic cells → multicellular plants
   (B) heterotrophic eukaryotic cells → anaerobic prokaryotic cells → autotrophic cyanobacteria → multicellular plants

   (C) aerobic eukaryotic cells → anaerobic eukaryotic cells → photosynthetic cells → multicellular plants
   (D) anaerobic prokaryotic cells → autotrophic cyanobacteria → aerobic eukaryotic cells → multicellular plants

5. Legumes perform a unique ecological function by

   (A) hosting nitrogen-fixing bacteria in their root nodules.
   (B) providing food for primary consumers.
   (C) releasing oxygen into the atmosphere.
   (D) attracting lightning.

6. Which of the following is found in a carbohydrate molecule?

   I.   N
   II. S
   III. NH_2
   IV. CH_2O

   (A) I and IV
   (B) I, III and IV
   (C) I and II
   (D) IV only

7. Each of the following statements regarding the hydrologic cycle is true EXCEPT:

   (A) Water evaporates from bodies of water and plant surfaces and forms clouds in the atmosphere.
   (B) The hydrologic cycle does not affect any of the other biogeochemical cycles.

(C) Water is released from clouds as precipitation.

(D) Water vapor in the atmosphere protects the Earth from rapid and extreme temperature changes.

8. Which of the following is a monosaccharide?

(A) Glucose
(B) Cellulose
(C) Amylase
(D) Starch

9. The study of the interaction of organisms with their living space is known as

(A) environmentalism.
(B) habitology.
(C) zoology.
(D) ecology.

10. Which of the following is likely to happen when a limited amount of enzyme is added to a reaction with an unlimited amount of substrate?

(A) The rate of the reaction increases, then levels off as the entire enzyme is engaged.
(B) The rate of the reaction rises steeply, and then the reaction stops completely.
(C) The rate of the reaction rises steeply and continues to rise.
(D) The rate of the reaction slowly decreases.

11. Which of the following organs DOES NOT function in immunity to defend the body from infection?

(A) Lymph nodes
(B) Spleen
(C) Spinal cord
(D) Thymus

12. A cell without a nucleus or membrane-bound organelles is

(A) prokaryotic.
(B) replicating.
(C) in telophase.
(D) eukaryotic.

13. Which of the following are found in the cells of fungi?

I.   Chloroplasts
II. Nucleus
III. Mitochondria
IV. Ribosomes

(A) I, II and III
(B) I, II, III and IV
(C) I only
(D) II, III, and IV

14. Grana are embedded within which part of the chloroplast?

(A) Stroma
(B) Pigments
(C) Chlorophyll
(D) Carotene

15. Anton van Leeuwenhoek is credited with inventing the first microscope in the 1600's. The invention of the microscope was most likely instrumental in which of the following?

(A) Development of the theory of natural selection
(B) Development of the laws of independent assortment
(C) Development of cell theory
(D) Development of the laws of motion

16. Charles Darwin described the laws concerning the change in species that occur over long periods of time.

(A) Common Descent
(B) Natural Selection
(C) Punctuated Equilibrium
(D) Acquired Characteristics

17. The correct measurement of the following graduated cylinder is best described as

(A) 29.35 mL.
(B) 30.55 mL.
(C) 29.40 mL.
(D) 29.30 mL.

18. Which of the following is NOT true of regulations regarding human research?

(A) The rights of the subject are paramount except in cases where the testing will benefit the greater good of a large human population.
(B) Prior to 1974, the rights of human subjects were not protected through federal regulations.
(C) All research involving human subjects that is carried out by any organization receiving federal funding must be approved through an Institutional Review Board (IRB).
(D) Informed consent is required from human subjects of any research carried out by any organization receiving federal funding.

19. The ultimate source of energy for most life on Earth is

(A) water.
(B) protein.
(C) the Sun.
(D) ATP.

20. The conversion of light energy into chemical energy is accomplished by

(A) catabolism.
(B) oxidative phosphorylation.
(C) metabolism.
(D) photosynthesis.

21. The sum total of a species' genetic information is known as its

(A) genes.
(B) chromosomes.
(C) inheritance.
(D) genome.

22. Which of the following is NOT a step in the translation part of protein synthesis?

(A) Free bases line up along the DNA template and are bonded together forming a single strand of RNA.
(B) A ribosome attaches to start a codon on mRNA and links a tRNA with its attached amino acid.
(C) The ribosome continues to link a sequence of tRNA molecules that correspond with the mRNA strand being encoded.
(D) A terminating codon stops the synthesis process and releases the newly formed protein.

23. Transduction refers to the process whereby a bacterium's genetic makeup is altered when

(A) genetic material is absorbed from dead cell debris in the cell's environment.
(B) some genetic material is transferred from one bacterium to another via a viral bacteriophage.

(C) genetic expression is suppressed by regulatory genes.

(D) a bacterium's chromatin is destroyed by high temperatures.

24. Chromosomes that are paired with another of similar size and shape within the nucleus are known as

(A) homologs.
(B) histones.
(C) genes.
(D) nucleosomes.

25. Restriction enzymes cut samples of DNA into fragments by

(A) binding to specific sequences of nucleotides and breaking the sugar-phosphate backbone.
(B) unwinding the DNA.
(C) breaking the base-to-base hydrogen bonds.
(D) transcribing the RNA sequences.

26. The figure below shows the exponential rise in world population in recent years. Which of the following are immediate implications that could impact the world in the next generation or two?

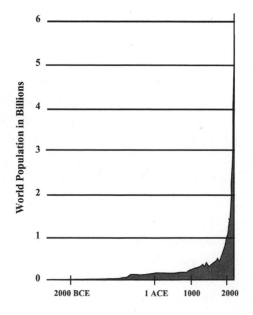

(A) Pollution from added use of vehicles
(B) Pandemic disease from overcrowding of cities
(C) Localized famine
(D) Global climate change

27. These pieces of equipment are

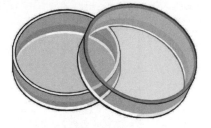

(A) graduated pipettes.
(B) beakers.
(C) Petri dishes.
(D) graduated cylinders.

28. The invention of the microscope was essential and preliminary to the development of cell theory, the discovery of bacteria, and the understanding of concepts relating to disease and sanitation. Which of the following best states the relationship between science and technology demonstrated by this example?

(A) Progress in gaining scientific knowledge is sometimes directly impacted by technological development.
(B) Technological development cannot happen without new scientific knowledge.
(C) Progress in scientific knowledge can only be advanced with the aid of technological advance.
(D) Technological development is a direct result of scientific progress.

29. Which of the following laboratory safety considerations are NOT accurate?

(A) It is the teacher's responsibility to be familiar with Material Safety Data Sheets (MSDSs) for any and all substances used in a laboratory activity.

(B) Clothing should be worn loose and baggy with long sleeves and pant legs.

(C) Never eat or drink anything in a laboratory situation.

(D) Be sure laboratory activities for students are age appropriate and that students are aware of safety procedures for all activities, equipment, and chemicals.

30. Which of the following best states the relationship, in science, between a law and a theory?

   (A) A theory is a law that has successfully undergone repeated experimental testing.
   (B) A law is a statement that can be tested; a theory cannot be tested.
   (C) A theory becomes a law when the experimental data supports its findings.
   (D) A law is a broad consistent statement; a theory explains an aspect of a law.

31. Each of the following statements about meiosis is true EXCEPT:

   (A) Meiosis produces two exact replica daughter cells.
   (B) The first phase of meiosis is known as reduction, which reduces the ploidy from 2N to N (diploid to haploid).
   (C) The second phase of meiosis, division, produces four haploid daughter cells, each with a different combination of chromosomes.
   (D) Meiosis begins with chromosome duplication.

32. The iron-containing molecule that carries oxygen within red blood cells throughout the body via the circulatory system is the

   (A) erythrocyte.
   (B) neutrophils.
   (C) lymphocyte.
   (D) hemoglobin.

33. When sodium (Na+) ion concentration outside a cell increases, water molecules travel out of the cell through the cell membrane. This process is known as

   (A) osmosis.
   (B) facilitated diffusion.
   (C) exocytosis.
   (D) endocytosis.

34. The_____ is the organ that prevents food from entering the bronchial tubes.

   (A) glottis
   (B) epiglottis
   (C) trachea
   (D) pharynx

35. The site of transfer for nutrients, water, and wastes between a mammalian mother and embryo is the

   (A) yolk sac membrane.
   (B) uterus.
   (C) placenta.
   (D) allantois.

36. The function of the gallbladder and pancreas is to aid digestion by producing digestive enzymes and secreting them into the

   (A) small intestine.
   (B) large intestine.
   (C) stomach.
   (D) colon.

37. Electrical shock can restart a heart that has stopped beating. Which of the following statements is a valid reason for this fact?

   (A) Electric shock stimulates the nervous system.
   (B) Electric shock causes smooth muscle to contract.
   (C) Electric shock pushes blood through a stopped heart.
   (D) Electric shock stimulates the cardiac muscle, causing it to contract.

38. All of the following may cause mutations in a DNA sequence EXCEPT

    (A) x-rays.
    (B) chemical exposure.
    (C) random copying error.
    (D) crossing over.

39. Bones perform many functions in the human body. All of the following are functions of bones EXCEPT

    (A) providing structure and support.
    (B) providing protection for organs.
    (C) producing red blood cells.
    (D) producing calcium and phosphate.

Use the following illustration to answer questions 40 through 44 below. In the illustration, "T" stands for tall and "t" for short.

	T	T
t	Tt	Tt
t	Tt	Tt

40. The illustration above is called a

    (A) Mendelian Diagram.
    (B) genotype.
    (C) Punnett square.
    (D) phenogram.

41. Which of the following genotypes are represented by the two parents?

    I.   tt
    II. Tt
    III. TT

    (A) II only
    (B) I only
    (C) I and III
    (D) I and II

42. The gametes for this cross will have which possible alleles?

    (A) T, T
    (B) T, t
    (C) TT, tt
    (D) t, t

43. What will be the phenotypic ratios of the offspring in this cross?

    (A) 4 tall: 0 short
    (B) 2 tall: 2 short
    (C) 4 tt: 0 tt
    (D) 0 tt: 4 tt

44. If two of the offspring are crossed what will the phenotypic ratio of the next generation be?

    (A) 1 tt: 2 tt; 1 tt
    (B) 4 tall: 0 short
    (C) 3 tall: 1 short
    (D) 0 tall: 4 short

45. All of the following are major structural regions of plant roots EXCEPT

    (A) the meristematic region.
    (B) the elongation region.
    (C) the epistematic region.
    (D) the maturation region.

46. Water molecules are attracted to each other due to which of the following?

    (A) Polarity, partial positive charge near hydrogen atoms, partial negative charge near oxygen atoms
    (B) Inert properties of hydrogen and oxygen
    (C) Ionic bonds between hydrogen and oxygen
    (D) Brownian motion of hydrogen and oxygen atoms

47. All of the following are true EXCEPT

    (A) animal cells have organized nuclei and membrane-bound organelles.

(B) animal cells do not have cell walls or plastids.

(C) animals only reproduce asexually.

(D) animals develop from embryonic stages.

48. Which of the following terms represent the movement of a species in or out of a given area?

I.   Dispersion
II. Emigration
III. Competition

(A) I only
(B) I and II
(C) I, II and III
(D) III only

49. An unknown plant found in the forest has five petals on its flower and a tap root system. Which of the following is most likely TRUE?

(A) The plant's seed has only one cotyledon.
(B) The plant is male.
(C) The leaves of the plant have parallel veins.
(D) The leaves of the plant have networked veins.

50. After school hours a student gained access to a teacher's classroom and took some Benedict's solution. The teacher was held responsible because

(A) anything that occurs in the room is the teacher's responsibility.
(B) although there was not specific liability, there was basic responsibility.
(C) all chemicals must be kept in locked storage facilities.
(D) Benedict's solution is a prohibited chemical.

51. Teachers should encourage students to present the results of a technology design or research project to students and teachers orally or in writing by means of all that follows EXCEPT

(A) diagrams.
(B) models.
(C) demonstrations.
(D) editorials.

52. The biogeography of a tropical island is affected by all of the following factors EXCEPT

(A) volcanic activity.
(B) distance from other landmasses.
(C) human population.
(D) fossil preservation within the geologic column.

53. A form of symbiosis in which one species benefits while the other is harmed is called

(A) parasitism.
(B) mutualism.
(C) amensalism.
(D) habituation.

54. All of the following are steps in the carbon cycle EXCEPT

(A) carbon is taken in by plants and used to form carbohydrates through photosynthesis.
(B) carbon dioxide is dissolved out of the air into ocean water, combined with calcium to form calcium carbonate.
(C) carbon is taken in by animal respiration and used to form carbohydrates.
(D) burning fossil fuels releases carbon dioxide into the atmosphere where it can be used by plants.

55. Large protein molecules may be secreted from a cell by the process of

(A) endocytosis.
(B) exocytosis.
(C) active transport.
(D) facilitated diffusion.

56. The enzyme amylase is present in saliva and is instrumental in the breakdown of starches in early digestion. Which of the following is the most likely reason for amylase's suitability to aid in the catalysis of starches?

    (A) The shape of the active site on the amylase molecule matches the shape of starch molecules.
    (B) The speed of the reaction is slowed by the ingestion of more starches.
    (C) The amount of substrate is limited.
    (D) All enzymes will aid in the catalysis of starches.

57. Which of the following are autotrophs?

    I.   *E. coli* bacteria
    II. Portobello mushroom
    III. Asparagus fern
    IV. A human fetus

    (A) I only
    (B) III only
    (C) II and IV
    (D) II and III

58. Which of the following elements is/are found in organic tissue?

    I.   Carbon and Argon
    II. Oxygen
    III. Nitrogen and Sulfur
    IV. Phosphorous and Hydrogen

    (A) I only
    (B) II and III
    (C) I and II
    (D) II, III and IV

59. Organisms store energy within

    (A) carbon.
    (B) chemical bonds.
    (C) phosphorous.
    (D) water.

60. The diploid generation in plants is known as the

    (A) spore.
    (B) sporophyte.
    (C) gametophyte.
    (D) adult.

61. Cells of eukaryotes have all of the following EXCEPT

    (A) membrane-bound organelles.
    (B) DNA organized into chromosomes.
    (C) a nucleus.
    (D) DNA floating free in the cytoplasm.

62. The process whereby molecules and ions flow through a cell membrane from an area of higher concentration to an area of lower concentration without an input of energy is known as

    (A) diffusion.
    (B) active transport.
    (C) endocytosis.
    (D) exocytosis.

63. A species' ecological niche is defined as including

    (A) only the physical features of its habitat.
    (B) all the biotic and abiotic factors that will support its life and reproduction.
    (C) the biotic features of its habitat.
    (D) only abiotic factors such as weather, temperature, etc.

64. A DNA strand in a double helix has a base sequence of ATACGT. The base sequence of its DNA complement is:

    (A) ACGUAU
    (B) ATACGT
    (C) TATGCA
    (D) UAUGCA

65. There are various types of plant stems that have different functions. All of the following are types of stems EXCEPT

   (A) corms.
   (B) nodes.
   (C) tubers.
   (D) rhizomes.

66. A gas that causes asphyxiation by binding to hemoglobin, thus preventing oxygen from doing so, is known as

   (A) carbon dioxide.
   (B) carbon monoxide.
   (C) nitrous oxide.
   (D) water vapor.

67. Which of the following factors exerts the most influence over limiting cell size?

   (A) A rigid cell wall
   (B) The ratio of surface area to volume of cytoplasm
   (C) The replication of mitochondria
   (D) The chemical composition of the cell membrane

68. When a hamburger is consumed by an individual, it passes through all the following organs EXCEPT the

   (A) mouth.
   (B) esophagus.
   (C) salivary gland.
   (D) small intestine.

69. In order for a species to be established on an island it must have all of the following features EXCEPT

   (A) a population large enough to ensure successful reproduction.
   (B) a food source for the species.
   (C) a predator of the species.
   (D) a source of moisture.

70. Which of the following are NOT involved in the immune system?

   (A) Antibodies
   (B) Stem cells
   (C) T cells
   (D) Epithelial cells

71. The process that releases energy for use by the cell is known as

   (A) photosynthesis.
   (B) anabolism.
   (C) anaerobic metabolism.
   (D) cellular respiration.

72. Which of the following are secreted by the stomach?

   I.   Digestive enzymes
   II.   Hydrochloric acid
   III. Mucus
   IV.   Gastric juices

   (A) II and III
   (B) I, II, III and IV
   (C) I, II, and IV
   (D) I and IV

73. Plants and animals obtain usable nitrogen through the action of

   (A) respiration.
   (B) nitrogen fixing by bacteria and lightning.
   (C) nitrogen processing in the atmosphere.
   (D) digestion.

74. All of the following statements about photosynthesis are true EXCEPT

   (A) photosynthesis occurs through numerous small steps.
   (B) photosynthesis can be summarized by the equation:
   $6CO_2 + 6H_2O + \text{light energy} \rightarrow C_6H_{12}O_6 + 6O_2$.

(C) chlorophyll is not harmed or used up by the photosynthetic process.

(D) chlorophyll speeds the photosynthetic process, but it is not required for photosynthesis to occur.

75. In Genetics, the Law of Segregation states that

(A) one gene is usually dominant over the other (expresses itself over the other).

(B) genes are inherited via a process of multiple alleles.

(C) genes are randomly separated in gamete formation and brought together in fertilization.

(D) gamete formation causes mutation in genetic material of both parents.

76. Sharks and dolphins have similar body shapes. Which of the following is the most likely explanation of this fact?

(A) Sharks and dolphins have a common ancestry.

(B) The similar body shape traits are the result of convergent evolution.

(C) Sharks and dolphins are competitors in their ocean communities.

(D) A species of shark evolved into the first dolphin species.

77. In humans, the ability to roll the tongue is an inherited trait and the allele for tongue-rolling is dominant. If 36% of the population cannot roll their tongue, what is the frequency of the heterozygous genotype within the population, according to the Hardy-Weinberg Equation?

(A) 0.06

(B) 0.04

(C) 0.48

(D) 0.36

78. The term *Homo sapiens* is an example of

(A) family and phylum names.

(B) a class name.

(C) a taxonomic key.

(D) binomial nomenclature.

79. Members of which of the following categories are most closely related?

(A) Phylum

(B) Genus

(C) Kingdom

(D) Class

80. Which of the following are included in the Oparin hypothesis?

I. H_2O once existed only in the form of ice.

II. The young Earth had very little oxygen present in the atmosphere.

III. The Earth is more than 4 billion years old.

IV. Heat energy was abundantly available because of the Earth's cooling.

(A) II, III, and IV

(B) I, II and III

(C) II and III

(D) I and IV

81. Which of the following is an explanation of how altruistic traits evolve?

(A) The presence of an altruistic trait in an individual decreases its fitness to survive.

(B) The process of kin selection preserves altruistic traits.

(C) Genetic drift accounts for the development of altruistic traits.

(D) Species that experience adaptive radiation also develop altruism.

82. *Streptococcus pyogenes* bacteria cause throat infections in humans, but can be killed with the antibiotic penicillin. If penicillin therapy is not administered correctly, some bacteria may survive. The surviving bacteria are those with a higher level of resistance to penicillin. The living resistant bacteria will reproduce, magnifying the traits of resistance in subsequent generations. This is an example of

(A) genetic drift.
(B) natural selection.
(C) mutation.
(D) genetic equilibrium.

83. The major driving force of the evolution of species is known as

    (A) the Oparin hypothesis.
    (B) natural selection.
    (C) allopatric speciation.
    (D) the Hardy-Weinberg Equilibrium.

84. A _____ is a distinct group of individuals that are able to mate and produce viable offspring.

    (A) class
    (B) community
    (C) phylum
    (D) species

85. Which of the following phylums of vertebrates contains animals with mammary glands?

    I.   Reptilia
    II. Amphibia
    III. Mammalia
    IV. Chondrichthyes

    (A) IV only
    (B) I, II and III
    (C) III and IV
    (D) III only

86. Which of the following kingdoms contains photosynthetic organisms?

    (A) Fungi
    (B) Protista
    (C) Animalia
    (D) Monera

87. There are three different genes that control skin color in humans. Each gene has a dominant and a recessive allele, so the possible alleles are A, a, B, b, C, c. The more dominant

alleles inherited by offspring, the darker the skin color. Skin color in humans is an example of

(A) a polygenic trait.
(B) an autosome.
(C) a sex-linked trait.
(D) a monohybrid cross.

88. The fossil of a fish is found in a limestone bed. The imprint of a skeleton is easily discernable, including several vertebrae. The fish most likely belonged to the class

    (A) Cephalochordates.
    (B) porifera.
    (C) Osteichthyes.
    (D) Cnidaria.

89. According to the Hardy-Weinberg Law, evolution can occur due to changes in allele frequencies. All of the following can contribute to changes in allele frequencies EXCEPT

    (A) mutations.
    (B) immigration.
    (C) emigration.
    (D) sexual recombination.

90. Protists are divided into two major subgroups by their

    (A) methods of locomotion.
    (B) methods of reproduction.
    (C) habitats.
    (D) method of nourishment.

91. Regarding the taxonomic classification of man,

    I.   its phylum is Mammalia
    II. its family is Hominidae
    III. its kingdom is Chordata

    (A) I only
    (B) II only
    (C) II and III
    (D) I, II, and III

92. The diversification of mammals that followed the extinction of dinosaurs is an example of

    (A) allopatric speciation.
    (B) sympatric speciation.
    (C) disruptive selection.
    (D) adaptive radiation.

93. Which of the following conducted early research into the process of genetic inheritance?

    (A) Hooke
    (B) Mendeleev
    (C) Schwann
    (D) Mendel

94. In what way may a mass extinction event allow for diversification of species?

    (A) Mass extinction opens up ecological niches, making conditions favorable for the establishment of new, diverse species.
    (B) Mass extinction encourages convergent evolution.
    (C) Mass extinction serves to magnify evolution of altruistic traits.
    (D) Mass extinction allows for preservation of genetic material through fossilization.

95. Which of the following elements may proteins contain?

    I.   Carbon
    II. Hydrogen
    III. Oxygen

    (A) I and II
    (B) II only
    (C) I, II, and III
    (D) I only

96. Which of the following are within the phylum Chordata?

    (A) Crabs
    (B) Flat worms
    (C) Nematodes
    (D) Snakes

97. Work in science and engineering requires all of the following EXCEPT

    (A) good general knowledge base.
    (B) imagination.
    (C) familiarity of science and engineering at home.
    (D) creativity.

98. Which of the following is NOT true about disease processes in humans?

    (A) Many diseases can be prevented, controlled, or cured by human measures.
    (B) Some diseases occur because of specific dysfunction in body cells and systems and are not transmitted from person to person.
    (C) Lack of sanitation has been eliminated as a cause of disease in the world.
    (D) Severity of specific cases of disease can be impacted by human resistance or organism virulence.

Use the following information to answer questions 99-101.

Students in Mr. Fernando's Biology class were learning about osmosis and diffusion, and how each relates to cell processes. They took part in the following laboratory experiment:

1) Slice a potato into 4 discs without skin.
2) Pour assigned solution into a beaker.
3) Measure and record the mass of each of the 4 discs. (Use the triple beam balance provided with markings to the nearest gram to measure mass.)
4) Put one of each of the 4 discs into one of each of the following solutions – 0.2 M sucrose, 0.4 M sucrose, 0.6 M sucrose, 0.8 M sucrose - and let sit overnight.
5) Remove discs. Measure and record their masses.
6) Calculate percentage change from initial to final and graph data.

Questions 99 - 101 refer to the following table and graphs.

Potato Core Results-Class Date 0.2 M Sucrose Solution									
	Group 1	Group 2	Group 3	Group 4	Group 5	Group 6	Group 7	Total	Class Average
Initial Mass	6.3	6.1	5.9	4.872	6.1	6	5.8	41.07	5.87
Final Mass	8	8	7.8	5.9001	8.1	7.9	7.9	53.60	7.66
Mass Difference	1.7	1.9	1.9	1.0281	2	1.9	2.1	12.53	1.79
Percent Change in Mass	26.98%	31.15%	32.20%	21.10%	32.79%	31.67%	36..21%	30.49%	30.49%

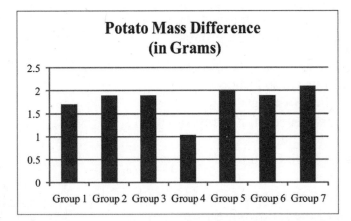

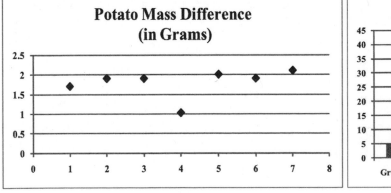

Scatter-plot of group values

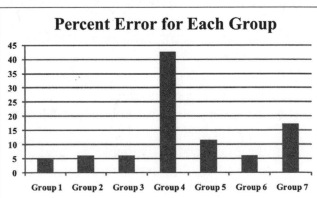

99. The data for the seven groups in Mr. Fernando's class are represented for the 0.2 M sucrose solution in the table. Looking at the data from Groups 1–7, which of the following statements is MOST LIKELY true?

    (A) Students in Group Four needed more assistance in measuring mass.
    (B) It would have been more appropriate to divide the class into fewer groups.
    (C) Group Four used the correct number of significant figures and will most likely get more accurate results.
    (D) The class average will be more accurate because Group Four used a higher number of significant figures.

100. Which of the following best represents the difference in accuracy of the seven groups' results?

    (A) Potato Core Results Class Data
    (B) Scatter Plot of Group Values
    (C) Potato Mass Difference in Grams of Each Group
    (D) Percent Error for Each Group

101. Regarding the experiment completed by Mr. Fernando's class, all of the following are true EXCEPT

    (A) the independent variable is the Group numbers (1-7).
    (B) the dependent variable is the potato mass difference in grams.
    (C) the independent variable is the percent error for each group.
    (D) the independent variable is also expressed in this experiment by percent change in mass.

Read the following passage and answer question 102 below.

The Sanghua River area of China has experienced a dramatic increase in population in the previous 50 years, resulting in increased industry and agriculture. Unfortunately, as a result, there have also been problems with the Sanghua River ecosystems. A study was done to consider the factors contributing to the decline in water quality.

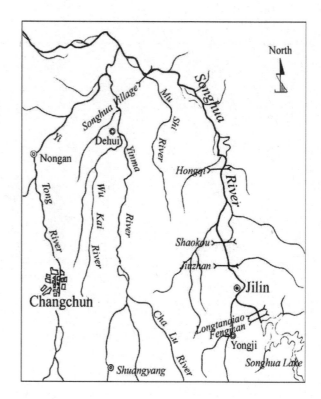

102. Which of the following factors would not contribute to poor water quality as a result of increased local population?

    (A) Factory waste
    (B) Lowered nitrogenous wastes
    (C) City sewage
    (D) Agricultural pesticides and fertilizers

103. Which of the following is the weakest type of chemical bonds?

    (A) Ionic bonds
    (B) Hydrogen bonds
    (C) Double bonds
    (D) Disulfide bonds

104. All of the following are myths or misconceptions about the evolution of *Homo sapiens* EXCEPT

    (A) *Homo sapiens* evolved from chimpanzees.
    (B) there is a linear sequence or ladder of different primates that leads to *Homo sapiens*.
    (C) the large brain and upright posture of *Homo sapiens* evolved together.
    (D) chimpanzees are more closely related to *Homo sapiens* than to other apes.

105. Algae and protozoa are organisms within which kingdom?

    (A) Plantae
    (B) Animalia
    (C) Mammalia
    (D) Protista

106. When the water pressure is equal inside and outside the cell, it is said to be

    (A) hydrostatic.
    (B) diffuse.
    (C) isohydric.
    (D) isotonic.

107. Energy transformations that occur as chemicals that are broken apart or synthesized within the cell are collectively known as

    (A) catabolism.
    (B) anabolism.
    (C) metabolism.
    (D) synthesis.

108. The largest number of ATP molecules are formed by

    (A) fermentation.
    (B) the electron transfer system.
    (C) glycolysis.
    (D) the Krebs cycle.

109. How does DNA produce particular genetic traits?

    (A) Through DNA replication
    (B) Through protein synthesis
    (C) Through genetic imprinting
    (D) Through genetic maintenance

110. A single DNA strand that has the sequence GATACCA would be complemented by a strand of DNA with which sequence?

    (A) GATACCA
    (B) CTATGGT
    (C) ACCATAG
    (D) CUAUCCU

111. The longest of the two major periods of the cell cycle in which the cell is carrying on its primary function is known as

    (A) interphase.
    (B) prophase.
    (C) telophase.
    (D) anaphase.

Read the following sentence and answer questions 112 through 114.

Normal skin color in mice is dominant to albino. In the following questions, N stands for normal skin color and n for albino.

112. Three offspring of two normal-skinned parents have normal skin, but one of the offspring is albino. Which of the following must be true?

(A) One parent must have the NN genotype.
(B) Both parents must have the NN genotype.
(C) One parent must have the nn genotype.
(D) Both parents must have the Nn genotype.

113. If these two normal-skinned parents have eight offspring, approximately how many are likely to be albino?

(A) 2
(B) 3
(C) 1
(D) 8

114. The albino offspring from the F_1 generation described above produces one albino offspring and one normal offspring in the F_2 generation. What must be the genotype of the albino's mate?

(A) Either Nn or NN
(B) Either Nn or nn
(C) Nn
(D) nn

115. What is 78°F in International System (SI) units?

(A) 25.6 K
(B) 25.6 °C
(C) 43.3 °C
(D) 46.0 °C

116. Which of the following natural hazards is MOST likely to be predicted in advance by modern technology and therefore allow for preventive measures to be taken to save life and property?

(A) Hurricane
(B) Earthquake
(C) Volcano
(D) Tsunami

117. Which of the following statements regarding the relationship of science, society, and technology is true?

(A) Understanding science will eventually resolve local, national, and global challenges.
(B) Progress in science and technology is not affected by social issues and challenges.
(C) Understanding about a technology should precede a political debate about that technology.
(D) Understanding about science is necessary for making all political and ethical decisions.

118. When scientists consider new research, they have to consider what risks are involved in conducting the research and if the purpose of conducting the research is worth the risk. Which of the following questions is LEAST important for a researcher to ask in assessing risk management?

(A) What will happen if the research is not successful? What are the odds of it failing?
(B) What are the risks and costs of the research that is being conducted?
(C) What is the literature basis for the research being conducted?
(D) What is the purpose of the research being conducted?

119. Ronda has taken a Biology teaching position in an urban school district. In her first week of classes she finds that one of her lab sessions has 32 students assigned to it. In addition, there is no fire blanket available in the room and the lab tables are too small to allow for each student to participate in the group work. Which of the following is NOT Ronda's responsibility?

(A) Notify district officials of potential safety issues that could impact learning.
(B) Document safety issues in the classroom.
(C) Notify the school administration of class size issues.
(D) Ensure that each student passes lab session regardless of the deficiencies.

120. Which of the following is NOT an energy storage molecule?

(A) Cellulose
(B) Ribonucleic acid
(C) Starch
(D) Lipid

121. The organelle of a cell that engages in both passive and active transport is the

(A) rough endoplasmic reticulum.
(B) smooth endoplasmic reticulum.
(C) Golgi complex.
(D) cell (plasma) membrane.

122. Stem tissue includes which of the following?

I. Vascular tissue
II. Xylem
III. Phloem
IV. Cuticle

(A) All of the above
(B) None of the above
(C) II and III
(D) I, II, and III

123. An ion that binds to an enzyme, making it more able to catalyze a reaction, is known as

(A) a protein.
(B) an inorganic cofactor.
(C) a coenzyme.
(D) a prosthetic group.

124. Which type of tissue is made up of stacked cells connected by sieve plates that allow nutrients to pass from cell to cell?

(A) Xylem
(B) Meristem
(C) Phloem
(D) Internodal

125. All of the following characteristics of water make it valuable to living organisms EXCEPT

(A) transparency.
(B) polarity.
(C) a lower density when solid than when liquid.
(D) a pH of 11.

126. Each ecosystem can support a certain number of organisms; this number is known as the

(A) natality.
(B) population.
(C) carrying capacity.
(D) community.

127. Many insects have special respiratory organs known as

(A) spiracles.
(B) alveoli.
(C) the cephalothorax.
(D) lungs.

128. What happens to most chemical pollutants that are accidentally ingested by a human?

(A) They are broken down, mixed with broken down pigment molecules in the bile, and excreted in the feces.
(B) They are attacked by the lymphatic system and recycled in protein synthesis.
(C) They are collected in lymph tissue and excreted through the skin.
(D) They build up in epithelial tissue until lethal levels are reached.

129. The process of forming egg and sperm cells in the reproductive organs is known as

(A) gametogenesis.

(B) spermatagonium.

(C) oogonium.

(D) gametocide.

130. The cells of a developing embryo (at the gastrula stage) differentiate into layers (called germ layers) that will later develop into various tissues and organs. Which layer will eventually form muscles, skeletal organs, and the circulatory, respiratory, reproductive, and excretory systems?

(A) Endoderm

(B) Ectoderm

(C) Blastula

(D) Mesoderm

131. Behavior that benefits the group at the individual's expense is known as

(A) imprinting.

(B) fixed action pattern.

(C) altruism.

(D) sacrificial.

132. Learned behavior that results in not responding to a stimulus is called

(A) circadian rhythm.

(B) habituation.

(C) imprinting.

(D) altruism.

133. The physical place where a particular organism lives is called its

(A) niche.

(B) biosphere.

(C) lithosphere.

(D) habitat.

134. All of the following are requirements of the habitat of an apple tree EXCEPT

(A) soil quality.

(B) available sunlight.

(C) seasonal temperature fluctuations.

(D) role in the food chain.

135. Sugars synthesized by photosynthesis travel through _____ _____ to various parts of the plant.

(A) epidermal tissue

(B) vascular bundles

(C) meristem tissue

(D) parenchyma tissue

136. Which of the following environmental factors are recycled?

I.   Nitrogen

II. Carbon

III. Phosphorous

(A) All of the above

(B) None of the above

(C) I and III

(D) I and II

137. As energy is transferred through the trophic levels, some energy

(A) is created by producers.

(B) is destroyed by producers.

(C) is destroyed by decomposers.

(D) becomes unusable.

138. Channels in cell membranes that carry water between cells are called

(A) guard cells.

(B) plasmodesmata.

(C) stomata.

(D) internodes.

139. All of the following are steps in the phosphorous cycle EXCEPT

(A) phosphorous becomes available for erosion as undersea sedimentary rocks are up-thrust by volcanic activity.

(B) phosphorous is returned to the ground through animal wastes.

(C) gaseous phosphorous is absorbed from the atmosphere by plant leaves.

(D) erosion releases phosphorous from rocks into streams where it combines with oxygen to form phosphates in lakes that are then absorbed by plants.

140. A bilayer of phospholipids with protein globules interspersed is characteristic of which of the following organelles?

(A) cell membrane
(B) mitochondria
(C) lysosome
(D) chromatin

141. A pond ecosystem has sharp boundaries at the shorelines. The sharp boundary of an ecosystem is known as

(A) a segregation point.
(B) a succession.
(C) an ecotone.
(D) a borderline.

142. Which of the following cell organelles is known as the cell's "powerhouse" because it produces energy for the cell's use?

(A) Nucleus
(B) Mitochondrion
(C) Smooth endoplasmic reticulum
(D) Ribosome

143. Which one of the following statements about cells is NOT true?

(A) All living things are made up of one or more cells.
(B) Cells may be seen with a microscope.
(C) Cells are the basic units of life.
(D) All cells have cell walls.

144. The bee belongs to which phylum?

(A) Arthropoda
(B) Aves
(C) Annelida
(D) Nematoda

145. Which of the following is a polymer of amino acids?

I. Lactose
II. Lactase
III. Glycogen
IV. Sucrose

(A) I only
(B) II only
(C) I and II
(D) II, III and IV

146. Vertebrates with no jaws belong to the super-class

(A) aganatha.
(B) gnathostomata.
(C) protista.
(D) cnidaria.

147. Which of the following structures provide rigidity to plant cells but not animal cells?

(A) Microtubules
(B) Cell walls
(C) Microfilaments
(D) Centrioles

148. The nervous system is an integrated circuit with many functions. Which of the following parts of the nervous system are matched with the wrong function?

(A) forebrain—controls olfactory lobes (smell)
(B) cerebrum—controls function of involuntary muscle
(C) hypothalamus—controls hunger and thirst
(D) cerebellum—controls balance and muscle coordination

149. Nitrogen is made available to organisms of the food chain through all of the following EXCEPT

(A) bacteria break ammonia into nitrites, then into nitrates that are usable by plants.
(B) volcanic activity produces ammonia and nitrates that enter the soil and can be absorbed by plants.
(C) lightning reacts with atmospheric nitrogen to form nitrates that are absorbed by plants.
(D) nitrogen is absorbed into ocean water.

150. Scurvy is a disease caused by a lack of vitamin C, leaving the body unable to build up enough collagen (a major component of connective tissue). The most plausible explanation for this malfunction is

(A) vitamin C is an amino acid component of collagen.
(B) vitamin C is a coenzyme required in the synthesis of collagen.
(C) vitamin C destroys collagen.
(D) vitamin C is produced by collagen.

Detailed Explanations to Answers for Practice Test 1

Praxis II: Biology
Core Content Knowledge

1. (B)	39. (D)	77. (C)	115. (B)
2. (C)	40. (C)	78. (D)	116. (A)
3. (C)	41. (C)	79. (B)	117. (C)
4. (D)	42. (B)	80. (A)	118. (C)
5. (A)	43. (A)	81. (B)	119. (D)
6. (D)	44. (C)	82. (B)	120. (B)
7. (B)	45. (C)	83. (B)	121. (D)
8. (A)	46. (A)	84. (D)	122. (D)
9. (D)	47. (C)	85. (D)	123. (D)
10. (A)	48. (A)	86. (B)	124. (C)
11. (C)	49. (D)	87. (A)	125. (D)
12. (A)	50. (C)	88. (C)	126. (C)
13. (D)	51. (D)	89. (D)	127. (A)
14. (A)	52. (D)	90. (D)	128. (A)
15. (C)	53. (A)	91. (B)	129. (A)
16. (B)	54. (C)	92. (D)	130. (D)
17. (A)	55. (B)	93. (D)	131. (C)
18. (A)	56. (A)	94. (A)	132. (B)
19. (C)	57. (B)	95. (C)	133. (D)
20. (D)	58. (D)	96. (D)	134. (D)
21. (D)	59. (B)	97. (C)	135. (B)
22. (A)	60. (B)	98. (C)	136. (A)
23. (B)	61. (D)	99. (A)	137. (D)
24. (A)	62. (A)	100. (D)	138. (B)
25. (A)	63. (B)	101. (C)	139. (C)
26. (D)	64. (C)	102. (B)	140. (A)
27. (C)	65. (B)	103. (B)	141. (C)
28. (A)	66. (B)	104. (A)	142. (B)
29. (B)	67. (B)	105. (D)	143. (D)
30. (D)	68. (C)	106. (D)	144. (A)
31. (A)	69. (C)	107. (C)	145. (B)
32. (D)	70. (D)	108. (B)	146. (A)
33. (A)	71. (D)	109. (B)	147. (B)
34. (B)	72. (B)	110. (B)	148. (B)
35. (C)	73. (B)	111. (A)	149. (D)
36. (A)	74. (D)	112. (D)	150. (B)
37. (D)	75. (C)	113. (A)	
38. (D)	76. (B)	114. (C)	

PRACTICE TEST 1: PROGRESS AND COMPETENCY CHART

Basic Principles of Science ____/12

15	16	17	27	29	30	50	99	100	101

115	119

Molecular & Cellular Biology ____/38

1	3	6	8	10	12	14	22	23	25

31	33	38	46	55	58	59	61	62	64

67	71	95	103	106	107	108	109	110	111

120	121	123	138	140	142	143	145

Classical Genetics & Evolution ____/23

4	21	24	40	41	42	43	44	75	76

78	80	81	82	83	87	89	92	93	104

112	113	114

Diversity of Life, Plants, and Animals

_____/45

2	11	13	20	32	34	35	36	37	39

45	47	49	56	60	65	66	68	70	72

73	74	77	79	84	85	86	88	90	91

96	105	122	124	125	127	128	129	130	135

144	146	147	148	150

Ecology

_____/22

5	7	9	19	48	52	53	54	57	63

69	94	126	131	132	133	134	136	137	139

141	149

Science, Technology, and Society

_____/10

18	26	28	51	97	98	102	116	117	118

1.   (B)

Inorganic cofactors are substances that promote enzyme catalysis. These molecules may bind to the active site or to the substrate itself. The most common inorganic cofactors are metallic elements such as iron, copper, and zinc. Coenzymes are organic in nature; thus, they are organic cofactors. Hormones are also organic and are not cofactors. Similarly, inorganic cofactors are minerals but not all minerals are inorganic cofactors.

2.   (C)

The filament and anther are parts of the male reproductive system in plants. The male structure is the stamen, consisting of the anther atop a long, hollow filament. The anther has four lobes and contains the cells that become pollen. The stigma is only found on female plants.

3.   (C)

Blue-green bacteria are prokaryotic organisms of the Kingdom Monera. Prokaryotes do not have a nucleus or any other membrane-bound organelles. The cells of mold, seaweed, and hydra all have membrane-bound organelles and are therefore classified as eukaryotes.

4.   (D)

Scientists conclude that in the evolution of life (including plants) the first cells were prokaryotic, and that eukaryotic cells developed as cells with varying functions were incorporated into more complex cells (the Endosymbiont Theory). In addition, the early Earth atmosphere was devoid of oxygen, so early cells were anaerobic, with aerobic cells evolving later. Cyanobacteria are autotrophic (photosynthetic) prokaryotes that are considered ancestors of multicellular plants. Both answers (A) and (B) wrongly place eukaryotes before prokaryotes. Answer (C) wrongly places aerobic cells before anaerobic cells.

5.   (A)

Types of nitrogen-fixing bacteria live in symbiosis on the nodules of the roots of legumes (beans, peas, clover, etc.), supplying the roots with a direct source of ammonia – nitrogen in a form usable by plants. This is a unique niche (changing nitrogen from an unusable to a usable form) filled by the symbiotic relationship of legumes with nitrogen-fixing bacteria.

6.   (D)

A carbohydrate molecule contains only carbon, hydrogen, and oxygen in the ratio CH_2O. Nitrogen, N, and sulfur, S, are elements that are not found in carbohydrates. Amine, NH_2, groups are found in other organic molecules, but not in carbohydrates. Therefore, only answer IV is correct.

7. (B)

The hydrologic cycle intersects with nearly all biogeochemical cycles. The cycle includes the evaporation from bodies of water and plant leaves; water vapor is then redistributed over land via clouds that release water as precipitation. Water flows back into waterways that eventually flow into the ocean. Water vapor in the air is a greenhouse gas that traps heat in the lower atmosphere and resists rapid cooling.

8. (A)

Glucose is the only monosaccharide listed. Cellulose and starch are both polysaccharides. Amylase is not a sugar at all. It is an enzyme important to the digestion of starches.

9. (D)

Ecology is literally "the study of" (-ology) a "place to live" (eco). It involves the study of all the living (including interaction with other organisms) and nonliving factors that contribute to an organism's life within its living space.

10. (A)

An enzyme is a special protein that acts as a catalyst for organic reactions. A catalyst is a substance that changes the speed of a reaction without being affected itself. The enzyme will speed up the initial reaction rate until all the enzymes are in use, and then the reaction rate will level off as all the limited amount of enzyme becomes engaged but substrate is still present. Enzymes will not decrease the reaction rate or stop the reaction completely. Furthermore, the reaction will not stop happening when all of the enzyme is engaged, but the reaction rate will level off. The rate cannot continue to rise after all of the enzyme is engaged.

11. (C)

The spinal cord is not directly involved with immunity. The organs of the immune system in humans and other higher invertebrates include all of the other organs listed in the question—the lymph nodes, spleen, and thymus.

12. (A)

The term *prokaryote* is derived from *pro* (meaning before) and *karyo* (meaning a nucleus), thus the literal definition is "before nucleus." Prokaryotic cells have no nucleus or any other membrane-bound organelles. The DNA in prokaryotic cells floats freely within the cytoplasm. Even though the nuclear membrane is absorbed during replication, other membrane-bound organelles still exist in replicating cells—including those in telephase. A eukaryotic cell, by contrast, contains a nucleus and other membrane-bound organelles.

13. (D)

Fungi are not photosynthetic—they absorb nutrients from their surroundings. Therefore, fungi cells do not have chloroplasts. The cells of fungi are eukaryotic and therefore do have a nucleus, mitochondria, and ribosomes. Therefore, choices II, III, and IV should be included in the answer.

14. (A)

Grana are within the stroma (or body) of the chloroplasts in plant cells. Pigments, including chlorophyll and carotene (when present), are found within the grana. Cristae are found in mitochondria, not in chloroplasts.

15. (C)

Cell theory refers to the cell, which is the foundational unit of all life. The theory was developed by Robert Hooke as a direct result of the invention of the microscope in the 1600's that allowed for the direct viewing of cells. (A) Natural selection is a law developed by Darwin much later in the 1850's. Mendel described the laws of independent assortment as part of his laws of inheritance in the 1800's. Newton developed the laws of motion (D). (A), (B), (D), were not connected to the invention of the microscope.

16. (B)

Natural selection describes the change in species characteristics over time. (A), (C), and (D) were other ideas of other scientists and philosophers that do not stand up to testing and observation and are not laws of science.

17. (A)

29.35 mL is correct because you can measure to one decimal place beyond the specificity given by the device. Since this device is marked in tenths of a mL you can measure to hundredths. (D) would be correct if it would only have measured to tenths. Also, you measure to the bottom of the meniscus; the top of the meniscus (the edges would be (C) 29.40 (B) is measuring upside down – incorrect.

18. (A)

The rights of the subject always take precedent in research, therefore the statement in option (A) is not true. In no case is the right of the subject not paramount. (B), (C), and (D), are all true – the Common Rule instituted in 1974 (B) was the beginning of regulation protecting the rights of human research subjects through requiring qualifications such as having IRB approval (C) and informed consent (D).

19. (C)

Nearly all life forms derive their energy from the Sun whether directly (through photosynthesis), or indirectly (by consuming other organisms).

20. (D)

The process of photosynthesis is the crucial reaction that converts the light energy of the Sun into chemical energy that is usable by living things. While catabolism, metabolism, and oxidative phosphorylation are necessary processes for most organisms, only photosynthetic organisms convert energy directly from light.

21. (D)

The sum total of genetic information of a species is its genome. Genes are portions of chromosomes that determine the inheritance of an organism's characteristics.

22. (A)

Free bases line up along the DNA template and are bonded together, forming RNA during transcription, not translation. Translation begins as a ribosome attaches to the mRNA strand at a particular codon known as the start codon. This codon is only recognized by a particular initiator tRNA. The ribosome continues to link tRNA whose anticodons complement the next codon on the mRNA string. A third type of RNA is utilized at this point, ribosomal RNA or rRNA. Ribosomal RNA exists in concert with enzymes as a ribosome. In order for the tRNA and mRNA to link up, enzymes connected to rRNA at the ribosome must be utilized.

At the end of the translation process, a terminating codon stops the synthesis process and the protein is released. Thus, answers (B), (C), and (D) represent steps in the translation process.

23. (B)

Transduction refers to the changing of a bacterium's genetic makeup by the transfer of a portion of genetic material from one bacterial cell to another. This is accomplished via a bacteriophage (a virus that targets bacteria). Transformation refers to the absorption and incorporation of pieces of DNA from a bacterium's environment (usually from dead bacterial cells).

24. (A)

Chromosomes that are paired with another of similar size and shape within the nucleus are known as homologous pairs or homologs. Each set of homologous chromosomes has a similar genetic constitution, but the genes are not necessarily the same.

25. (A)

Restriction enzymes cut out sections of DNA molecules by cleaving the sugar-phosphate backbone. In most cases, a particular enzyme cuts the strands of the double helix DNA within a length of a few bases.

26. (D)

Global climate change would not be an immediate result of overpopulation. It may be a long-term impact of over-population and carbon emissions. However, pollution (A), disease (B), and localized famine (C) can all be exacerbated by increased population.

27. (C)

The picture is of Petri dishes. (A), (B), and (D) are pictured here:

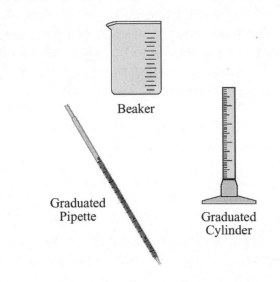

Beaker

Graduated Pipette

Graduated Cylinder

28. (A)

Students and teachers are often used to thinking that scientific progress influences technological advancement, but the reverse is also true, and the example of the microscope shows this clearly. Progress in scientific knowledge was directly positively impacted by the technological advancement of the invention of the microscope. (B) While technological advancement benefits with new scientific knowledge it is not completely dependent upon it. Neither is scientific knowledge, completely stymied by lack of technological advance (C), and neither is shown in this example. Further, (D) technological development is not always a direct result of scientific progress – and this case of the microscope does not show that.

29. (B)

Clothing should NOT be loose or baggy and sleeves should be short or rolled up out of the way to reduce fire hazard and contamination risk. In addition, hair should be tied back and in most cases gloves worn. (A), (C), and (D) are proper safety ideas.

30. (D)

Scientific laws are broad generalizations related to an aspect of how the natural world behaves under certain conditions. A scientific law must be testable, internally consistent, and compatible with available evidence and phenomena. For example, Newton's Laws of Motion are well established as scientific laws. A theory is an explanation of a particular phenomenon of the natural world. Theories explain aspects of laws, but not all laws have corresponding theories. Theories do not become laws with increasing testing or evidence. Rather, theories are a separate type of explanation, therefore a theory does not become a law (C), and neither does a law become a theory (A). A theory can be tested, and since it is a portion of a law, technically a law, in part may also be tested (B).

31. (A)

Mitosis produces two exact copies of the original cell as daughter cells. Meiosis, on the other hand, is the process of producing four daughter cells that have single unduplicated chromosomes (haploid). The parent cell is diploid, that is, it has duplicated sets of chromosomes. Meiosis also results in the production of four new cells, rather than two (as in mitosis), and each cell has half the chromosomes of the parent. Meiosis, like mitosis, begins with chromosome duplication. In meiosis, two distinct nuclear divisions occur: the first is known as reduction (or meiosis 1) and the second, division (or meiosis 2). Reduction affects the ploidy (referring to haploid or diploid) level, reducing it from 2n to n (i.e., diploid to haploid). Division then distributes the remaining set of chromosomes in a mitosis-like process among four daughter cells.

32. (D)

Oxygen is carried by hemoglobin molecules (that contain iron) in red blood cells. Lymphocytes, erythrocytes, and neutrophils are all non-oxygen-carrying types of blood cells.

33. (A)

Osmosis is a type of diffusion (passive transport) that occurs only with water molecules. The water on the side of the membrane with the highest water pressure will cross through the membrane until the concentration is equalized on both sides. Facilitated diffusion is the movement of substances across the cell membrane with the help of specialized proteins. Exocytosis is the process where large molecules are engulfed in a pocket of cell membrane and exported from the cell. Endocytosis also involves large molecules that are engulfed in a pocket of membrane, but in this case the molecules are imported into the cell.

34. (B)

The epiglottis is the flap of tissue that covers the glottis, preventing food particles from entering the bronchial tubes. Before reaching the glottis (the opening that allows gases to pass into the bronchi), air passes through the pharynx and into the trachea. The glottis is the lower portion of the trachea.

35. (C)

The placenta is the connection between the mother and embryo; it is the site of transfer for nutrients, water, and wastes between them. The yolk sac stores nutrients for the embryo and the yolk sac membrane encloses the yolk sac. The uterus is the organ in the female body that houses the developing embryo. A portion of the uterine lining becomes a part of the placenta, but the entire uterus is not involved. The allantois, contained by the allantoic membrane, develops into part of the umbilical cord.

36. (A)

Digestive enzymes are released by the pancreas and gallbladder into the small intestine. Digesting food then passes from the small intestine to the large intestine. Food travels through the esophagus on its way to the stomach, where food is digested through mechanical means as well as chemical means, but not with enzymes released by the pancreas and gallbladder. The stomach produces its own enzymes, mucus, and gastric juices. The rectum connects the large intestine with the anus where waste products are transported out of the body.

37. (D)

The heart is made of cardiac muscle. The electrical properties of cardiac muscle tissue cause the beating of the heart muscle that results in the pumping of blood through the body. When a heart stops beating, stimulating the cardiac muscle with electric shock can sometimes restart it. Smooth muscle tissue is not found in the heart.

38. (D)

All the DNA of every cell of every organism is copied repeatedly to form new cells for growth, repair, and reproduction. A mutation can be an error that occurs randomly during one of the many copying sequences that occur within the cell. Mutations can also be the result of damage to DNA through environmental agents such as sunlight, cigarette smoke, chemical exposure, or x-rays. Crossing over is a process that may occur during meiosis, resulting in exchange of corresponding portions between homologous chromosomes. Crossing over is not a mutation.

39. (D)

In addition to being the primary structure and support for the human frame, the 206 bones of the skeleton protect the soft internal organs of the human body, produce red blood cells from its marrow, and allow for movement by providing a base for muscles and ligaments. While the bones do store calcium and phosphates, they do not produce them.

40. (C)

The illustration is called a Punnett square and is used to illustrate genetic crosses. The genotype is the representation of the alleles present in a particular organism (for example, Tt, where uppercase T stands for the dominant allele for "tall" and lowercase t stands for the recessive allele for short). While Mendel was instrumental in the study of genetics, Reginald Punnett, not Mendel, developed the Punnett square; thus, it is not called a "Mendelian Diagram." *Phenogram* is not a term that is used in genetics.

41. (C)

Since the genotypes of the parents are always listed on the side and top of a Punnett square, the genotypes of the parents are tt and TT.

42. (B)

Every gamete will have either the T allele or the t allele since those are the only possibilities of gametes from the parents.

43. (A)

All offspring will have a genotype Tt; all have a dominant gene for tallness (T) so all will have a phenotype of tall; thus the ratio is 4 tall: 0 short.

44. (C)

The Punnett square for a cross of two of the offspring would be:

	T	t
T	TT	Tt
t	Tt	tt

The genotype ratio will be 1 TT: 2 Tt: 1 tt. Since T (tall) is dominant to t (short), only one out of four will be short. The phenotypic ratio will be 3 tall; 1 short.

45. (C)

There is no epistematic region in plant roots. Roots have four major structural regions that run vertically from bottom to top. The root cap (not an answer choice) is composed of dead, thick-walled cells and covers the tip of the root, protecting it as the root pushes through soil. The meristematic region is just above the root cap. It consists of undifferentiated cells that carry on mitosis, producing the cells that grow to form the elongation region. In the elongation region, cells differentiate, large vacuoles are formed, and cells grow. As the cells differentiate into various root tissues, they become part of the maturation region.

46. (A)

The hydrogen atoms in water molecules have a partial positive charge and the oxygen atoms a partial negative charge, causing polarity. This polarity allows the oxygen of one water molecule to attract the hydrogen of another. The partial charges attract other opposite partial charges of other water molecules, allowing for weak (hydrogen) bonds between the molecules. *Inert* means non-reactive; it does not explain the attraction between H and O. There are no ionic bonds within water molecules, only covalent bonds. Brownian motion is the random movement of atoms or particles caused by collisions between them; it does not explain attraction between atoms or molecules.

47. (C)

Animal species are capable of sexual reproduction, though some, such as the hydra and other invertebrates, asexually reproduce. All animal cells are eukaryotic (have nuclei and membrane-bound organelles). Only plants and blue-green bacteria have cell walls and/or plastids. Animals do develop from embryos.

48. (A)

Competition occurs when niches overlap between two species in the same community. The term *competition* does not indicate movement in or out of an area. Emigration (one-way movement out of the original range) is a form of dispersion (movement of species).

49. (D)

Five petals indicates that the plant is a dicot (a plant with two cotyledons in each seed). Dicots also have taproot systems and leaves with networked or branching veins. A monocot would have random arrangement of its vascular bundles and leaves with parallel veins. There was no indication from the given information whether the plant was male or female.

50. (C)

Teachers are responsible to keep all chemicals in locked storage facilities when not in use. Benedict's solution may or may not be a prohibited chemical in your school or locale (D), but regardless it needs to be locked up. (A) The teacher cannot be expected to be in the room and responsible (B) 24/7 but there are basic safety protocols for which the teacher *is* responsible.

51. (D)

An editorial would not be an appropriate manner of presenting the results of a technology design or research project as it expresses opinion, not data. (A), (B), and (C) are correct . . . "Students should present their results to students, teachers, and others in a variety of ways, such as orally, in writing, and in other forms—including models, diagrams, and demonstrations." (NSES, 1996, p.192)

52. (D)

Dispersal of species to an island is dependent on geographic as well as historical factors. Distance from other landmasses, prevailing winds, and ocean currents are also geographic factors that will affect species introduction. Historical factors such as climate shifts (for instance, the shift to an ice age), drought, volcanic action, plate shifting, and human intervention will also affect what species are able to travel to a given island. Fossil preservation or lack thereof would not affect any current conditions of biogeography.

53. (A)

Parasitism is symbiosis in which one organism benefits, but the other is harmed. Mutualism is symbiosis that benefits both organisms. Amensalism is symbiosis where one organism is neither helped nor harmed but the growth of the other is inhibited. Habituation is not a form of symbiosis; it is a behavioral response where there is less and less response by an individual to a stimulus over time.

54. (C)

Animal respiration releases carbon dioxide back into the atmosphere in large quantities; it does not take in carbon dioxide for use. Most of the carbon within organisms is derived from the production of carbohydrates in plants through photosynthesis. Carbon dioxide is dissolved directly into the oceans, where it is combined with calcium to form calcium carbonate—used by mollusks to form their shells. Organic matter that is left to decay may, under conditions of heat and pressure, be transformed into coal, oil, or natural gas—the fossil fuels. When fossil fuels are burned for energy, the combustion process releases carbon dioxide back into the atmosphere, where it is available to plants for photosynthesis.

55. (B)

Large molecules (such as proteins) are not able to pass through the cell membrane, but are instead engulfed by it. Endocytosis is the process whereby large molecules (i.e., some sugars, or proteins) are taken up by a sack of membrane and delivered to the interior of the cell where it can be used. (This process, for instance, is used by white blood cells to engulf bacteria.) Exocytosis uses the same process but exports substances to the exterior of the cell. Active transport and facilitated diffusion are processes that involve passing substances through the cell membrane by various means.

56. (A)

It is the shape of the active site of the enzyme that allows the enzyme to work on the substrate to form product(s). The active site of the amylase molecule matches the shape of starch molecules. The speed of the reaction and the amount of substrate do not enhance amylase's enzymatic functions. Specific enzymes are needed for specific reactions.

57. (B)

Plants (including asparagus ferns) produce their own food through photosynthesis and are known as autotrophs. Fungi, human fetuses, and bacteria do not produce their own food. Therefore, only answer choice (B) is correct.

58. (D)

Argon is a noble gas; it does not occur naturally in organic tissue. All organic molecules contain carbon, but because answer choice I includes argon, this choice is eliminated. Also commonly found in organic molecules are oxygen, nitrogen, sulfur, hydrogen, and phosphorous. Therefore, choice (D) which contains II, III and IV is correct.

59. (B)

Chemical bonds are where energy is stored within cells.

60. (B)

The diploid (2n)generation in plants is known as the sporophyte. The gametophyte is always haploid (n). What we consider the adult generation in a plant's life cycle may be haploid (ex. mosses) or diploid (ex. ferns). Spores are male haploid gametes.

61. (D)

The DNA of eukaryotes is organized into chromosomes within the nucleus.

62. (A)

Diffusion is the process whereby molecules and ions flow through the cell membrane from an area of higher concentration to an area of lower concentration. Where the substance exists in higher concentration, collisions occur that tend to propel them away toward lower concentrations. Active transport requires added energy to move substances across a membrane. In endocytosis and exocytosis the cell membrane surrounds the substance and moves it either into (endo) or out of (exo) a cell.

63. (B)

A species' habitat must include all the factors that will support its life and reproduction including biotic factors (i.e., living—food source, predators, place in the food chain, etc.) and abiotic factors (i.e., nonliving—weather, temperature, soil features, etc.).

64. (C)

Two base-pairing rules must be memorized for DNA strands: A-T and C-G. Thus, the given DNA strand of six bases dictates only one possible complement.

65. (B)

There are many types of stems that have specialized functions. The functions of stems generally may include transport of water and food between root and leaves, leaf support, and food storage. Underground stems include tubers, rhizomes and corms. Tubers, found in the potato, function to store starch. Rhizomes, in ferns, function in vegetative propagation. Corms are found in gladiolus and are actually fleshy leaves that store food. Nodes are not stems, but rather are the site on the stem at which the leaves attach. Internodes are thus the region between nodes.

66. (B)

Carbon monoxide is a colorless, odorless gas that can bind to hemoglobin without the subject's awareness. As hemoglobin in red blood cells transports oxygen, oxygen's unavailability due to CO binding causes internal suffocation, or asphyxiation.

67. (B)

The size of a cell is limited by the ratio of its surface area to volume. A cell will remain stable only if the surface area of the plasma membrane maintains a balance with the volume of cytoplasm. Only plant cells (and some bacteria) have cell walls. The replication of mitochondria and the chemical composition of the cell membrane do not specifically limit cell size.

68. (C)

Ingested food does not pass through the salivary gland; rather, the saliva secreted from this gland enters the digestive tract and helps digest the food. Food does pass through mouth, esophagus, stomach, and small intestine.

69. (C)

In order to become an established part of the island ecosystem it must find a suitable ecological niche. Ultimately the species must be able to reproduce in its new setting, or it will not remain a part of the ecosystem. Organisms do not require a predator, though one may be necessary in some cases for population control. But many thriving organisms, including those that are at the highest trophic level, have no predators.

70. (D)

Epithelial (skin) cells have no direct function in immunity. Cells involved in immunity are called lymphocytes and are produced in bone marrow as stem cells. T cells are one of two classes of lymphocytes, B cells and T cells. Some T cells patrol the blood for antigens, but T cells are also equipped to destroy antigens themselves. T cells also regulate immune responses.

71. (D)

Cellular respiration is the process that releases energy for use by the cell. There are several steps involved in cellular respiration; some require oxygen (aerobic) and some do not (anaerobic). Photosynthesis is a type of anabolism, a reaction that harnesses and stores solar energy in chemical bonds.

72. (B)

The stomach secretes digestive enzymes, hydrochloric acid, and gastric juices, which all aid in digestion. The stomach also secretes mucus, which protects the stomach lining from the acids and gastric juices.

73. (B)

Neither plants nor animals are able to use nitrogen directly from the air. Instead, a process known as nitrogen fixing makes nitrogen available for absorption by the roots of plants. Nitrogen-fixing is the process of combining it with either hydrogen or oxygen. Nitrogen fixing is accomplished in one of two ways—either by nitrogen-fixing bacteria or by the action of lightning. Nitrogen is present in the atmosphere (including the air we breathe), but it is not used in the process of respiration. Digestion does not render nitrogen useful to living things.

74. (D)

Though the process of photosynthesis actually occurs through numerous small steps, the entire process can be summed up with the following equation:

$$6CO_2 + 6H_2O + \text{light energy} \rightarrow C_6H_{12}O_6 + 6O_2$$

Chlorophyll is a green pigment that must be present in order for photosynthesis to occur. Chlorophyll has the ability to absorbe a photon of light and is found in the grana of the chloroplast. Chlorophyll is not used up in the photosynthetic process.

75. (C)

The first law of Mendelian genetics is the Law of Segregation, stating that traits are expressed from a pair of genes in the individual, one of which came from each parent. The alleles are randomly separated as gametes are formed and are brought together in varying combinations through fertilization.

Not all genetic crosses involve an allele that is dominant over the other, and not all crosses involve multiple alleles. Also, mutations may occur during the DNA replication process of gamete formation, however, gamete formation itself does not cause mutation.

76. (B)

The similarity of body shapes between sharks and dolphins most likely results from the convergent evolution of traits that are favorable to sur-

vival in the ocean. Sharks (cartilaginous fish) and dolphins (mammals) do not share a common ancestry, nor did one evolve into the other. Sharks and dolphins have different niches in the ocean community, so they are not in competition.

77. (C)

According to the Hardy-Weinberg Law, $p + q = 1$, where p and q represent the frequencies of two alleles. Also, $p^2 + 2pq + q^2 = 1$, where the frequency of homozygous dominant genotypes is represented by p^2, the homozygous recessive by q^2, and the heterozygous genotype by 2pq. So, in the case of tongue-rolling, if the frequency of non-tongue-rollers is 36% or 0.36, then the frequency of the recessive allele (q) is 0.6 (the square root of 0.36). Therefore, the frequency of the dominant allele (p) is 0.4 (since $p + q = 1$). The heterozygous genotype is represented by 2pq, which equals 2(0.6)(0.4) or 0.48.

78. (D)

The term *Homo sapiens* is an example of binomial nomenclature, the use of the genus and species names together.

79. (B)

The order of classification from least specific to most specific is kingdom, phylum, class, order, family, genus, and species, so of those listed, genus is the most specific, with members most closely related to each other.

80. (A)

Oparin's hypothesis included the idea that most water on Earth was in the form of water vapor and steam, not ice. Answer choices (II) – (IV) are all consistent with Oparin's hypothesis that proposed the Earth was approximately 4.6 billion years old and had a reducing atmosphere with very little oxygen present. There was an abundance of ammonia, hydrogen, methane, water vapor, and steam (H_2O). There was a great deal of heat energy available as the Earth was cooling. Recurring violent lightning storms also provided energy. The cooling of the Earth also caused much of the water vapor surrounding the Earth to condense, forming hot seas.

81. (B)

Though the presence of altruistic traits may actually decrease the individual's fitness to survive, it increases the survival rate of the population. Altruistic traits are preserved through kin selection. Kin selection accounts for the expression of altruistic traits toward close relatives, thus increasing the probability for those relatives to survive and to pass on their genetic traits.

82. (B)

Natural selection occurs when the surviving species is the one that is most adapted to the environment (in this case, resistant to penicillin). Clearly, only the surviving competitors reproduce. Therefore, traits that provide the competitive edge will be represented most often in succeeding generations. The survival of resistant bacteria does not represent genetic drift.

Genetic drift is random fluctuation in allele frequency, including loss of alleles. It is most pronounced in small populations and therefore in populations that have become separated from a main population. In this example, mutation does not contribute to the survival of resistant bacteria; the genetic material has not changed. There is no genetic equilibrium, since a certain trait (resistance) is favored by the environment.

83. (B)

The driving mechanism of evolution is natural selection. The Oparin hypothesis involved only the earliest forms of organic life and does not involve speciation. Allopatric speciation depends upon natural selection. Hardy-Weinberg Equilibrium explains the preservation of genes within a population in spite of the occurrence of natural selection.

84. (D)

By definition, a species is a distinct group of individuals that are able to mate and produce viable offspring. Class and phylum are taxonomic groups. A community includes all the species that interact in a particular area.

85. (D)

Only mammals (mammalia) have mammary glands. So (D), or III, is the only correct choice.

86. (B)

Photosynthetic organisms are found in the Kingdom Plantae and the Kingdom Protista, and are not found in the Kingdom Fungi, Kingdom Animalia, or Kingdom Monera.

87. (A)

When more than one gene controls a particular genetic trait, that trait is called *polygenic*. An autosome is any chromosome that does not determine the sex of an individual. A sex-linked trait is one whose genes are found on one of the sex chromosomes. A monohybrid cross is a genetic cross where only one trait is considered.

88. (C)

Since the skeleton of the fish was easily identifiable, the fish must belong to the class of bony fish—Osteichthyes. Cephalochordates have a notochord, but no vertebrae. Porifera is the phylum including sponges; Cnidaria is the phylum including jellyish and hydra.

89. (D)

Hardy-Weinberg Equilibrium only occurs when mutation, immigration, emigration, as well as natural selection (not an answer choice), are not happening in a population. When mutation, immigration, emigration, and natural selection are occurring, evolution is possible as allele possibilities are changed. Sexual recombination is a factor that will reinforce Hardy-Weinberg Equilibrium.

90. (D)

Members of the kingdom Protista may be autotrophic, heterotrophic, or a combination of both depending on the presence or absence of chloroplasts. This criterion can be applied to the three types of protists: algae, slime molds, and protozoa.

91. (B)

Taxonomy refers to the scientific classification of all living things into a systematic scheme. It is based on evolutionary relationships.

The largest category of classification is the kingdom, of which there are five: Monera (bacteria and blue-green algae), Protista, Fungi, Plantae, and Animalia. Within a kingdom, there are phyla (or divisions as in Fungi and Plantae). Phyla are divided into classes, classes into orders and orders into families. Families are divided into genera. Each genus is then divided into species. When we refer to a specific organism, we usually give its binomial name, the genus and species. Hence, man is called *Homo sapiens*. Note that by convention, the genus name is capitalized and the specific epithet is not; the binomial name is underlined or italicized.

The specific epithet <u>never</u> stands alone. Thus, man's species name is *Homo sapiens,* not *sapiens*. The specific name could be given to organisms of other genera. For example, *multilora* is a specific name. When used alone, you could be referring to *Rosa* or *Begonia*, clearly two different species. By saying *Rosa multilora*, you are referring to one and only one species.

Man's complete taxonomic classification is as follows:

kingdom - Animalia

phylum - Chordata

class - Mammalia

order - Primates

family - Hominidae

genus - *Homo*

species - *Homo sapiens*

There are also sub-groups. For instance, man belongs in the subphylum Vertebrata. For other species, there may be subclasses, suborders, etc.

92. (D)

Adaptive radiation is a pattern that occurs when a lineage (single line of descent) branches into two or more lineages, and these further branch out. This pattern can occur when a species is able to invade environments that have previously been occupied by other species. In this case, when the dinosaurs became extinct, mammals invaded their vacated ecological niches and quickly diversified to adapt to the living conditions of the niches. In addition to invading vacant ecological niches, species can undergo adaptive radiation when they partition existing environments.

93. (D)

Gregor Mendel studied the relationships between traits expressed in parents and offspring and the genes that caused the traits to be expressed. Hooke, Mendeleev, and Schwann were all scientists not directly involved with genetics.

94. (A)

Extinction events cause ecological niches to be available for other, newer species to fill. None of the other answer choices is a true statement.

95. (C)

Carbon, hydrogen, and oxygen are all common elements found in proteins.

96. (D)

Chordata have four defining characteristics: a notochord, a dorsal hollow nerve cord, pharyngeal gill slits, and a postanal tail during some point of their development. Of the given choices, only snakes have these characteristics during some point of their development.

97. (C)

It is not necessary for students to have a familiarity with science and engineering at home in order to become successful engineers. (A), (B), and (D) are required according to the NSES, "Creativity, imagination, and a good knowledge base are all required in the work of science and engineering." (1996, p.193)

98. (C)

Unfortunately, even though there are technological answers that can provide sanitation in any situation, there are certain places in the world where these answers have yet to be applied. Further, when natural disasters hit, sanitation issues are always a problem that spreads disease such as dysentery and typhus. (A), (B), and (D) are true statements.

99. (A)

The students in Group Four likely needed more assistance in measuring mass as evidenced by the fact that their measurements are much different from the rest of the groups' measurements. Also, since the instructions note that the balance was marked to the nearest gram, the measurements should have been to the nearest tenth. The teacher could likely have helped this group to avoid some of these errors with some attention to their measuring procedures during the lab. (B) It is not evident from the figure that having fewer (or more) groups would impact the results in any way. (C) While Group Four had more significant figures, since the instructions state that the balance has markings to the nearest gram, the measurements should only be to the nearest tenth in significant figures. Therefore these are not more accurate, they are inappropriately measured. (D) The class average would be less accurate due to Group Four's inappropriate measurement techniques.

100. (D)

The graph, Percent Error for Each Group, best represents accuracy as it graphs percent error for each group and shows that Group Four has a 42.6% error in comparison to much lower percentages of the other groups. The Potato Core Results table (A), Scatter Plot (B), and Potato Mass Bar Graph (C) represent the data directly and the information can be inferred from them, but (D) has the accuracy clearly defined numerically.

101. (C)

The percent error is not the independent variable for this experiment, rather it is a function of the dependent variable. Statements (A, B, and D) are correct. Choice (C) is correct.

102. (B)

Nitrogenous wastes would go up, not down with increased population. With increased population comes increased industry, thus increased factory waste (A), sewage (C) and agriculture with corresponding pesticides and fertilizers (D) which *raise* nitrogenous wastes; they do not lower them.

103. (B)

A hydrogen bond involves the attraction of atoms of different polarity and can be easily broken. Ionic bonds (where electrons are transferred), as well as double bonds and disulfide bridges, are all stronger than hydrogen bonds.

104. (A)

Chimpanzees are more closely related to *Homo sapiens* than to other apes but *Homo sapiens* did not evolve from chimpanzees. About five million years ago, the lineage that led to the modern *Homo sapiens* diverged from the lineage that led to the modern chimpanzee. It is a common misconception that the evolution leading to *Homo sapiens* occurred like a series of steps on a ladder. It is more like a branching tree with dead ends and new branches appearing simultaneously. The large brain and upright posture are important features of *Homo sapiens* but the early hominoids stood upright before there was an increase in brain size.

105. (D)

Algae and protozoa are within the Kingdom Protista, which contains one-celled eukaryotes. Kingdom Animalia contains organisms that are multicellular eukaryotes (including vertebrates and invertebrates). Mammalia is not a kingdom; it is a class within the subphylum vertebrata. Kingdom Plantae contains organisms that are multicellular, photosynthetic eukaryotes (including gymnosperms, angiosperms, etc.).

106. (D)

When the water concentration inside and outside the cell is equal, it is said to be in an isotonic state. Water will pass through the cell membrane by osmosis from an area of higher concentration to an area of lower concentration in order to produce isotonic conditions.

107. (C)

Cellular metabolism is a general term that includes all types of energy transformation processes, including photosynthesis, respiration, growth, movement, etc. Energy transformations occur as chemicals are broken apart (catabolism) or synthesized within the cell (anabolism).

108. (B)

The electron transfer system (ETS) produces the most ATP molecules, yielding 34 ATPs per glucose molecule. Fermentation and glycolysis each produce two ATPs per glucose molecule. Some of the products of the Krebs cycle are easily converted to ATP, but the main energy products of the Krebs cycle are those that liberate electrons that are then used in the electron transfer reactions.

109. (B)

The primary role of DNA in the cell is the control of protein synthesis. Genetic traits are expressed and specialization of cells occurs as a result of the combination of proteins produced by the DNA of a cell. DNA replication allows for the genetic code to be preserved in future generations of cells. When expression of genetic traits is determined by whether the trait is inherited from the mother or the father, it is called genetic imprinting. Genetic maintenance simply refers to the preservation of the integrity of genetic information from one generation to another.

110. (B)

In DNA, guanine (G) pairs with cytosine (C) and thymine (T) with adenine (A). Therefore, the sequence GATACCA would pair with the sequence CTATGGT.

111. (A)

There are two major periods within the cell cycle: interphase and mitosis. Interphase is the period when the cell is active in carrying on the function it was designed to perform within the organism. Cells spend much more time in interphase than in the cell division portion of their cycle, which includes the prophase, telophase, anaphase, and metaphase phases of mitosis plus cytokinesis.

112. (D)

As shown in the following Punnett square, the only way offspring could be albino is if each parent has at least one recessive gene for albinism. Since both have a normal phenotype, both must have the Nn genotype.

	N	n
N	NN	Nn
n	Nn	nn

113. (A)

The phenotype ratio for this generation of offspring will be 3 normal: 1 albino, so out of 8 offspring 2 are likely to be albino.

114. (C)

The albino parent from the F_1 cross must have the nn genotype. As shown in the following Punnett square, if the mate was albino (nn) all the offspring would be albino, and if the mate was homozygous (NN) then all the offspring would be normal. In order to produce both phenotypes, the second parent must be heterozygous (Nn).

	n	n
N	Nn	Nn
n	nn	nn

115. (B)

(B) is correct. (78 -32)/18 = 25.6 °C. (A) While K is an SI unit, 78°F does not convert to 25.6K. (C) 78/1.8 = 43.3 but you must subtract 32 first. (D) 78-32 = 46 but you also must divide by 1.8.

116. (A)

There is the most opportunity to predict landfall of a hurricane even though they can still be devastating. Unfortunately, most lives are lost in hurricanes from those not following evacuation procedures. Property damage cannot always be avoided. (B) Earthquakes are the least likely to be predicted, though scientists are working on technology to do this. (C) and (D) While there is some predictability to volcanoes and tsunamis in that there may be some warning signs, there is still a great amount of unpredictability, making them deadly hazards.

117. (C)

Policy makers and voters should have a basic understanding about a technology before debating about or voting on a particular technology-related issue. (A), (B), (D) are not true . . . rather—understanding basic concepts and principles of science and technology should precede active debate about the economics, policies, politics, and ethics of various science – and technology-related challenges. However, understanding science alone will not resolve local, national, or global challenges. Progress in science and technology can be affected by social issues and challenges.

118. (C)

In determining risk, the literature basis is the least important factor. Literature review is important to other factors of research, but for risk assessment other questions such as (A), (B), and (D) come to the forefront.

119. (D)

Choice (D) is correct since only the students can ensure that they meet expectations to pass the class. (A), (B), (C) are all true as the teacher is responsible to identify, document, and notify school and district officials about existing or potential safety issues that impact the learning environment, including hazards such as class-size overcrowding. Research shows that classes containing more than 24 students engaged in science activities cannot safely be supervised by one teacher.

120. (B)

Ribonucleic acid (RNA) is a molecule that stores information for protein synthesis and genetic coding, not energy. Cellulose, starch, lipid, and sugar molecules all store energy within their chemical bonds.

121. (D)

The selective permeability of the cell membrane serves to manage the concentration of substances within the cell, preserving its health. There are two methods by which substances can cross the cell membrane, passive transport and active transport. The rough endoplasmic reticulum and smooth endoplasmic reticulum serve as channels for moving molecules through a cell. The Golgi complex stores and packages proteins and lipids for transport and use throughout the cell.

122. (D)

Stem tissue does not include the cuticle. The cuticle is found covering the leaf. The stem is made of vascular tissue, including both xylem and phloem.

123. (D)

Prosthetic groups, which may be ions or non-protein molecules, are similar to cofactors in that they facilitate the enzyme reaction. However, prosthetic groups are tightly attached by covalent bonds to the enzyme, rather than being separate atoms or molecules. The enzyme itself is a protein; the prosthetic group is not. An inorganic cofactor does not bind with the enzyme. A coenzyme also does not bind to the enzyme itself and is not an ion.

124. (C)

Phloem tissue, made of stacked cells connected by sieve plates (that allow nutrients to pass from cell to cell), transports food made in the leaves (by photosynthesis) to the rest of the plant. Xylem tissue transfers water and does not require sieve plates to allow nutrients through. Meristem is the tissue that is found in the root cap and is responsible for quick growth in the roots. Internodal tissue is found on the stem between nodes.

125. (D)

Water has a pH of approximately 7, making it neither basic (under 7) nor alkaline (over 7). Transparency, polarity, and density are characteristics that make water valuable to living things.

126. (C)

Carrying capacity is the number of organisms that can be supported within a particular ecosystem. The term *natality* refers to the birthrate of a population. The population includes the number of organisms in a given community, whether or not the community is at its carrying capacity. The community is comprised of all the organisms that interact within a given ecosystem whether or not it is at carrying capacity or not.

127. (A)

Insects use spiracles for gas exchange. Alveoli are found within the lungs (lungs are not found in insects). The cephalothorax is the head and thorax of arachnids and crustaceans, and is not found in insects.

128. (A)

The liver filters out most chemical pollutants, which are then mixed with broken-down pigments in the bile. Bile is secreted into the small intestine, then proceeds to the large intestine and is expelled in the feces.

129. (A)

Egg and sperm cells are called gametes and are formed in the process of gametogenesis. Spermatogonium are cells that eventually may become sperm cells, and oogonium are cells that eventually may become egg cells. Gametocide refers to the destruction of gametes.

130. (D)

The mesoderm (between the ectoderm and endoderm) layer will eventually form muscles, and organs of the skeletal, circulatory, respiratory, reproductive, and excretory systems. The endoderm will become the gut lining and some accessory structures. The ectoderm will become the skin, some endocrine glands, and the nervous system. The blastula develops into a thin layer of cells surrounding an internal cavity.

131. (C)

Altruism is a social behavior of an organism that is beneficial to the group at the individual's expense. Imprinting is a behavior that is learned during a critical period of an organism's life. Fixed Action Pattern (FAP) is an innate behavior that is independent of the organism's environment. Sacrificial behavior is not a term that is used in this context.

132. (B)

Habituation occurs when an individual learns not to respond to a particular stimulus, for instance when a stimulus is repeated many times without consequence. Circadian rhythm is a cycle of daily behavior based on an internal clock and environmental cues. Imprinting is a behavior that is learned during a critical period of an organism's life, and altruism is a social behavior of an organism that is beneficial to the group at the individual's expense.

133. (D)

A habitat refers to the physical place where an organism lives. A species' habitat must include all the factors that will support its life and reproduction. The niche also includes the role played by the organism in its food chain. The biosphere is the part of the Earth that contains all living things. The lithosphere (Earth) is a part of the biosphere.

134. (D)

A species' role in the food chain is a part of its niche, not its habitat. The niche includes the habitat, but the habitat is within the niche. A species' habitat includes all the factors that will support its life and reproduction. These factors may be biotic (population, food source, etc.) and abiotic (i.e., nonliving—weather, temperature, soil features, sunlight, etc.).

135. (B)

The sugars produced by photosynthesis are transported throughout the plant via the vascular bundles. The vascular bundles make up the veins in the leaf and are also distributed throughout the stem. Epidermal tissue is the outermost layer of cells of the stem. Meristem tissue consists of undifferentiated cells capable of quick growth and specialization. Meristem tissue is responsible for elongation of the stem. Parenchyma tissue has loosely packed cells that allow for gas and moisture exchange.

136. (A)

Carbon, nitrogen, and phosphorous are all recycled through biogeochemical cycles, so (A) or "all of the above" is correct.

137. (D)

The energy cycle of the food chain is subject to the laws of thermodynamics—no energy can be created or destroyed, and as energy changes form and passes from one level to another, some becomes unusable.

138. (B)

One pathway for water to pass through cell walls and plasma membranes toward xylem tissue is through an intercellular route through channels in the cell membranes known as plasmodesmata. Guard cells and stomata are whole cells that regulate the intake and outflow of water, whereas plasmodesmata are channels within a cell membrane. Internodes are the areas on the stem between nodes (places on the stem where leaves can begin to grow).

139. (C)

Phosphorous is nearly always found in solid form, within rocks and soil. Phosphorous gas is very rare and is not absorbed by plant leaves. The usable reservoir of Earth's phosphorous is found within rocks and soil. Water dissolves phosphorous from rocks by erosion, and carries it into rivers and streams. Here phosphorous and oxygen unite to form phosphates that end up in bodies of water. Phosphates are absorbed by plants in and near the water and are used in the synthesis of organic molecules. As in the carbon and nitrogen cycles, phosphorous is then passed up the food chain and returned through animal wastes and organic decay of dead matter. New phosphorous enters the cycle as undersea sedimentary rocks are upthrust during the shifting of the Earth's tectonic plates. New rock-containing phosphorous is then exposed to erosion and enters the cycling process.

140. (A)

The cell membrane is composed of a double layer (bilayer) of phospholipids with protein globules imbedded within the layers. The construction of the membrane allows it to aid cell function by permitting entrance and exit of molecules as needed by the cell. Mitochondria are the organelles where cellular respiration occurs. A lysosome is a packet of digestive enzymes that destroy cellular wastes. Chromatin is disorganized DNA with histones attached.

141. (C)

The sharp boundary of a community is called an ecotone. None of the other terms applies to the boundary of an ecological community.

142. (B)

Mitochondria are called the cell's "powerhouses," as they constitute the center of cellular respiration. (Cellular respiration is the process of breaking up covalent bonds within sugar molecules

with the intake of oxygen and release of energy in the form of ATP [adenosine tri-phosphate] molecules. ATP is the energy form used by all cell processes.) Mitochondrion (singular: mitochondria) are found wherever energy is needed within the cell, and are more numerous in cells that require more energy (muscle, etc.). The nucleus contains mitochondria, but mitochondria also exist outside the nucleus. The smooth endoplasmic reticulum is a system of channels for moving substances within the cell. Ribosomes are the site of protein synthesis within the cell.

143. (D)

Only plant cells have cell walls, but all cells have a cell/plasma membrane.

144. (A)

Insects (including bees) are within the phylum Arthropoda. Aves is the class composed of birds. Annelida is the phyla composed of segmented worms. Nematoda is the phyla of roundworms.

145. (B)

Enzymes are proteins, which are polymers of amino acids. Enzymes generally have names ending in -ase—thus lactase is an enzyme. Lactose, glycogen and sucrose are carbohydrates, not proteins, and are not made of amino acids. Lactose is the sugar that lactase acts upon. Glycogen and sucrose are saccharides.

146. (A)

Vertebrates are divided into two main groups, the Aganatha (animals with no jaws) and the Gnathostomata (animals with jaws). Protista is a kingdom that includes algae and protozoa. Cnidaria is a phylum that contains jellyish, hydra, etc.

147. (B)

While microtubules, microfilaments, and centrioles all provide structure to cells of plants and animals, cell walls provide structure to plant cells (and some bacteria). Animal cells do not have a cell wall.

148. (B)

The cerebrum controls sensory and motor responses, and it controls memory, speech, and intelligence factors. It does not control involuntary muscles.

149. (D)

Nitrogen is not absorbed into the ocean as part of the nitrogen cycle. Each of the other steps is included in the nitrogen cycle.

150. (B)

Vitamins are organic cofactors or coenzymes that are required by some enzymatic reactions. Vitamin C is required for collagen to be synthesized.

dom that includes algae and protozoa. Cnidaria is a phylum that contains jellyish, hydra, etc.

147. (B)

While microtubules, microfilaments, and centrioles all provide structure to cells of plants and animals, cell walls provide structure to plant cells (and some bacteria). Animal cells do not have a cell wall.

148. (B)

The cerebrum controls sensory and motor responses, and it controls memory, speech, and intelligence factors. It does not control involuntary muscles.

149. (D)

Nitrogen is not absorbed into the ocean as part of the nitrogen cycle. Each of the other steps is included in the nitrogen cycle.

150. (B)

Vitamins are organic cofactors or coenzymes that are required by some enzymatic reactions. Vitamin C is required for collagen to be synthesized.

Practice Test 2

Praxis II: Biology
Core Content Knowledge (0235)

This test is also on CD-ROM in our special interactive TestWare® for the PRAXIS II: Biology Core Content Knowledge. It is highly recommended that you first take this exam on computer. You will then have the additional study features and benefits of enforced time conditions and instantaneous, accurate scoring. See page 4 for instructions on how to get the most out of REA's TestWare®.

ANSWER SHEET FOR PRACTICE TEST 2

1. Ⓐ Ⓑ Ⓒ Ⓓ	39. Ⓐ Ⓑ Ⓒ Ⓓ	77. Ⓐ Ⓑ Ⓒ Ⓓ	115. Ⓐ Ⓑ Ⓒ Ⓓ
2. Ⓐ Ⓑ Ⓒ Ⓓ	40. Ⓐ Ⓑ Ⓒ Ⓓ	78. Ⓐ Ⓑ Ⓒ Ⓓ	116. Ⓐ Ⓑ Ⓒ Ⓓ
3. Ⓐ Ⓑ Ⓒ Ⓓ	41. Ⓐ Ⓑ Ⓒ Ⓓ	79. Ⓐ Ⓑ Ⓒ Ⓓ	117. Ⓐ Ⓑ Ⓒ Ⓓ
4. Ⓐ Ⓑ Ⓒ Ⓓ	42. Ⓐ Ⓑ Ⓒ Ⓓ	80. Ⓐ Ⓑ Ⓒ Ⓓ	118. Ⓐ Ⓑ Ⓒ Ⓓ
5. Ⓐ Ⓑ Ⓒ Ⓓ	43. Ⓐ Ⓑ Ⓒ Ⓓ	81. Ⓐ Ⓑ Ⓒ Ⓓ	119. Ⓐ Ⓑ Ⓒ Ⓓ
6. Ⓐ Ⓑ Ⓒ Ⓓ	44. Ⓐ Ⓑ Ⓒ Ⓓ	82. Ⓐ Ⓑ Ⓒ Ⓓ	120. Ⓐ Ⓑ Ⓒ Ⓓ
7. Ⓐ Ⓑ Ⓒ Ⓓ	45. Ⓐ Ⓑ Ⓒ Ⓓ	83. Ⓐ Ⓑ Ⓒ Ⓓ	121. Ⓐ Ⓑ Ⓒ Ⓓ
8. Ⓐ Ⓑ Ⓒ Ⓓ	46. Ⓐ Ⓑ Ⓒ Ⓓ	84. Ⓐ Ⓑ Ⓒ Ⓓ	122. Ⓐ Ⓑ Ⓒ Ⓓ
9. Ⓐ Ⓑ Ⓒ Ⓓ	47. Ⓐ Ⓑ Ⓒ Ⓓ	85. Ⓐ Ⓑ Ⓒ Ⓓ	123. Ⓐ Ⓑ Ⓒ Ⓓ
10. Ⓐ Ⓑ Ⓒ Ⓓ	48. Ⓐ Ⓑ Ⓒ Ⓓ	86. Ⓐ Ⓑ Ⓒ Ⓓ	124. Ⓐ Ⓑ Ⓒ Ⓓ
11. Ⓐ Ⓑ Ⓒ Ⓓ	49. Ⓐ Ⓑ Ⓒ Ⓓ	87. Ⓐ Ⓑ Ⓒ Ⓓ	125. Ⓐ Ⓑ Ⓒ Ⓓ
12. Ⓐ Ⓑ Ⓒ Ⓓ	50. Ⓐ Ⓑ Ⓒ Ⓓ	88. Ⓐ Ⓑ Ⓒ Ⓓ	126. Ⓐ Ⓑ Ⓒ Ⓓ
13. Ⓐ Ⓑ Ⓒ Ⓓ	51. Ⓐ Ⓑ Ⓒ Ⓓ	89. Ⓐ Ⓑ Ⓒ Ⓓ	127. Ⓐ Ⓑ Ⓒ Ⓓ
14. Ⓐ Ⓑ Ⓒ Ⓓ	52. Ⓐ Ⓑ Ⓒ Ⓓ	90. Ⓐ Ⓑ Ⓒ Ⓓ	128. Ⓐ Ⓑ Ⓒ Ⓓ
15. Ⓐ Ⓑ Ⓒ Ⓓ	53. Ⓐ Ⓑ Ⓒ Ⓓ	91. Ⓐ Ⓑ Ⓒ Ⓓ	129. Ⓐ Ⓑ Ⓒ Ⓓ
16. Ⓐ Ⓑ Ⓒ Ⓓ	54. Ⓐ Ⓑ Ⓒ Ⓓ	92. Ⓐ Ⓑ Ⓒ Ⓓ	130. Ⓐ Ⓑ Ⓒ Ⓓ
17. Ⓐ Ⓑ Ⓒ Ⓓ	55. Ⓐ Ⓑ Ⓒ Ⓓ	93. Ⓐ Ⓑ Ⓒ Ⓓ	131. Ⓐ Ⓑ Ⓒ Ⓓ
18. Ⓐ Ⓑ Ⓒ Ⓓ	56. Ⓐ Ⓑ Ⓒ Ⓓ	94. Ⓐ Ⓑ Ⓒ Ⓓ	132. Ⓐ Ⓑ Ⓒ Ⓓ
19. Ⓐ Ⓑ Ⓒ Ⓓ	57. Ⓐ Ⓑ Ⓒ Ⓓ	95. Ⓐ Ⓑ Ⓒ Ⓓ	133. Ⓐ Ⓑ Ⓒ Ⓓ
20. Ⓐ Ⓑ Ⓒ Ⓓ	58. Ⓐ Ⓑ Ⓒ Ⓓ	96. Ⓐ Ⓑ Ⓒ Ⓓ	134. Ⓐ Ⓑ Ⓒ Ⓓ
21. Ⓐ Ⓑ Ⓒ Ⓓ	59. Ⓐ Ⓑ Ⓒ Ⓓ	97. Ⓐ Ⓑ Ⓒ Ⓓ	135. Ⓐ Ⓑ Ⓒ Ⓓ
22. Ⓐ Ⓑ Ⓒ Ⓓ	60. Ⓐ Ⓑ Ⓒ Ⓓ	98. Ⓐ Ⓑ Ⓒ Ⓓ	136. Ⓐ Ⓑ Ⓒ Ⓓ
23. Ⓐ Ⓑ Ⓒ Ⓓ	61. Ⓐ Ⓑ Ⓒ Ⓓ	99. Ⓐ Ⓑ Ⓒ Ⓓ	137. Ⓐ Ⓑ Ⓒ Ⓓ
24. Ⓐ Ⓑ Ⓒ Ⓓ	62. Ⓐ Ⓑ Ⓒ Ⓓ	100. Ⓐ Ⓑ Ⓒ Ⓓ	138. Ⓐ Ⓑ Ⓒ Ⓓ
25. Ⓐ Ⓑ Ⓒ Ⓓ	63. Ⓐ Ⓑ Ⓒ Ⓓ	101. Ⓐ Ⓑ Ⓒ Ⓓ	139. Ⓐ Ⓑ Ⓒ Ⓓ
26. Ⓐ Ⓑ Ⓒ Ⓓ	64. Ⓐ Ⓑ Ⓒ Ⓓ	102. Ⓐ Ⓑ Ⓒ Ⓓ	140. Ⓐ Ⓑ Ⓒ Ⓓ
27. Ⓐ Ⓑ Ⓒ Ⓓ	65. Ⓐ Ⓑ Ⓒ Ⓓ	103. Ⓐ Ⓑ Ⓒ Ⓓ	141. Ⓐ Ⓑ Ⓒ Ⓓ
28. Ⓐ Ⓑ Ⓒ Ⓓ	66. Ⓐ Ⓑ Ⓒ Ⓓ	104. Ⓐ Ⓑ Ⓒ Ⓓ	142. Ⓐ Ⓑ Ⓒ Ⓓ
29. Ⓐ Ⓑ Ⓒ Ⓓ	67. Ⓐ Ⓑ Ⓒ Ⓓ	105. Ⓐ Ⓑ Ⓒ Ⓓ	143. Ⓐ Ⓑ Ⓒ Ⓓ
30. Ⓐ Ⓑ Ⓒ Ⓓ	68. Ⓐ Ⓑ Ⓒ Ⓓ	106. Ⓐ Ⓑ Ⓒ Ⓓ	144. Ⓐ Ⓑ Ⓒ Ⓓ
31. Ⓐ Ⓑ Ⓒ Ⓓ	69. Ⓐ Ⓑ Ⓒ Ⓓ	107. Ⓐ Ⓑ Ⓒ Ⓓ	145. Ⓐ Ⓑ Ⓒ Ⓓ
32. Ⓐ Ⓑ Ⓒ Ⓓ	70. Ⓐ Ⓑ Ⓒ Ⓓ	108. Ⓐ Ⓑ Ⓒ Ⓓ	146. Ⓐ Ⓑ Ⓒ Ⓓ
33. Ⓐ Ⓑ Ⓒ Ⓓ	71. Ⓐ Ⓑ Ⓒ Ⓓ	109. Ⓐ Ⓑ Ⓒ Ⓓ	147. Ⓐ Ⓑ Ⓒ Ⓓ
34. Ⓐ Ⓑ Ⓒ Ⓓ	72. Ⓐ Ⓑ Ⓒ Ⓓ	110. Ⓐ Ⓑ Ⓒ Ⓓ	148. Ⓐ Ⓑ Ⓒ Ⓓ
35. Ⓐ Ⓑ Ⓒ Ⓓ	73. Ⓐ Ⓑ Ⓒ Ⓓ	111. Ⓐ Ⓑ Ⓒ Ⓓ	149. Ⓐ Ⓑ Ⓒ Ⓓ
36. Ⓐ Ⓑ Ⓒ Ⓓ	74. Ⓐ Ⓑ Ⓒ Ⓓ	112. Ⓐ Ⓑ Ⓒ Ⓓ	150. Ⓐ Ⓑ Ⓒ Ⓓ
37. Ⓐ Ⓑ Ⓒ Ⓓ	75. Ⓐ Ⓑ Ⓒ Ⓓ	113. Ⓐ Ⓑ Ⓒ Ⓓ	
38. Ⓐ Ⓑ Ⓒ Ⓓ	76. Ⓐ Ⓑ Ⓒ Ⓓ	114. Ⓐ Ⓑ Ⓒ Ⓓ	

Directions: Each of the questions or incomplete statements below is followed by four possible answers or completions. Select the best choice in each case and fill in the corresponding oval on the answer sheet.

1. What percentage of the off-spring of two albino mice parents would most likely be normal?

   (A) 100%
   (B) 50%
   (C) 25%
   (D) 0%

2. What are the chances that two normal parents, each carrying recessive genes for albinism, could have a heterozygous normal offspring?

   (A) 1 out of 2
   (B) 3 out of 4
   (C) 2 out of 3
   (D) 0 out of 4

3. A _____ is a length of DNA (with corresponding histones) that is responsible for the production of a particular protein that causes a particular trait to be expressed in an organism.

   (A) chromosome
   (B) mutation
   (C) genome
   (D) gene

4. The synthesis of ATP molecules to store energy is an example of

   (A) anabolism.
   (B) catabolism.
   (C) adaptive radiation.
   (D) lysis.

5. Which of the following reactions will NOT occur after glycolysis?

   (A) photolysis.
   (B) aerobic respiration.
   (C) the Krebs cycle.
   (D) the electron transport cycle.

6. What type of organic molecule has this group attached?

$$-\overset{\displaystyle \underset{\displaystyle O}{\|}}{C}-OH$$

   (A) Aldehyde group
   (B) Hydroxyl group
   (C) Carbonyl group
   (D) Carboxyl group

7. Which of the following represents an opportunistic life strategy (r-selection)?

   (A) Lichens invade a bare rock area after a volcanic eruption.
   (B) Coniferous trees spread to an adjacent area.
   (C) Lightning wipes out a forest of deciduous trees.
   (D) A species of mice emigrates into a forest community.

8. Which of the following statements about the cell theory is NOT true?

   (A) It was developed by the German scientists Schleiden and Schwann.
   (B) It states that all living things are made up of cells.

(C) It states that cells are the basic units of life.

(D) It states that anaerobic cells existed before aerobic cells.

9. Each of the following statements about enzymes is true EXCEPT

(A) High temperatures destroy most enzymes.

(B) Enzymes only function within living things.

(C) An enzyme is unaffected by the reactions it catalyzes, so it can be used over and over again.

(D) Enzymes are usually very specific to certain reactions.

10. In ferns, the individual we generally recognize as an adult fern is really which structure?

(A) A mature gametophyte

(B) A prothallus

(C) A mature sporophyte

(D) A young sporophyte

11. When a stem bends toward the light, it is due to the

(A) increased level of auxin on the light side of the shoot tip.

(B) migration of auxin toward the dark side of the shoot tip.

(C) migration of auxin toward the light side of the shoot tip.

(D) elongation of cells on the light side of the shoot tip.

12. The theory of punctuated equilibrium assumes that

I. there are periods of stability during which little evolutionary change occurs.

II. speciation can occur rapidly over a very short period of time.

III. evolution occurs gradually within lineages.

(A) I only

(B) I, II, & III

(C) III only

(D) I & II only

13. Hemophilia is a disease caused by a sex-linked recessive gene on the x chromosome; therefore,

(A) females have twice the likelihood of having the disease, since they have two x chromosomes.

(B) mothers can pass the gene with probability to either a son or daughter.

(C) females can never have the disease, but can only be carriers.

(D) inbreeding has no effect on the incidence of the disease, since it is purely sex-linked.

14. Because fungi can obtain nutrients from non-living organic matter, they are referred to as

(A) parasitic.

(B) saprophytic.

(C) eukaryotic.

(D) heterotrophic.

15. Restriction enzymes are used in genetic research to

(A) cleave DNA molecules at certain sites.

(B) produce individual nucleotides from DNA.

(C) slow down the reproductive rate of bacteria.

(D) remove DNA strands from the nucleus.

16. Of the following, which is the most abundant element of protoplasm?

(A) Calcium

(B) Carbon

(C) Phosphorus

(D) Sulfur

17. The site of photosynthetic reactions within plant cells is the stacked disk-like plates embedded within the stroma of the chloroplast known as

    (A) bodies.
    (B) cytosomes.
    (C) flora.
    (D) grana.

18. The combination of DNA with histones is called

    (A) a centromere.
    (B) chromatin.
    (C) a nucleosome.
    (D) an amino acid.

19. A corn seed is planted and left to grow. After three weeks, no sprout has appeared. Which of the following is most likely the problem?

    (A) The corn seed did not contain a cotyledon.
    (B) The seed coat was damaged.
    (C) The weather was too cold and dry.
    (D) Corn seeds only sprout biennially.

20. After a forest fire, a meadow community develops and is later replaced by a temperate forest community. This process is called

    (A) commensalism.
    (B) succession.
    (C) dynamic equilibrium.
    (D) alternation of generations.

21. The discovery and manufacture of pharmaceuticals to treat disease and physical ailments has been a societal advance that has occurred in the past 150 years. However, there are some negative impacts that use of drugs can also cause to humans. Which of the following is LEAST important for students to understand regarding pharmaceutical drugs?

    (A) Pharmaceuticals may modify mood and behavior which can be beneficial or detrimental depending on circumstances and motives.
    (B) Inappropriate use of pharmaceuticals can lead to an increased risk of injury, accident, and death.
    (C) Appropriate use of pharmaceuticals can lead to beneficial relief from harmful effects of disease and physical ailments.
    (D) Some pharmaceuticals require a prescription.

22. One role of the science educator is to help the high school students differentiate science and technology. Which of the following is an effective teaching tool to accomplish this task?

    (A) Lecturing on the invention of the microscope and having students take two column notes
    (B) Assigning groups to complete projects for a science and engineering fair where they are guided to meet a need through designing a technology
    (C) Assigning students to complete a report on the history of science and technology
    (D) Taking students on a field trip to see science and technology in action at a local hospital

23. Chorionic Villus Sampling (CVS) is one of several methods of prenatal testing used to collect test the DNA of unborn fetuses for genetic abnormalities. Which of the following is NOT true of prenatal DNA testing such as Chorionic Villus Sampling (CVS)?

    (A) Only DNA chromosomal and genetic abnormalities such as disease can be determined through CVS, not matters of choice such as eye color or gender.
    (B) Both abnormalities and genetic information such as gender and eye color may be determined from CVS.

(C) CVS is controversial because some believe it is leading to a form of eugenics where certain types of people with certain diseases will be eliminated, or others will be selected by choice.

(D) CVS is controversial because if abnormalities are found, the choice may be made to terminate the pregnancy, which may be against the moral beliefs of some.

24. In considering ecological concerns of the modern society, sustainability is becoming a key term. Which of the following is the LEAST important component of ecological sustainability?

(A) Economic viability
(B) Environmentally bearable
(C) Aesthetically plausible
(D) Socially equitable

25. Which of the following is NOT a characteristic of the nature of scientific knowledge?

(A) Generation of scientific knowledge involves inquiry and is bounded by the natural world.
(B) Generation of scientific knowledge does not involve human imagination or creativity.
(C) Scientific knowledge tends to be durable and tentative.
(D) Scientific knowledge tends to be empirical and testable.

26. Which of the following is an International System (SI) unit?

(A) Ounce
(B) Pound
(C) Second
(D) Foot

27. Which of the following chemical equations represents a replacement reaction?

(A) $A + C \rightarrow AC + B$
(B) $A + B \rightarrow AB$
(C) $AB + C \rightarrow AC + B$
(D) $AB \rightarrow A + B$

28. The molecule that stores energy short-term in muscle and liver tissue is

(A) glycogen.
(B) adipose.
(C) sucrose.
(D) fat.

29. Which of the following statements is TRUE?

(A) Primary consumers are mostly carnivores.
(B) Bacteria recycle nutrients from organisms they decompose.
(C) Secondary consumers are mostly herbivores.
(D) There are exactly five trophic levels in every food chain.

30. Which system is only found in vertebrates?

(A) Gas exchange (respiratory)
(B) Circulatory
(C) Musculoskeletal
(D) Nervous

31. Multiple sclerosis is a disease that destroys the myelin sheath around nerve bodies. All of the following would be affected by losing the myelin sheath EXCEPT

(A) nerve tissue loses its white color.
(B) nerve impulses are impaired.
(C) sensory input is increased.
(D) senses such as sight may be adversely affected.

32. Cyanobacteria (blue-green bacteria) provide which of the following ecologic functions?

(A) Releasing carbon dioxide into the atmosphere
(B) Decomposing dead organisms

(C) Consuming lichen

(D) Combining nitrogen with hydrogen-forming ammonium ions

33. There are many types of nerves; nerves that transmit impulses from the central nervous system to skeletal muscle are called

(A) somatic sensory nerves.

(B) sympathetic nerves.

(C) autonomic nerves.

(D) somatic motor nerves.

34. Energy flows through the food chain from

(A) producers to consumers to decomposers.

(B) producers to secondary consumers to primary consumers.

(C) decomposers to consumers to producers.

(D) secondary consumers to producers.

35. Which group contains organisms with prokaryotic cells?

(A) Protista

(B) Archaea

(C) Fungi

(D) Plantae

36. All of the following are organs of the excretory system EXCEPT

(A) skin.

(B) heart.

(C) liver.

(D) lungs.

37. A person who has been exercising vigorously begins to sweat and breathe quickly. These reactions are involuntary responses known as

(A) fight or flight instincts.

(B) feedback controls.

(C) equilibrium responses.

(D) fixed action patterns.

38. All of the following are part of a DNA molecule EXCEPT

(A) nucleotide.

(B) sugar.

(C) phosphate group.

(D) an alcohol.

39. The first scientist to use the term "cells" as he described the appearance of cell walls and spaces within organic matter (cork) was

(A) Newton.

(B) Schwann.

(C) Smith.

(D) Hooke.

40. Temporary movement of a species from one range to another, then back to the original, is known as

(A) immigration.

(B) migration.

(C) emigration.

(D) dispersion.

41. All of the following are true statements regarding the scientific method EXCEPT

(A) The scientific method is characterized by a particular set of steps constituting inquiry in any discipline.

(B) Scientific ideas are tested and retested over time through methodical processes.

(C) There are many valuable ways to investigate the natural world in a scientific manner through methods such as direct observation, modeling, testing hypotheses, etc.

(D) Methods of gathering knowledge are subject to scrutiny by a body of knowledgeable individuals that belong to the scientific community.

42. Ms. Shuh's AP Biology lab's cultures of bacteria yielded class averages of 4,500,000 bacteria after 20 generations. Represented in scientific notation, this would be

    (A) 4.5×10^6
    (B) 45×10^5
    (C) 4.5×10^5
    (D) 4.5×10^{-6}

43. The human genome project, which has identified the entire genetic makeup of the all human chromosomes, has made it possible for incredible medical breakthroughs and research. It has also caused ethical dilemmas. Which of the following is of LEAST ethical concern as a result of the mapping of the human genome?

    (A) DNA testing can reveal gender early in pregnancy leading to
    (B) social issues – DNA testing can reveal parental connections such as paternal testing
    (C) reproductive issues – DNA testing and mapping allows for parents to choose certain types of acceptable offspring
    (D) privacy issues – since it is now possible to know if a person carries genes for certain diseases, testing for them raises issues of concern regarding whether insurance companies and employers have a right to know about these conditions

44. One of the greatest economic issues in the field of biology is agriculture and the economics of feeding the world. All of the following are likely to impact agriculture as a field of biology EXCEPT

    (A) genetic engineering of new seed types.
    (B) advancements in biotechnology.
    (C) development of new biofuels.
    (D) cloning of new animal species.

45. Which of the following personal and social factors is LEAST likely to impact a person's food choices and/or eating patterns?

    (A) Family income
    (B) Transportation methods
    (C) Advertising
    (D) Ethnic heritage

46. Cyclooxygenase-2 (COX-2) is an enzyme vital to the production of the prostaglandins, but also contributes to the inflammation of joints in medical conditions such as arthritis. New medications that block the production of prostaglandins by COX-2 enzymes and thereby relieve the symptoms of arthritis are a type of

    (A) hormone.
    (B) chemical inhibitor.
    (C) ion.
    (D) prosthetic group.

47. What is the most likely outcome when the gene frequency within a given population remains constant?

    (A) The rate of evolution within the population will increase.
    (B) Expression of dominant traits will increase within the population.
    (C) Evolution will not take place within this population.
    (D) There will be an increase in the recessive traits within the population.

48. All of the following about viruses are true EXCEPT

    (A) viruses often kill their host cell.
    (B) viruses consist of a protein capsule, DNA, RNA, and sometimes enzymes.
    (C) viruses cannot carry on metabolic functions without a host organism.
    (D) scientists are agreed that viruses are the smallest living organisms.

49. All of the following are members of the phylum Chordata EXCEPT

    (A) snail.
    (B) crocodile.
    (C) trout.
    (D) platypus.

50. All of the following may inhibit enzymatic reactions EXCEPT

    (A) temperature.
    (B) pH level.
    (C) particular chemical agents.
    (D) excess of substrate.

51. Which of the following statements is NOT true about electrons?

    (A) Electrons have a negative charge.
    (B) Electrons have greater mass than neutrons.
    (C) Electrons are found orbiting the nucleus of atoms.
    (D) The number of electrons is equal to the number of protons in an uncharged atom.

52. Most photosynthesis occurs in the uppermost layer of mesophyll tissue that contains vertically aligned cells with numerous chloroplasts. This layer is called the

    (A) epidermis.
    (B) parenchyma.
    (C) meristematic region.
    (D) palisade layer.

53. All of the following are lipids EXCEPT

    (A) fat.
    (B) steroid.
    (C) triglyceride.
    (D) cellulose.

54. A double-helix structure is characteristic of which molecule(s)?

    (A) Water
    (B) Deoxyribonucleic acid
    (C) Carbohydrate
    (D) Lipid

55. The female plant structure includes all of the following parts EXCEPT

    (A) ovary.
    (B) style.
    (C) stigma.
    (D) filament.

56. In order to clearly view the organelles of a cell you must use

    (A) a light microscope.
    (B) a compound microscope.
    (C) an electron microscope.
    (D) staining procedures.

57. Mitochondria are likely to be most abundant in which type of tissue?

    (A) Red blood cells
    (B) Bone tissue
    (C) Epithelial tissue
    (D) Cardiac tissue

58. Photosynthesis would NOT proceed without which of these structures that allow moisture and gases to pass in and out of the leaf?

    (A) Surface hairs
    (B) Stomata
    (C) Cuticles
    (D) Epidermal cells

Use the figure below to answer Question 59.

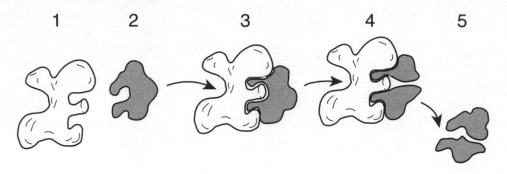

59. In the picture above, step Number 3 represents

    (A) a substrate.
    (B) an enzyme.
    (C) the products.
    (D) the enzyme-substrate complex.

60. In which stage of interphase are the centrioles replicated and proteins necessary for cell division synthesized?

    (A) G_1 phase
    (B) Mitosis
    (C) S phase
    (D) G_2 phase

Questions 61-65

In snapdragons, a red flower crossed with a white flower produces a pink flower. In this illustration, R stands for red color and W for white color. The Punnett square for a cross between a white snapdragon and a red snapdragon is shown here:

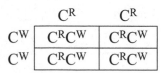

	C^R	C^R
C^W	C^RC^W	C^RC^W
C^W	C^RC^W	C^RC^W

61. The cross illustrated in this punnett square is an example of

    (A) a sex-linked trait.
    (B) multiple alleles.
    (C) incomplete dominance.
    (D) a dihybrid cross.

62. The symbol C^RC^W represents which of the following?

    (A) The allele for red
    (B) The genotype for pink
    (C) The phenotype for pink
    (D) The allele for white

63. In this cross, both parents have genotypes that are

    (A) heterozygous for color.
    (B) homozygous for color.
    (C) recessive for pink color.
    (D) dominant for pink color.

64. Which of the following statements about this cross MUST be true?

    (A) Both parents of the red snapdragon must have had the genotype C^RC^R.
    (B) One of the parents of the red snapdragon must have had the genotype C^RC^R.
    (C) Both parents of the red snapdragon must have been pink.
    (D) Neither parent of the red snapdragon could be white.

65. If two of the heterozygous offspring (C^RC^W) of this cross are bred, what will be the ratio of phenotypes of the offspring?

    (A) 0 red: 4 pink: 0 white
    (B) 2 red: 2 pink: 0 white
    (C) 1 red: 1 pink: 1 white
    (D) 1 red: 2 pink: 1 white

66. Which of the following is part of the alimentary canal?

    (A) Artery
    (B) Sinus
    (C) Vagus nerve
    (D) Mouth

67. Vertebrates that consume large amounts of vegetation and chew cud are known as

    (A) annelids.
    (B) ruminants.
    (C) chordates.
    (D) arthropods.

68. Which of the following embryonic membranes is matched correctly with its function?

    (A) yolk sac—heart protection
    (B) allantois—gas exchange
    (C) chorion—food storage
    (D) amnion—energy transfer

69. In which step of the nitrogen cycle do bacteria and fungi break excess nitrates back into their elements and release elemental nitrogen back into the atmosphere?

    (A) Ammonification
    (B) Denitrification
    (C) Nitrogen ixing
    (D) Decomposition

70. The father of our modern taxonomic key was

    (A) Carolus Linnaeus.
    (B) Robert Hooke.
    (C) Charles Darwin.
    (D) Gregor Mendel.

71. The leaves of an Easter Lily have parallel veins. The Easter Lily will have all of the following characteristics EXCEPT

    (A) an Easter Lily has seeds with double cotyledons.
    (B) an Easter Lily has vascular bundles arranged randomly in its stem.
    (C) the roots of the Easter Lily are ibrous.
    (D) the lower of the lily has three petals.

72. Water's ability to regulate environmental temperatures within a small range conducive to life is partially due to its

    (A) function as a universal solvent.
    (B) high heat capacity.
    (C) nonpolarity.
    (D) viscosity.

73. The cycle of daily behavior that is based on an internal clock and environmental clues is known as

    (A) imprinting.
    (B) fixed–action pattern.
    (C) circadian rhythm.
    (D) habituation.

74. _____ is an innate behavior that is independent of the environment.

    (A) Altruism
    (B) Fixed–action pattern
    (C) A reflex
    (D) Habituation

75. Which of the following is defined as a behavior that is learned only during a critical period of an organism's life?

    (A) Instinct
    (B) Habitat
    (C) Imprinting
    (D) Habituation

76. _____ are nonvascular plants that lack special tissue for conducting water or food.

    (A) Bryophytes
    (B) Angiosperms

(C) Conifers

(D) Cycads

77. The portion of the throat that includes the windpipe and the glottis is the

(A) pharynx.

(B) larynx.

(C) trachea.

(D) epiglottis.

78. Structural genes are responsible for coding the proteins necessary for

(A) developing organization of body structure.

(B) determining the timing of eye formation.

(C) synthesizing epithelial tissue.

(D) determining the sequence of neural development.

79. All of the following describe conditions in a taiga EXCEPT

(A) low precipitation levels.

(B) variety of animal life.

(C) coniferous forests.

(D) cold.

80. The derived characteristic of which of the following groups is the amniotic egg?

(A) Osteichthyes

(B) Reptilia

(C) Mammalia

(D) Aves

81. Which of the following describes the main function(s) of adipose tissue?

(A) It covers the outside of internal organs.

(B) It lines the interior of internal organs.

(C) It insulates and cushions.

(D) It reduces friction between bones.

82. Which of the following describes a sporophyte?

(A) A plant that produces only one type of spore

(B) The diploid generation, which becomes more dominant in the evolution of plants

(C) The multicellular structure that produces megaspores and microspores

(D) Haploid and may be either male or female

83. The multicellular structure that produces megaspores and/or microspores is called a

(A) sporangia.

(B) gametophyte.

(C) zygote.

(D) spore mother cell.

84. Which of the following describe(s) the structure or function of alveoli?

I. Located at the end of bronchioles

II. Small branch-like tubules

III. Where gas exchange occurs

(A) I and II only

(B) II only

(C) I and III only

(D) I, II, and III

85. An automatic response to an environmental signal is a

(A) releaser.

(B) fixed action pattern.

(C) reflex.

(D) stimulus.

86. A population's carrying capacity is

(A) an abiotic limiting factor.

(B) the total area occupied by a particular species.

(C) a permanent one-way movement out of the original range.

(D) the maximum population level where a population will continue to thrive.

87. A plant that can produce megaspores as well as microspores is

(A) diploid.
(B) heterosporous.
(C) homosporous.
(D) haploid.

88. In the 1700's, the French scientist Lamarck proposed the idea that animals develop characteristics over the course of their lives that help them adapt to their environment. These characteristics are then passed on to the next generation and adapted further. For instance, Lamarck suggested that giraffes developed long necks over their lifespan in order to enable them to reach food on high tree branches. The parents passed these traits on to the next generation. Over many generations, the giraffe species had changed to better survive in its environment. This now-discredited theory (which was replaced by Darwin's model of natural selection) is known as the theory of

(A) acquired characteristics.
(B) genetic drift.
(C) special isolation.
(D) genetic mutation.

89. Cytokinesis is the stage of mitosis during which

(A) kinetochore forms.
(B) paired chromosomes separate at the kinetochore, and each chromosome travels along the spindle fibers to opposite ends of the cell.
(C) the nuclear membrane forms around new groups of single-stranded chromosomes.
(D) cytoplasm splits forming two distinct cells.

90. Extreme heat or cold, sparse vegetation, and very low precipitation describes which of the following?

(A) Tundra
(B) Taiga
(C) Savanna
(D) Desert

91. A learned behavior that results in not responding to a stimulus is

(A) habituation.
(B) altruism.
(C) instinct.
(D) reflex.

92. The vocal chords are located within the

(A) glottis.
(B) larynx.
(C) esophagus.
(D) pharynx.

93. Abiotic-limiting factors are associated with which of the following?

I. Density-independent factors
II. Density-dependent factors
III. Pollution
IV. Symbiosis

(A) I and IV only
(B) I and III only
(C) II and III only
(D) II and IV only

94. All of the following are parts of prophase EXCEPT the

(A) condensation of chromatin.
(B) movement of the centrioles to opposite ends of the cell.
(C) dissolvation of the nuclear membrane.
(D) separation of chromatids.

95. Which of the following climates describes a chaparral?

(A) Moderate seasonal temperatures, low precipitation most of the year, grassland, shrubs, rodents, carnivores

(B) Many trees (which lose leaves in cold season), mosses, grasses, shrubs, abundant animal life, moderate rainfall, moderate seasonal temperatures

(C) Hot summers, temperate winters, precipitation varies from low in summer to high in winter, trees, shrubs, small animals, prolonged summer

(D) Dense forest, heavy rainfall, abundant vegetation, warm temperatures

96. One of Mendel's experiments involved pea plant color and pea plant height. He wanted to determine whether all green plants would be tall if the parent plant was green and tall. In these experiments, Mendel demonstrated that traits are not always inherited together; that is, a pea plant could be green and tall or green and short, yellow and tall or yellow and short. This demonstrated Mendel's

(A) Law of Independent Assortment.

(B) Law of Dependent Variables.

(C) Law of Inherited Recessives.

(D) Law of Dominance.

97. Which group has members that were most likely to have evolved earlier than members of any of the other groups listed?

(A) Protista

(B) Plantae

(C) Eubacteria

(D) Animalia

98. Chromosomes align along the equatorial plane of the cell during

(A) metaphase.

(B) anaphase.

(C) telophase.

(D) None of the above.

99. When a yellow pea plant is crossed with a green pea plant, all the offspring are yellow. The law that best explains this is the

(A) Law of Intolerance.

(B) Law of Dominance.

(C) Law of Interference.

(D) Law of Relative Genes.

100. Which of the following statements are true regarding primary oocytes?

I. Undergo meiosis II

II. Are present in reproductive organs at birth

III. Result in the formation of a secondary oocyte and a polar body

(A) I and II only

(B) II and III only

(C) I, II, and III

(D) None of the above.

101. Which of the following experimental evidence was NOT considered to support the Oparin Hypothesis?

(A) Amino acids can be produced in the laboratory by exposing simple inorganic molecules to electrical charge.

(B) Guanine can be formed in the laboratory by thermal polymerization of amino acids.

(C) Ultraviolet light induces the formation of dipeptides from amino acids in laboratory experiments.

(D) In the laboratory, proteins. are not useful as catalysts, indicating that early proteins were stable.

102. Cytochromes (pigment molecules that are found on the cristae of mitochondria) are the site of which one of the following processes?

    (A) The Krebs cycle
    (B) The electron transfer cycle
    (C) Photosynthesis
    (D) Fermentation

103. The first cells to evolve on Earth were most likely all of the following EXCEPT

    (A) anaerobic.
    (B) specialized.
    (C) prokaryotic.
    (D) aquatic.

104. A female haploid cell that is ready for fertilization is called a(n)

    (A) polar body.
    (B) zygote.
    (C) egg cell.
    (D) oocyte.

105. Which of the following are contained within both plant and animal cells?

    (A) Chloroplasts
    (B) Ribosomes
    (C) Cell wall
    (D) Grana

106. A mistake in the replication of DNA is known as a

    (A) chromosome.
    (B) mutation.
    (C) genome.
    (D) gene.

107. The organelle that takes up the most surface area in a plant cell is the

    (A) nucleolus.
    (B) chloroplast.
    (C) stroma.
    (D) central vacuole.

108. Which of the following is an infertile cell that results from meiosis II in females?

    (A) Polar body
    (B) Gamete
    (C) Zygote
    (D) Morula

109. Of the following, which is NOT true regarding secondary spermatocytes?

    (A) They contain haploid cells.
    (B) They develop into male gametes.
    (C) They undergo meiosis II.
    (D) They contain two sets of chromosomes.

110. Vitamin D is an example of

    (A) a protein.
    (B) an inorganic cofactor.
    (C) a coenzyme.
    (D) a prosthetic group.

111. The green color of plants is due to

    (A) chloroplasts.
    (B) verdine.
    (C) protein.
    (D) chlorophyll.

112. Ms. Ricardo's class is practicing calculations of forest biomass using the following equation:

Aboveground biomass density = VOB $\times$ WD $\times$ BEF = 150 m^3/ha $\times$ 0.55 t/m^3 = 82.5 t/ha.

VOB = Volume of Biomass
WD = volume-weighted average wood density (average of oven-dry biomass per m^3 green volume)
BEF = biomass expansion factor (ratio of aboveground oven-dry biomass of trees to oven-dry biomass of inventoried volume)
t = metric ton
ha = hectare

Which of the following is true about the class calculations?

(A) The numerical answer is correct; however, the units are incorrect.

(B) The numerical answer and the units are both correct.

(C) The answer is incorrect because it should be rounded to the nearest whole number.

(D) There is a calculation error in the numerical answer and the units are incorrect.

Directions for Question 113: The following question asks you to analyze teacher goals and actions intended to lead to the achievement of the goal. Decide whether the action makes it likely or unlikely to lead to the achievement of the goal.

113. GOAL: To increase student understanding of osmosis/diffusion and cell membranes.

ACTION: Teacher divides students into groups and makes available a variety of lab equipment (including beakers, dialysis tubing, distilled water, salt, sucrose solution in two strengths, and a balance scale), conductivity probe, and some basic information and reference materials regarding osmosis and cell membranes. After conducting an initial experiment that demonstrates osmosis of the sucrose solutions, the teacher asks students to design an additional experiment that demonstrates diffusion of salt.

(A) Likely, because students who experience anxiety about answering quiz questions are not required to take part in the experiment

(B) Likely, because research supports the idea that inquiry activities help students make sense of new ideas and construct new understanding

(C) Unlikely, because students in the science classes prefer steps clearly outlined and processes explained

(D) Unlikely, because students will likely be confused by the amount of equipment and the different processes that have to be undertaken

114. The cell that results from the combination of an egg cell of one individual with the sperm of another is called a

(A) gamete.
(B) zygote.
(C) morula.
(D) blastula.

115. As a result of the Common Rule, all of the following are required in any research involving human subjects connected to a federal agency EXCEPT which of the following?

(A) All research is subject to review by an Institutional Review Board (IRB).

(B) Research subjects are to be given an opportunity for informed consent before being asked to participate in any research.

(C) Research subjects must be compensated for their time and any inconvenience they may suffer as part of the study.

(D) Research subjects are to be given an opportunity to remove themselves from the research study at any time.

116. Gel electrophoresis is a process for analyzing a sample of DNA and identifying individual marker sections allowing a sample to be identified as a particular individual. The applications for this technology have had several impacts. Which of the following impacts would be of MOST ethical concern?

(A) Electrophoresis can be used to identify genetically undesirable fetuses prenatally, which may then be aborted, allowing parents to select eye, hair color, gender, etc.

(B) Electrophoresis is used to confirm or deny paternity in questionable cases.

(C) Electrophoresis is used in identifying DNA samples in forensic applications to apprehend criminals and/or free falsely accused individuals.

(D) Electrophoresis can be used to confirm the identity of historical remains or remains of lost individuals.

117. Which of the following is NOT considered a biology process skill?

(A) Analyzing data
(B) Designing investigations
(C) Conducting experiments
(D) Adjusting data

Questions 118 and 119 refer to the following:

A student wants to perform an experiment involving mold growth on solid nutrient agar for a science fair project.

118. Which type of glassware is most appropriate for this procedure?

(A) Graduated cylinder
(B) Test tube
(C) Watch glass
(D) Petri dish

119. What safety procedures should be observed?

(A) Be sure the student grows the mold in a lab environment in covered glassware and follows all IRB procedures.

(B) No special precautions are needed as mold is a common agent found in most refrigerators.

(C) Do not allow student to experiment with mold because it is too dangerous and may cause damage to the student or others.

(D) Do not allow student to experiment with model because it is a living organism and students at the high school level should be prohibited from experimentation with all living things.

120. Which of the following is NOT an appropriate means of disposal of infectious microbial waste?

(A) Steam autoclave sterilization at 15 psi and 121° C for at least 15 minutes

(B) Placement of waste in specially marked infectious material bags then seal in second layer of plastic for disposal with standard waste

(C) Dry heat sterilization at temperatures of 160-170°C (320-338°F) for 2-4 hours

(D) Immersion in household bleach for 6-10 hours

121. Which of the following events impacted the development of modern scientific ideals the LEAST?

(A) Piaget's development of the Theory of Cognitive Development

(B) Newton's development of the Law's of Motion and Gravity

(C) Einstein's development of the Theory of Special Relativity

(D) Darwin's development of the Theory of Natural Selection

122. Climate change is one man-made/natural hazard that this generation of students will have to debate. They will have to determine exactly how and if it is happening and what to do about it. Which of the following is NOT a mitigative effort currently being investigated to combat climate change?

(A) Research into use of alternative energy sources (solar, wind, fuel cells)

(B) Research into carbon capture

(C) Research into cutting greenhouse gas emissions

(D) Research into use of fossil fuels

123. The change in frequency of particular genes in a population over time due to chance fluctuations is known as

    (A) Genetic drift
    (B) Sympatric speciation
    (C) Kin selection
    (D) Punctuated equilibrium

124. All of the following are tracheophytes EXCEPT

    (A) moss.
    (B) roses.
    (C) corn.
    (D) ferns.

125. Which of the following statements LEAST expresses best biology teaching practice?

    (A) Biology students should spend about half of their instructional time in laboratory, inquiry, or field experiences.
    (B) It is better for some students, according to ability, to not be required to participate in laboratory or field biology experiences according to teacher discretion.
    (C) Research shows that beginning a unit of study with experiences in a laboratory or field setting allows students to construct new knowledge for themselves.
    (D) Biology instruction should provide opportunity for student involvement that shows the tentative nature of science.

126. Which of the following statements describes the concept of adaptive radiation?

    (A) Short period of quick mutation and change resulting in new species
    (B) Process whereby one species can evolve into several new species over time as migration to new areas occurs and traits are specialized to fit new habitat
    (C) The development of members within a population that possess differences preventing successful reproduction with the original population

    (D) The tendency for an individual to express altruistic traits toward close relatives, thus preserving the genes that produce altruistic traits

127. Natality is defined as a population's

    (A) birth rate.
    (B) overall growth rate.
    (C) population growth.
    (D) death rate.

128. Which of the following is NOT characteristic of a cell membrane?

    (A) Measures 500-1000 nanometers thick
    (B) Can be viewed only with an electron microscope
    (C) Embedded protein globules
    (D) Double phospholipid layer

129. In glycolysis, a molecule of glucose is broken down into all of the following EXCEPT

    (A) pyruvic acid.
    (B) ATP.
    (C) CO_2.
    (D) H^+.

130. Of the following, which are characteristics of gymnosperms?

    I.   Seed producing
    II. Flower producing
    III. Cone-bearing

    (A) I, II, and III
    (B) I and II only
    (C) II and III only
    (D) I and III only

131. All of the following are part of the transcription step in protein synthesis EXCEPT that

    (A) DNA molecule "unzips," exposing a sequence of nucleotides that corresponds to a certain amino acid or protein.
    (B) RNA polymerase matches RNA nucleotides to their corresponding DNA nucleotides.

(C) mRNA strand is formed as RNA nucleotides join together and uncoil from DNA.

(D) Ribosome attaches to start codon on mRNA.

132. The exothermic breakdown of ATP into ADP plus a phosphate group is an example of

(A) anabolism
(B) catabolism
(C) enzyme response
(D) lysis

133. The modern synthesis concept of evolution stresses that

(A) evolution represents gradual change in traits across populations
(B) evolution is only seen on the species level
(C) evolution may occur in bursts over a short period of time
(D) evolution represents the presence of acquired characteristics in individuals

134. The _____ within a population is represented by the birth rate minus the death rate.

(A) mortality rate
(B) rate of increase
(C) exponential curve
(D) logistic curve

135. Regulatory genes are responsible for coding the proteins that

(A) form bone tissue
(B) determine eye color
(C) determine the sequence of neural development
(D) synthesize cardiac muscle

136. All of the following are steps of photosynthesis EXCEPT

(A) chlorophyll is absorbed through plant roots.
(B) during photolysis a photon of light is absorbed by the chlorophyll pigment,

which then is in an excited (higher energy) state.
(C) water is separated into hydrogen and oxygen atoms.
(D) an ADP molecule is phosphorylated to ATP.

137. ATP (adenosine triphosphate) is known as the energy currency of cellular activity because

I. the amount of energy stored in a carbohydrate molecule is more than is usable by a single cell
II. ATP can be broken down into ADP plus a phosphate group yielding a small packet of energy usable by a cell
III. ATP contains three high-energy bonds making it an efficient energy storage molecule
IV. green plants produce ATP molecules during photosynthesis

(A) I only
(B) II only
(C) II and III only
(D) I, II, III, IV

138. Which of the following is characteristic of an equilibreal life strategy (k-selection)?

(A) Short maturation time
(B) Long life span
(C) Asexual reproduction
(D) Do not parent young

139. All of the following are true about glycolysis EXCEPT

(A) glycolysis breaks down glucose into smaller molecules.
(B) glycolysis only occurs in plant cells.
(C) the process of respiration always begins with glycolysis.
(D) glycolysis occurs in the cytoplasm of all living cells.

140. Plants may use any of the following structures for vegetative propagation EXCEPT

    (A) cones.
    (B) tubers.
    (C) rhizomes.
    (D) bulbs.

141. Which of the following hormones regulates the opening and closing of stomata as well as the formation of winter buds?

    (A) Cytokinin
    (B) Auxin
    (C) Gibberellins
    (D) Abscisic acid

142. Populations in which no environmental or social limits are present that affect population size would result in which of the following?

    (A) Logistic population growth
    (B) S-curve population growth
    (C) J-curve population growth
    (D) None of the above.

143. Which of the following eras in the geological time scale is correctly matched to the type of animal that dominated it?

    (A) Cenozoic - Age of reptiles
    (B) Mesozoic - Age of amphibians
    (C) Paleozoic - Age of fish
    (D) Precambrian - Age of mammals

144. Darwin's theory of natural selection includes all of the following stipulations EXCEPT

    (A) every organism produces more organisms that can survive.
    (B) due to competition, not all organisms survive.
    (C) some organisms are more it, i.e., they are able to survive better in the environment.
    (D) variation is due, at least in part, to mutations.

145. The filtering of inhaled debris that travels through the upper respiratory tract occurs through the action of

    (A) cilia.
    (B) goblet cells.
    (C) Leidig cells.
    (D) phagocytes.

146. Which of the following diseases is caused by a protozoa?

    (A) Chicken pox
    (B) Common cold
    (C) Malaria
    (D) Measles

147. Which of the following is NOT a cofactor?

    (A) Mn^{2+}
    (B) NAD^+
    (C) ATP
    (D) FAD

148. The animals of this group (extinct and living) are the first tetrapods, are ectotherms, and use the skin as an important organ for respiration

    (A) Amphibia
    (B) Reptilia
    (C) Chondrichthyes
    (D) Aves

149. Which of the following is a terrestrial biome that has warm temperatures, moderate precipitation, and grassland?

    (A) Tundra
    (B) Chaparral
    (C) Tropical rain forest
    (D) Savanna

150. The part of a leaf responsible for maintaining moisture balance is the

    (A) epidermis.
    (B) cuticle.
    (C) palisade layer.
    (D) guard cells.

Detailed Explanations to Answers for Practice Test 2

Praxis II: Biology
Core Content Knowledge

ANSWER KEY FOR PRACTICE TEST 2

1.	(D)	39.	(D)	77.	(C)	115.	(C)
2.	(A)	40.	(B)	78.	(C)	116.	(A)
3.	(D)	41.	(A)	79.	(A)	117.	(D)
4.	(A)	42.	(A)	80.	(B)	118.	(D)
5.	(A)	43.	(A)	81.	(C)	119.	(A)
6.	(D)	44.	(D)	82.	(B)	120.	(B)
7.	(A)	45.	(B)	83.	(A)	121.	(A)
8.	(D)	46.	(B)	84.	(C)	122.	(D)
9.	(B)	47.	(C)	85.	(C)	123.	(A)
10.	(C)	48.	(D)	86.	(D)	124.	(C)
11.	(B)	49.	(A)	87.	(B)	125.	(B)
12.	(D)	50.	(D)	88.	(A)	126.	(B)
13.	(B)	51.	(B)	89.	(D)	127.	(A)
14.	(B)	52.	(D)	90.	(D)	128.	(A)
15.	(A)	53.	(D)	91.	(A)	129.	(C)
16.	(B)	54.	(B)	92.	(B)	130.	(D)
17.	(D)	55.	(D)	93.	(B)	131.	(D)
18.	(B)	56.	(C)	94.	(D)	132.	(B)
19.	(C)	57.	(D)	95.	(C)	133.	(A)
20.	(B)	58.	(B)	96.	(A)	134.	(B)
21.	(D)	59.	(D)	97.	(C)	135.	(C)
22.	(B)	60.	(D)	98.	(A)	136.	(A)
23.	(A)	61.	(C)	99.	(B)	137.	(D)
24.	(C)	62.	(B)	100.	(B)	138.	(B)
25.	(B)	63.	(B)	101.	(D)	139.	(B)
26.	(C)	64.	(D)	102.	(B)	140.	(A)
27.	(C)	65.	(D)	103.	(B)	141.	(D)
28.	(A)	66.	(D)	104.	(C)	142.	(C)
29.	(B)	67.	(B)	105.	(B)	143.	(C)
30.	(C)	68.	(B)	106.	(B)	144.	(D)
31.	(C)	69.	(B)	107.	(D)	145.	(A)
32.	(D)	70.	(A)	108.	(A)	146.	(C)
33.	(D)	71.	(A)	109.	(D)	147.	(C)
34.	(A)	72.	(B)	110.	(C)	148.	(A)
35.	(B)	73.	(C)	111.	(D)	149.	(D)
36.	(B)	74.	(B)	112.	(C)	150.	(B)
37.	(B)	75.	(C)	113.	(B)		
38.	(D)	76.	(A)	114.	(B)		

PRACTICE TEST 2: PROGRESS AND COMPETENCY CHART

Basic Principles of Science ____/12

25	26	41	42	112	113	117	118	119	120

121	125

Molecular & Cellular Biology ____/38

4	5	6	8	9	15	18	27	38	39

48	50	51	53	54	56	57	59	60	89

94	98	102	105	106	107	110	111	128	129

131	132	135	136	137	139	141	147

Classical Genetics & Evolution ____/23

1	2	3	7	12	13	61	62	63	64

65	88	96	97	99	101	103	123	126	133

138	143	144

Diversity of Life, Plants, and Animals _____/45

10	11	14	16	17	28	29	30	31	33

35	36	37	46	49	52	55	58	66	67

68	70	71	76	77	78	80	81	82	83

84	87	92	100	104	108	109	114	124	130

140	145	146	148	150

Ecology _____/22

19	20	32	34	40	47	69	72	73	74

75	79	85	86	90	91	93	95	127	134

142	149

Science, Technology, and Society _____/10

21	22	23	24	43	44	45	115	116	122

1. (D)

All offspring of two albino parents (each must have the geno type nn) will be albino, so the answer is 0%.

2. (A)

As seen in the following Punnett square, it is clear that the Nn × Nn cross would yield 1 out of 4 albino (homozygous), 1 out of 4 homozygous normal (NN), and 2 out of 4 heterozygous normal (Nn) children.

	N	**n**
N	NN	Nn
n	Nn	nn

3. (D)

A gene is the portion of DNA that produces a particular expressed trait. A chromosome contains many genes and is a structure comprised of linear DNA and associated proteins. A mutation is a mistake in DNA replication. The genome is the total amount of genetic information available for a given species.

4. (A)

The process whereby cells build molecules and store energy (in the form of covalent chemical bonds) is called *anabolism*. Catabolism is when molecules are broken apart. Adaptive radiation refers to an evolutionary process. Lysis is a sufix meaning "to break apart."

5. (A)

Photolysis does not occur after glycolysis; rather it is the first step in photosynthesis. Aerobic respiration occurs after glycolysis if oxygen is present in the cell. There are two steps in aerobic respiration for most organisms: the Krebs cycle (also known as the citric acid cycle) and electron transport. The first step, the Krebs cycle, occurs in the matrix of a cell's mitochondria and breaks down two pyruvic acid molecules into two CO_2 molecules, plus four H+ (protons), and one molecule of ATP. The second step occurs along the electron transport system (or ETS) that captures the energy (in the form of electrons) that the Krebs cycle releases.

6. (D)

The group is a carboxyl group and is the signature group found within organic acids.

7. (A)

Lichens are often the first pioneer species to enter a rocky area after a volcanic eruption. Lichens break up the rock surfaces into soil, making the environment more hospitable for species of plants and animals. This represents and opportunistic life strategy or r-selection. Choices (B) and (D) represent equilibreal or k-selected life strategies that tend to remain long-term in a stable ecosystem. Choice (C) may be a precursor to the invasion of an r-selected species.

8. (D)

While this statement is considered scientifically accurate, it is not a tenet of the cell theory. Choice (A) is a true statement about the cell theory, and choices (B and C) represent tenets of the cell theory.

9. (B)

Enzymes catalyze reactions in both living and nonliving environments.

10. (C)

The individual we recognize as an adult fern is actually the mature sporophyte. The mature gametophyte is a heart-shaped haploid structure that does not resemble an adult fern. The young sporophyte develops into the mature sporophyte, but while young it does not have the leaf structure characteristic of an adult fern.

11. (B)

This response to a light stimulus is called phototropism. The hormone auxin, in response to the light, migrates from the light to the dark side of the shoot tip. The cells on the dark side now contain more auxin, which causes the cells on that side to elongate more rapidly than cells on the light side. The result is that the plant bends toward the light.

12. (D)

The theory of punctuated equilibrium can account for the sudden appearance and disappearance of fossil species. The fossil record shows periods of stability with regard to appearance and disappearance of species as well as periods of sudden change.

13. (B)

Hemophilia is a sex-linked recessive disease. Like color-blindness, the gene for hemophilia, h, is carried on the X-chromosome. If a male inherits the gene, he will have the genotype X^hY and will be a hemophiliac (a normal male is X^HY) since the recessive gene will be expressed. If a female inherits the gene, she will have the genotype X^HX^h and will carry the trait since her other X chromosome has the normal dominant gene, H. The common pattern of transmittal is from carrier mothers to their sons. Note that a carrier mother X^HX^h has an equal (50%) chance of passing the gene on to either a son (X^hY) or a daughter (X^HX^h); however the daughter will not express the disease. It is unlikely for a female to be a hemophiliac, X^hX^h, since she must have acquired the recessive gene from both her carrier mother and her hemophiliac father. However, this is possible, and as expected, the incidence increases when there is marriage between relatives. If the gene were Y-linked, then a diseased father would always produce a hemophiliac son. However, a son inherits the gene only from his mother, since the mother contributes his sole X chromosome.

14. (B)

The fungi encompass an entire kingdom in the classification scheme. They function as decomposers of organic matter and hence aid in the carbon, nitrogen, and phosphorus cycles. Of interest, fungi decompose both living and nonliving matter. The term *saprophytic* refers to its ability to decompose dead matter. This is in contrast to parasitic behavior, exhibited by some fungi, which refers to decomposition of living matter.

15. (A)

Restriction enzymes cleave strands of DNA segments at certain sites, thus yielding uniform fragments to be studied in the laboratory. The DNA molecule is not cleaved straight across by restriction enzymes; rather, these enzymes leave "sticky ends" that are complementary to another molecule cleaved by the same enzyme.

16. (B)

Of the choices given, carbon is the most abundant element found in protoplasm. Together with oxygen, hydrogen, and nitrogen, it composes over 90% of cellular structure. Calcium, phosphorus, and sulfur are found in varying amounts, depending upon the nature of the cell. Zinc is found in trace amounts.

17. (D)

The body (or stroma) of the chloroplast contains imbedded grana (stacked, disk-like plates) that are the site of photosynthetic reactions. Bodies, cytosomes, and chlorosites are not organelles of plant cells.

18. (B)

The combination of DNA with histones is called *chromatin*. A centromere is the connecting point of a chromosome. A nucleosome is one monomer of a nucleic acid (DNA or RNA). An amino acid is a building block (monomer) of a pro-

tein. RNA is a different nucleic acid with ribose as its sugar as well as other differences from DNA.

19. (C)

The most likely explanation of those listed is that the seed will only germinate when it is exposed to proper moisture, temperature, and oxygen. Corn is not a biennial plant.

20. (B)

When one community completely replaces another over time in a given area it is known as *succession*. *Commensalism* is a type of symbiosis where one organism is helped and the other is neither helped nor harmed. *Dynamic equilibrium* refers to chemical reactions or homeostatic mechanisms in animals. Alternation of generations is a feature of plant life cycles.

21. (D)

While this statement is true, it is of least importance to teach. Students need to know choices (A), (B), and (C), as these facts are scientific points that are important to their own health and safety and in making informed life decisions.

22. (B)

According to the National Science Education Standards (Content Standard E: Science and Technology), it is more effective for students to have fewer but more integrated and long term experiences with science and technology in the high school years. Choices (A), (C), and (D) are reinforcements of teaching practices that do not differentiate between the concepts of science and the uniquenesses and interconnectedness of technology.

23. (A)

Choice (A) is an incorrect statement since eye color and gender can also be determined through CVS and other prenatal DNA testing. Choices (B), (C), and (D) are all considerations of the controversies that should be considered in the Biology classroom of the 21st century.

24. (C)

Aesthetics are important, but this is not a key to sustainability. In the diagram below, notice that choices (A), (B), and (D) are all interlinked in the concept of ecological sustainability.

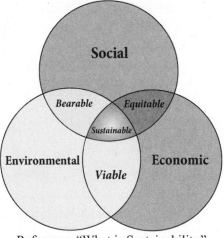

Reference: "What is Sustainability."
www.sustainability.umd.edu

25. (B)

Generation of scientific knowledge uniquely involves human imagination and creativity as much as other types of knowledge in the arts and other areas. Mendeleev, Mendel, Newton, Einstein, and Watson and Crick all had to access abilities of creativity and imagination to allow them to envision the models and discoveries they made. Choices (A), (C), and (D) are similarly important tenets of the nature of science.

26. (C)

The second choice is the standard SI unit of time. Choices (A), (B), and (D) are English system units and not SI.

27. (C)

A replacement reaction occurs when a compound is broken down into its components and recombined with another reactant, as shown by the equation $AB + C \rightarrow AC + B$. The reaction $A + B \rightarrow AB$ represents a combination reaction; $AB \rightarrow A + B$ is a decomposition reaction; $A + C \rightarrow AC + B$ is not a possible reaction since it is not consistent with the first law of thermodynamics—matter cannot be created nor destroyed in a chemical reaction. Since (B) was not a reactant, it cannot be a product.

28. (A)

Adipose, sucrose, and fat molecules store energy, but glycogen is the short-term energy storage molecule commonly found in muscle and liver tissue.

29. (B)

The only true statement is that bacteria are decomposers that recycle some of the nutrients from dead organisms to be reused by plants.

30. (C)

The musculoskeletal system provides the body with structure, stability, and the ability to move. By definition, the musculoskeletal system is unique to vertebrates, although some invertebrates (such as mollusks and insects) have external support structures (exoskeletons) and muscle. Invertebrates may have a gas exchange system, a circulatory system, and/or a nervous system.

31. (C)

Sensory input depends on healthy function of nerves, which requires the myelin sheath to be intact. Sensory input would be impaired by the loss of the myelin sheath. Damage to the myelin sheath causes all of the other problems listed.

32. (D)

Cyanobacteria (or blue-green bacteria) perform the task of combining gaseous nitrogen from the atmosphere with hydrogen, forming ammonium (NH_{4+}) ions. Ammonium ions are then available to be absorbed and used by plants. Blue-green bacteria do not perform any of the other tasks listed.

33. (D)

The somatic motor nerves carry impulses from the CNS to skeletal muscle. Somatic sensory nerves carry impulses from body surface to CNS. Sympathetic nerves carry impulses that stimulate organs. Autonomic nerves carry impulses to and from organs.

34. (A)

Energy flows through the entire ecosystem in one direction, from producers to consumers and on to decomposers through the food chain.

35. (B)

Archaea is a domain that contains organisms with prokaryotic cells. Protista, Fungi, Plantae, and Animalia are all kingdoms within the domain Eukaryota. Eukaryota contains only organisms with eukaryotic cells.

36. (B)

The heart is the only organ listed that is not a part of the excretory system. The skin excretes salts, urea, and other wastes as sweat; the lungs excrete carbon dioxide; the liver produces bile from broken down pigments and chemical pollutants (from medications, etc.) and secretes it into the small intestine where it proceeds to the large intestine and is expelled in the feces.

37. (B)

Feedback controls respond to stimulus conditions such as temperature, pH, water balance, sugar levels, etc. Environmental stimuli are monitored and controlled in order to keep the body and cells within the accepted ranges that will not inhibit life. Cells and living organisms have homeostatic mechanisms (including feedback controls) that serve to keep body conditions within normal ranges. Fight or flight instincts occur in response to imminent danger, not body conditions. The term "homeostatic mechanisms" is used rather than "equilibrium responses." Fixed action patterns are a type of instinctive behavior; they are not internal functions and are not necessarily involuntary.

38. (D)

A DNA molecule is a long chain of nucleotides, each of which is composed of a sugar, a phosphate group, and a nitrogen base. Alcohol is not a component of DNA.

39. (D)

Robert Hooke was the first to use the term *cells* to describe his observation of the cell walls of cork under a microscope.

40. (B)

Temporary movement into a new range and back again is known as migration. Immigration occurs when an organism permanently moves into a new area and emigration occurs when an organism permanently moves out of an area. Dispersion is the spreading of a species over a broader range via immigration, emigration, and/or migration.

41. (A)

Choice (A) is not a true statement since there is not any one particular scientific method with any given particular set of steps. Rather, choices (B), (C), and (D) are more accurate representations of characteristics of the scientific method. Choice (D) represents the concept of peer review – an important concept in the scientific world.

42. (A)

4.5×10^6 is correct. To express in scientific notation, place the decimal point after the first significant digit (making the absolute value between 1 and 10) and then multiply by a factor of 10 to equate to original number.

43. (A)

DNA testing indeed can reveal gender early in pregnancy which is of little ethical concern in most cases. Choices (B,) (C), and (D) all can lead to larger ethical concerns.

44. (D)

Advancements in the cloning of animal species is not likely to impact agriculture whereas (A), (B), and (C) will have a direct impact on agriculture.

45. (B)

Of the choices given, transportation methods are the least impactful of the items listed in a person's food choices and eating patterns. Choices (A), (C), and (D) are each likely to impact food selection.

46. (B)

Substances that compete to attach to an enzyme's active site are called inhibitors. If they attach to the enzyme first, the cellular reaction (in this case the synthesis of prostaglandins) will not take place. A hormone is a specific chemical messenger used throughout the endocrine system. The COX-2 inhibitor is a molecule, not an ion. Prosthetic groups are substances that work with enzymes to enhance certain reactions, whereas an inhibitor will limit the reaction.

47. (C)

Evolution of traits depends on the shifting of certain gene frequencies within a population. If gene frequencies remain constant, evolution does not occur. It then follows that the rate of evolution within the population will not increase. The expression of dominant or recessive traits will not be affected—it will neither increase nor decrease.

48. (D)

Viruses are the smallest organisms in the world, by far, but scientists disagree as to whether they can be considered "living" at all. Their structure consists of only a protein capsule, DNA, or RNA, and sometimes enzymes. Viruses do not have any organelles or metabolic capability of their own, so they survive and replicate by invading a living cell of another organism and taking over its metabolic functions for their own use. The virus then utilizes the cell's mechanisms to reproduce itself, often destroying the cell in the process. This invade-and-destruct operation of viruses causes the organism containing the infected cells to sicken and sometimes die as the virus overtakes more and more of its cells. Scientists do not agree as to whether viruses are actually "alive," since they do not have the ability to conduct metabolic functions on their own.

49. (A)

A snail is found in the phylum Mollusca.

50. (D)

Environmental conditions such as heat or acidity inhibit enzymatic reactions by changing the shape of the active site and render the enzyme ineffective. Certain chemicals inhibit enzymatic reactions by changing the shape of the enzyme's active site. If there is a lack of substrate, the enzyme will have no substance to affect. Thus all of these factors may inhibit enzymatic reactions, except an excess of substrate, which would not inhibit those reactions.

51. (B)

Electrons have very small mass, much less than either protons or neutrons.

52. (D)

The mesophyll is comprised of several layers of tissue between the upper and lower epidermis. The uppermost of these, the palisade layer, contains vertically aligned cells with numerous chloroplasts. The arrangement of these cells maximizes the potential for exposure of the chloroplasts to needed sunlight. Most photosynthesis occurs in

this layer. The epidermis is the outermost layer of the plant tissue that serves as a protective coating. Parenchyma cells are found in many plant tissues; their function is to allow for gas and moisture exchange. The meristematic region is in the roots, and therefore is not active in photosynthesis.

53. (D)

All of the choices are lipids, except cellulose, which is a long chain of water insoluble polysaccharides, a starch that is a common energy storage molecule within plants.

54. (B)

A double helix is the signature formation (spiral staircase) of DNA, as modeled by scientists Watson and Crick.

55. (D)

The pistil is the female plant structure and includes the stigma, style, and ovary. The stigma is a sticky surface at the top of the pistil that traps pollen grains. The stigma sits above a slender vase-like structure, the style, which encloses the ovary. The ovary is the hollow bulb-shaped structure in the lower interior of the pistil. (After seeds have formed, the ovary will ripen and become fruit.) Within the ovary are the ovules; small round cases each containing one or more egg cells. The filament is part of the male plant structure, the stamen.

56. (C)

The light microscope is useful in distinguishing most cells; however the cell organelles, which are much smaller, are only clearly visible with the use of an electron microscope.

57. (D)

Since mitochondria produce energy for cellular function, you would expect to find more mitochondria in tissue that require a lot of energy, such as cardiac tissue.

58. (B)

Stomata are openings in the leaf surface that allow for exchange of water and gases.

59. (D)

Step Number 3 shows the enzyme and substrate joined to become the enzyme-substrate complex. Number 1 is the enzyme, Number 2 the substrate, and Number 5 is the products.

60. (D)

The G_2 phase is the final stage of interphase, in which proteins and centrioles are produced in preparation for cell division. The G_1 phase is the first part of interphase, where metabolism, protein synthesis, and growth are occurring at a high rate. Mitosis includes prophase, metaphase, anaphase, and telophase. Mitosis produces two daughter cells identical to the parent cell. In the S phase, the cell begins to prepare for cell division by replicating the DNA and proteins necessary to form a new set of chromosomes.

61. (C)

This is known as incomplete dominance. Neither white nor red is dominant over the other.

62. (B)

$C^R C^W$ is a symbol for genotype and in this case the $C^R C^W$ genotype produces a pink pheno-

type. C^R and C^W represent the alleles for red and white, respectively.

63. (B)

Both parents have two alleles that are the same, thus they have homozygous genotypes for color.

64. (D)

While (A), (B), (C), and (E) could have been true, a red snapdragon could have been produced by any of those choices. However, a white snapdragon cannot produce a red snapdragon as an offspring even if paired with a red.

65. (D)

If two of the heterozygous offspring of an incomplete dominant trait are bred, the Punnett square would be:

	C^R	C^W
C^R	$C^R C^R$	$C^R C^W$
C^W	$C^R C^W$	$C^W C^W$

The phenotypic ratio of the offspring then is one-fourth red, one-half pink, and one-fourth white, a 1:2:1 ratio—1 red: 2 pink: 1 white.

66. (D)

The alimentary canal is also known as the gastrointestinal (or GI) tract and includes the mouth, pharynx, esophagus, stomach, small intestine, and large intestine.

67. (B)

Food in the rumen mixes with bacteria and is regurgitated as the cud for chewing. Chewed vegetation is regurgitated from the first two chambers of the complex stomach as cud and is chewed again. Chewing mechanically breaks down the food, thereby increasing the surface area available for action of digestive juices and bacteria.

68. (B)

The allantois appears in the third week of development and becomes part of the umbilical cord. It contains blood vessels that function to exchange gases and nutrients between the embryo and the mother.

69. (B)

Various species of bacteria and fungi break excess nitrates back down into elements, a process that releases elemental nitrogen back into the air. This process is called denitrification.

70. (A)

Our current taxonomic key is based on one first developed by Carolus Linnaeus, who published *Systema Naturae* in 1735. Linnaeus based his taxonomic keys on the morphological (outward anatomical) differences seen among species. Linnaeus designed a system of classification for all known and unknown organisms according to their anatomical similarities and differences.

71. (A)

The seeds of Easter Lilies are monocotyledenous (single). They also have leaves with parallel veins, lowers with petals in a multiple of three, a fibrous root system, and random arrangement of vascular bundles in their stems.

72. (B)

The heat capacity is the amount of heat energy (calories) required to raise the temperature of one gram (g) of substance one degree Celsius (°C). It is expressed as cal/g/°C. The higher the heat capacity of a substance, the more stable its temperature when the external (environmental) temperature changes, and the more stable its molecules. Water has a high heat capacity (1 cal/g/°C) and therefore is relatively unaffected by changes in environmental temperatures and is highly stable.

73. (C)

Circadian rhythms consist of an organism's daily repeated behavior such as wake and sleep cycles that function according to its internal clock. The internal clock is affected by environmental cues such as hours of sunlight per day, etc.

74. (B)

A Fixed Action Pattern (FAP) is a type of innate behavior, or instinct. The FAP is a pre-programmed response to a particular stimulus (known as a *releaser* or a *sign stimulus*). FAPs include courtship behaviors and feeding of young. Organisms automatically perform FAPs without any prior experience (FAPs are not learned).

75. (C)

Imprinting is behavior that is learned during a critical point (often very early) in an individual's life. For instance, a gosling is imprinted with the impression of its mother immediately after hatching. Imprinting enables the young to recognize members of their own species.

76. (A)

Nonvascular plants are known as bryophytes (ex. mosses). They lack tissue that will conduct water or food. Plants can also be categorized by their method of reproduction. Angiosperms and gymnosperms (conifers and cycads) are examples of plants categorized by this method.

77. (C)

The trachea includes the windpipe (larynx) in its upper portion and the glottis, an opening that allows the gases to pass into the two branches known as the bronchi.

78. (C)

Structural genes are not involved in timing and development, but rather produce the actual proteins that form structures such as tissues and organs. Regulatory genes, on the other hand, determine functional or physiological events, such as growth. These specific genes control (regulate) when other genes are turned on or off, thus regulating when certain proteins that produce a specific trait will be synthesized. Thus, structural genes would be involved in synthesizing epithelial tissue.

79. (A)

Taiga is a type of biome that consists of cold temperatures with snow most of the year, thick coniferous forests, large variety of animals, and moderate precipitation.

80. (B)

The amniotic egg with its yolk sac and three extra embryonic membranes is first found in Reptilia. The extra embryonic membranes are the amniotic membrane, the allantoic membrane, and the chorionic membrane. The amnion protects the embryo from mechanical shock and dehydration. The allantois stores wastes and acts with the chorion in gas exchange. The chorion is important in gas exchange. The amniotic egg is important in the evolution of vertebrates because it allowed for eggs to be laid out of the water. In mammals and other vertebrates that have live births, the extra embryonic membranes are frequently part of the connection between the mother and embryo. Reptilia include species that lay eggs (e.g., turtles, crocodiles, and many lizards and snakes) and produce live offspring (e.g., alligator lizards, garter snakes, rattlesnakes).

81. (C)

Adipose tissue is found beneath the skin and outside the organs to provide cushioning, insulation, and fat storage. Connective tissue covers internal organs and comprises ligaments and tendons. Epithelial tissue covers the body (skin) and lines internal organs. Found at the end of bones and in the ears and nose, cartilage tissue reduces friction between bones and supports and connects them.

82. (B)

The diploid (2n) generation plant is called a sporophyte, a spore-producing plant. The haploid (1n) generation is the gametophyte plant. the gamete-producing plant. In the evolution of plants, the sporophyte generation becomes increasingly dominant.

83. (A)

The life cycle of plants is illustrated starting with the sporophyte generation. The sporophyte plant has multi-cellular structures called sporangia. The spore mother cells within undergo meiosis and produce haploid spores.

84. (C)

Alveoli are found at the end of the bronchioles, which are smaller, branch like tubules that extend from the bronchi. Alveoli are thin-walled air sacs that are the site of gas exchange.

85. (C)

A reflex is an automatic movement of a body part in response to an environmental signal.

86. (D)

Within a given area, the maximum level the population may reach where it will continue to thrive is known as the *carrying capacity*. Carrying capacity is a biotic limiting factor. Choice (B) is the population's range. Emigration is described by (C).

87. (B)

If a plant can produce both types of spores, (megaspores and microspores) it is a heterosporous plant. If it produces only one type of spore, it is homosporous.

88. (A)

Lamarck's ideas were known as "the theory of acquired characteristics." It was later discredited, but it got scientists thinking about possible alternatives to explain the origins of biological life. Natural selection was the process proposed by Darwin as the mechanism of evolution. Genetic drift describes a particular means of changing the genetic information of a population undergoing evolution. Special isolation can cause certain types of genetic changes within a population. Genetic mutations are accidental changes in the DNA code of an organism that over time can produce changes in the species' population.

89. (D)

The process of cytokinesis occurs at the end of telophase and involves the splitting of the cytoplasm into two distinct cells.

90. (D)

Desert has extreme hot or cold temperatures, with very low precipitation, sandy or rocky terrain, and sparse vegetation (mainly succulents).

91. (A)

Habituation occurs when an individual learns not to respond to a particular stimulus, for instance when a stimulus is repeated many times without consequence.

92. (B)

The vocal chords are found in the larynx. The pharynx is located just above the larynx. The glottis is an opening that allows air to pass into the bronchi. The esophagus is the passage for food to travel from the throat to the stomach.

93. (B)

Abiotic limiting factors are also known as *density-independent* factors. They are independent of population density and involve factors that are non-living, such as fire, pollution, sunlight, soil, precipitation, etc. Density-dependent factors, such as symbiosis and overpopulation, are also known as biotic factors.

94. (D)

During prophase, the first stage of mitosis, the chromatin condenses into chromosomes; the centrioles move to opposite ends of the cell, and spindle fibers begin to extend from the centromeres of each chromosome toward the center of the cell. In the second part of prophase, the nuclear membrane dissolves and the spindle fibers attach to the centromeres at the kinetochore. It is during anaphase that the chromatids are separated from each other as the centromere divides at the kinetochore.

95. (C)

A chaparral biome has hot summers, temperate winters, and precipitation that varies from low in summer to high in winter, with a prolonged summer. Trees, shrubs, and small animals are common. Choice (A) describes a temperate grassland. Temperate deciduous forest includes the climate described in choice (B). Choice (D) describes a tropical rain forest biome.

96. (A)

In this case Mendel demonstrated that gametes sort independently of one another in most cases, an idea known as the *law of independent assortment*.

97. (C)

The domain Eubacteria contains prokaryotic bacteria, which evolved before any of the eukaryotic organisms, including those of all four kingdoms – Plantae, Animalia, Protista, and Fungi (not listed).

98. (A)

Metaphase is the stage of mitosis where the spindle fibers pull the chromosomes into alignment along the equatorial plane of the cell, ensuring that one copy of each chromosome is distributed to each daughter cell.

99. (B)

Mendel determined that one gene is sometimes dominant over another gene for the same trait (that is, it expressed itself over the other). This is known as the *law of dominance*, Mendel's second law of inheritance. Since the offspring were all yellow it would indicate that yellow genes are dominant over the green.

100. (B)

Primary oocytes are formed in the ovaries of females before birth, usually in great number. Primary oocytes go through meiosis I, forming a secondary oocyte and a smalleer polar body. Numerals II and III are correct choices.

101. (D)

Proteins may be used as catalysts in the laboratory, so the formation of proteins in the laboratory under conditions presumed to be representative of early earth history is key evidence of the evolution of life on earth. Stanley Miller provided support for Oparin's hypotheses in experiments where he succeeded in producing amino acids by exposing simple inorganic molecules to electrical charges similar to lightning. Sidney Fox conducted experiments that proved ultraviolet light may induce the formation of dipeptides from amino acids. Researcher Cyril Ponnamperuma demonstrated that small amounts of guanine formed from the thermal polymerization of amino acids.

102. (B)

The electron transfer system utilizes cytochromes (pigment molecules) that exist on the cristae of the mitochondria.

103. (B)

The first cells to evolve were most likely unspecialized. Since Earth's atmosphere was most likely lacking in much oxygen, it is presumed that pre-plant cells were also anaerobic. Early cells were also aquatic and prokaryotic.

104. (C)

The egg cell is the female gamete (haploid) ready for fertilization. Primary oocytes go through meiosis I to become a secondary oocyte and a polar body. The polar body goes through meiosis II forming two more polar bodies, and the secondary oocyte then goes through meiosis II to form one egg cell and one polar body.

105. (B)

Grana is a part of the chloroplasts. These and cell walls are features of plant cells, but not animal cells.

106. (B)

The process of DNA replication is occasionally subject to a mistake known as a mutation.

107. (D)

The central vacuole is a membrane-bound, fluid-filled space that stores water and soluble nutrients for the plant's use. The tendency of the central vacuole to absorb water provides for the turgidity (or rigid shape) of plant cells.

108. (A)

Three polar bodies are formed when primary oocytes undergo meiosis I and II. An egg cell is also formed through this process. However, polar bodies are infertile.

109. (D)

Primary spermatocytes undergo meiosis I to form secondary spermatocytes with a single chromosome set (haploid). These secondary spermatocytes then go through meiosis II, forming spermatid, which are haploid. Spermatid develop into male gametes (sperm cells).

110. (C)

Most vitamins are coenzymes or parts of coenzymes.

111. (D)

Chlorophyll is the green pigment found in the chloroplasts of plant cells.

112. (C)

The choice is incorrect only because in the problem the least number of significant figures among the multiplicands is two, therefore you can not go beyond two in the answer. Because 82.5 has three significant figures, this should be rounded to 82. Otherwise, the units are correct and the calculation is correct so (A), (B), and (D) are incorrect choices.

113. (B)

The National Science Education Standards and many research documents support inquiry activities as one of the most effective teaching methods in science education. When students are allowed to construct knowledge themselves rather than being told the answers or given the steps (C), (D) they are more likely to raise their own good questions and internalize the information. Further, participation is shown to increase when students are given an opportunity to participate in hands on activities (A) and it is the teacher's responsibility to insure that participation occurs.

114. (B)

Sperm (male gamete) and egg cells (female gametes) combine to form the what is known as a zygote. A zygote then undergoes a series of cell divisions to form a cluster of cells called a morula. The morula continues through further cell division and forms the blastula.

115. (C)

The Common Rule does not require compensation of subjects. It does however require all of the details mentioned in choices (A), (B), and (D).

116. (A)

Identifying prenatal genetic traits in order to abort imperfect combinations and create the perfect child is practicing eugenics and a highly ethically controversial practice. Choices (B) and (C) are routinely carried out in the forensic world. Choice (D) is occasionally used and becoming more popular as a means of identification of remains.

117. (D)

Adjusting data would not be appropriate. Choices (A), (B), and (D) are process skills.

118. (D)

A covered Petri dish is the appropriate glassware for this procedure.

119. (A)

Be sure the student follows careful safety protocols including only experimenting in a laboratory environment (such as school lab), uses covered glassware, researches appropriate techniques for species grown, and follows IRB rules. Choice (B) is incorrect since even though mold does commonly grow in various places, it is dangerous. While mold can be dangerous, with proper supervision and following safety protocols, it is age appropriate for Biology students to experiment with mold according to teacher discretion (C). Experimentation with certain living things is appropriate according to teacher discretion and with appropriate precautions for educational purposes (D).

120. (B)

Infectious waste cannot be placed in normal waste at all whether wrapped and labeled or not. Choices (A), (C), and (D) are all appropriate disposal methods.

121. (A)

While Piaget's work is certainly monumental in the field of cognitive psychology, it did not have the all-encompassing impact of the overall scientific world that the other three in choices (B), (C), and (D) had. Thus, choice (A) had the LEAST impact on modern scientific ideals as a whole.

122. (D)

Use of fossil fuels is status quo and while some new biofuel technologies and cleaner fuel technologies are helpful, in the long run fossil fuels are unlikely to provide long term answers. Choices (A), (B), (C) are all high yield research fields regarding pollution reduction, clean energy, and climate sustainability as a whole.

123. (A)

Genetic drift occurs as a gene pool experiences a change in frequency of particular genes due to chance fluctuation. Over time the genetic pool within this finite population changes.

124. (C)

Trachcophytes is the name for vascular plants, such as roses, corn and ferns. Mosses are nonvascular (bryophytes).

125. (B)

According to the National Association of Biology Teachers, "Every student should have direct, hands-on experiences with laboratory materials. Resources should be available to allow all students, regardless of ability, to experience laboratory and field instruction in a safe environment." Further, the NABT document at goes on to affirm statements (A), (B), and (D).

126. (B)

When populations of an organism in a given area grow and move into new geographical areas, some discover niches and advantageous conditions. Traits possessed by this traveling population will grow more common over several generations through the process of natural selection. Over time, the species will specially adapt to live more effectively in the new environment. Through this process known as adaptive radiation, a single species can develop into several diverse species over time.

127. (A)

Natality is the birth rate within a population.

128. (A)

The cell membrane is only 5-10 nanometers thick.

129. (C)

CO_2 is not a product of glycolysis. Each molecule of glucose is broken down into two molecules of pyruvic acid (pyruvate), two ATP molecules, and two hydrogen atoms.

130. (D)

Gymnosperms produce seeds in cones or cone-like structures. They do not produce flowers. Answers I and III are correct but II is incorrect.

131. (D)

The ribosome does not attach to the mRNA until the second phase of protein synthesis—translation. Rather, transcription involves the formation of an RNA molecule that corresponds to the DNA strand. The DNA encodes an RNA strand that will produce the desired amino acids and/or protein. The DNA strand "unzips" as in the replication process, then individual RNA nucleotides are matched to the DNA sequence using the enzyme RNA polymErase. The RNA strand is then joined together and it uncoils from the DNA. This particular RNA strand is known as messenger RNA or mRNA. The mRNA then migrates from the nucleus to the cytoplasm, where it is modified in a process known as post-transcriptional processing. This processing prepares the mRNA for protein synthesis and the non-coding sequences are removed. Each mRNA coding sequence consists of a unit of three nucleotides known as a *codon*. Each codon corresponds to a particular amino acid (though an amino acid may correspond to more than one codon).

However, in order for the protein synthesis process to continue, a second type of RNA is required, transfer RNA or tRNA. Transfer RNA exists as a chain of about 80 nucleotides arranged in a clover-like shape. At one point along the tRNA chain there are three unattached bases, which are called the anticodon. This anticodon will line up with a corresponding codon during translation. Each tRNA molecule also has an attached specific amino acid. This ends the transcription process and translation then begins.

132. (B)

Catabolism is the process of breaking down molecules and releasing stored energy. Anabolism is the synthesizing of a molecule.

133. (A)

The modern synthesis focused on the concept that evolution was a process of gradual adaptive change in traits across populations.

134. (B)

The birth rate in a population minus that population's death rate represents the rate of increase for that group. When the birth rate of a population equals the death rate, the population remains at a constant level. The exponential curve and the logistic curve are two models that represent the effects of different circumstances on populations.

135. (C)

Determining the sequence of neural development is a function of a regulatory gene. Structural genes are responsible for coding proteins that will form actual tissues, organs, and structural characteristics. Regulatory genes, on the other hand, determine functional or physiological events, such as growth. These specific genes control (regulate) when other genes are turned on or off, thus regulating when certain proteins that produce a specific trait will be synthesized.

136. (A)

Chlorophyll is not absorbed through plant roots, it is synthesized within plant cells. Photolysis, where a photon of light is absorbed by the chlorophyll pigment, which then is in an excited (higher energy) state, is the first step in the photosynthetic process. The light reaction is a decomposition reaction that separates water molecules into hydrogen and oxygen atoms utilizing the energy from the excited chlorophyll pigment. Oxygen that is not needed by the cell combines to form O_2 (gas) and is released into the environment. The free hydrogen is grabbed and held by a particular molecule (called the hydrogen acceptor) until it is needed. This reaction then yields energy, which converts a molecule of ADP plus a phosphate to ATP (phosphorylation). The dark reaction (CO_2 fixation) then occurs in the stroma of the chloroplast. This second phase of photosynthesis does not require light, however it does require the use of the products of the light reaction (photolysis).

137. (D)

Energy from the sun is transformed by green plants into chemical energy in the form of ATP. ATP (adenosine triphosphate) is known as the energy currency of cellular activity. While energy is stored in the form of carbohydrates, in order to be used by cells, the energy must be released in small packets. Since ATP contains three high-energy bonds, it is an efficient storage molecule for the energy needed for cellular processes. ATP consists of a base (adenine) and a simple sugar (ribose) and three phosphate groups. When a cellular process requires energy, a molecule of ATP can be broken down into ADP (adenosine diphosphate) plus a phosphate group. The energy that was stored in the bond between the phosphate and ADP is released into the cell, and is available to fuel other reactions. Even more energy is released when ATP is decomposed into AMP (adenosine monophosphate) and two phosphate groups.

138. (B)

Species with *equilibreal* life strategies (k-selected) are those organisms that overtake the opportunistic pioneer species. These tend to have long life spans with a long maturation time and corresponding low mortality rate. They reproduce sexually and they tend to parent their offspring. They tend to stay within their established borders rather than dispersing. These characteristics form the basis for particular species to dominate in varying ecosystems.

139. (B)

Glycolysis is the reaction that breaks down glucose into smaller molecules. Unlike photosynthesis (which only occurs in plant cells), respiration occurs in all cells. Glycolysis is the first step in all respiration pathways and occurs in the cytoplasm of all living cells, not just plant cells.

140. (A)

Cones are a product of sexual reproduction not asexual reproduction (vegetative propagation). There are several types of plants that produce structures specifically designed to carry on vegetative propagation. These structures include tubers (potatoes), rhizomes (irises), and bulbs (amaryllis).

141. (D)

Abscisic acid is a hormone that regulates the opening and closing of stomata, thus controlling how much water is lost through transpiration. Abscisic acid also stimulates the formation of winter buds, putting the plant into a dormant state. Cytokinins regulate cell division and fruit development. The gibberellins include 65 hormones that regulate cell division and elongation. Auxins control growth factors (i.e., tropisms).

142. (C)

J-curve population growth (exponential curve) shows the rate of growth accelerating over time and occurs when there are no environmental or social limits on populations size. Logistic population growth and S-curve population growth are synonymous and represent the effects of limiting factors on population size.

143. (C)

The geological time scale is divided into four Eras: The Precambrian Era is the period of Earth's history prior to 600 million years ago. Prokaryotic life existed, and eukaryotes began to evolve. The Paleozoic Era lasted from 225 to 600 million years ago. Marine invertebrates were dominant in the oldest period within this Era. Dominance of fish and amphibians followed. The Mesozoic Era extended from 65 to 225 million years ago. Dinosaurs were abundant. This was the age of reptiles. The modern Era, the Cenozoic, which dates back to 65 million years ago, is characterized by the dominance of mammals, birds, and insects.

144. (D)

Charles Darwin is credited with formulating the most widely supported theory of evolution. The postulates of his theory came together in his book *On the Origin of Species by Means of Natural Selection* in 1859, and are recapitulated below.

All organisms overproduce gametes. Not all gametes form offspring, and of the offspring formed, not all survive. Those organisms that are most competitive (in various different aspects) will have greater likelihoods of survival. These survival traits vary from individual to individual but are passed on to the next generation, and thus over time, the best adaptions for survival are maintained. The environment determines which traits will be selected for or against, and these traits will change in time. A selected trait may be disadvantageous later.

The key drawback to Darwin's theory is that he did not suggest the key to variation in traits. It is now known that variation may be due to genetic mutations, gene low due to migration, genetic drift (especially in small populations) and natural selection of genotypes, i.e., a differential ability to survive and/or reproduce.

145. (A)

Cilia line the upper respiratory tract, waving against air inlow to filter out unneeded debris. They increase surface area to facilitate absorption of digested nutrients. Goblet cells line the same region and secret mucus. Leidig cells are in the male testis.

146. (C)

Malaria is caused by protozoans of the genus *Plasmodium*, of the Sporozoa. The other choices represent diseases caused by viruses.

147. (C)

A cofactor is a nonprotein substance that helps an enzyme to catalyze a reaction. Ions, such as manganese ions (Mn^{2+}), can be cofactors for certain enzymes. A coenzyme is a type of cofactor, and more specifically, is a nonprotein organic molecule that can function as an electron acceptor. NAD^+ and FAD are electron acceptors and are bound to enzymes.

148. (A)

Amphibians were the first animals with two pairs of limbs. Fish have fins, not limbs. Amphibians depend on their environment to obtain and lose heat (ectotherms) and there is significant exchange of gases across the skin. One group of salamanders does not have lungs and depends exclusively on the sking for respiration.

149. (D)

Savannah is a kind of plain characterized by a warm climate, grassland, and seasonally dry climatic conditions.

150. (B)

The waxy coating on leaves that keeps moisture balanced is the cuticle. The epidermis is the outermost layer of the cross-section of a leaf, which secretes the cuticle. The palisade layer and the spongy layer are additional layers of cells of a plant leaf.

Index

Installing REA's TestWare®

SYSTEM REQUIREMENTS

Pentium 75 MHz (300 MHz recommended) or a higher or compatible processor; Microsoft Windows XP or later; 64 MB available RAM; Internet Explorer 5.5 or higher.

INSTALLATION

1. Insert the Praxis II: Biology Core Content Knowledge CD-ROM into the CD-ROM drive.

2. If the installation doesn't begin automatically, from the Start Menu choose the RUN command. When the RUN dialog box appears, type d:\setup (where d is the letter of your CD-ROM drive) at the prompt and click OK.

3. The installation process will begin. A dialog box proposing the directory "C:\Program Files\REA\Praxis_Bio\" will appear. If the name and location are suitable, click OK. If you wish to specify a different name or location, type it in and click OK.

4. Start the Praxis II: Biology Core Content Knowledge TestWare® application by double-clicking on the icon.

REA's Praxis II: Biology Core Content Knowledge TestWare® is **EASY** to **LEARN AND USE**. To achieve maximum benefits, we recommend that you take a few minutes to go through the on-screen tutorial on your computer. The "screen buttons" are also explained here to familiarize you with the program.

SSD ACCOMMODATIONS FOR STUDENTS WITH DISABILITIES

Many students qualify for extra time to take the Praxis II Biology exam, and our TestWare® can be adapted to accommodate your time extension. This allows you to practice under the same extended-time accommodations that you will receive on the actual test day.

TECHNICAL SUPPORT

REA's TestWare® is backed by customer and technical support. For questions about **installation or operation of your software**, contact us at:

> **Research & Education Association**
> **Phone: (732) 819-8880 (9 a.m. to 5 p.m. ET, Monday–Friday)**
> **Fax: (732) 819-8808**
> **Website: *www.rea.com***
> **E-mail: info@rea.com**

Note to Windows Users: In order for the TestWare® to function properly, please install and run the application under the same computer administrator-level user account. Installing the TestWare® as one user and running it as another could cause file-access path conflicts.